Antoine Joseph Pernety

The History of a Voyage to the Malouine or Falkland Islands

Antoine Joseph Pernety

**The History of a Voyage to the Malouine or Falkland Islands**

ISBN/EAN: 9783743319240

Manufactured in Europe, USA, Canada, Australia, Japa

Cover: Foto ©ninafisch / pixelio.de

Manufactured and distributed by brebook publishing software (www.brebook.com)

Antoine Joseph Pernety

**The History of a Voyage to the Malouine or Falkland Islands**

THE

# HISTORY of a VOYAGE

TO THE

## Malouine (or Falkland) Iſlands,

Made in 1763 and 1764,

Under the Command of M. de BOUGAINVILLE,
in Order to form a Settlement there:

AND OF

Two Voyages to the STREIGHTS of MAGELLAN,

WITH AN

Account of the PATAGONIANS.

Tranſlated from Dom PERNETY's HISTORICAL JOURNAL,
written in French.

---

ILLUSTRATED WITH COPPER-PLATES.

---

THE SECOND EDITION.

---

LONDON:

Printed for WILLIAM GOLDSMITH, Number 24, PATER-NOSTER
Row; and DAVID STEEL, Number 1, UNION-Row, the
Lower-End of the MINORIES, LITTLE TOWER-HILL.
M.DCC.LXXIII.

ADVERTISEMENT to the READER.

THE Editor thinks it neceſſary to acquaint the Reader, that, in this tranſlation of Dom Pernety's Journal, nothing has been omitted, but the detail of ordinary occurrences, which appeared common to every voyage. Whatever ſeemed in any view peculiar to this expedition has been retained.

In reſpect to the cuts and plans, ſome alterations and additions have been made. A general chart ſhewing the ſituation of Falkland's Iſlands in the Southern Ocean, which was not given in the original, is here inſerted. Plans of the iſlands of St. Catherine, and of Buenos Ayres, are alſo added. The birds, fiſh, &c. are claſſed in their proper order, and placed at the end of the book with references to the page in which they are mentioned.

The Editor hopes the work will meet with the approbation of the public, as he has ſpared neither coſt nor pains to make it uſeful and exact.

Note of the Tranflator omitted in page 242.

The Pinguin here mentioned, is different from that which is defcribed by our Ingenious countryman Mr. Pennant, under the name of the Patagonian Pinguin; and anfwers more exactly to the fecond fpecies or leffer Pinguin fpoken of by that gentleman, and which is otherwife called, Anfer Magellanicus Clufii, &c. It is probable that Don Pernety never faw the Patagonian Pinguin, fince he fays nothing of it. The Reader will find an accurate account of the different fpecies of this fingular bird, in the 58th volume of the Philofophical Tranfactions, which contains Mr. Pennant's paper on that fubject.

Directions to the Book Binder for placing the PLATES.

|     |                                  | Page |
|-----|----------------------------------|------|
| 1.  | The general Chart to front the Title. |   |
| 2.  | St. Catherines Ifland, &c.       | 41   |
| 3.  | Rio de la Plata                  | 101  |
| 4.  | Plan of Montevideo               | 139  |
| 5.  | Spaniards at Montevideo          | 142  |
| 6.  | Spanifh Lady of Montevideo       | 143  |
| 7.  | A Spaniard of Montevideo         | 144  |
| 8.  | A Spanifh Gentleman of Montevideo | 145  |
| 9.  | An Indian of Montevideo          | 163  |
| 10. | Malouine or Falkland Iflands     | 177  |
| 11. | Plan and View of Acarron Bay     | 189  |
| 12. | Streights of Magellan            | 263  |
| 13. | The Patagonians                  | 273  |
| 14. | Fifhes found in this Voyage      |      |
| 15. | Birds, ditto                     | at the End of the Book. |
| 16. | Sea Lyons, &c.                   |      |

THE

AUTHOR's

PREFACE.

THE difcovery and knowledge of the Malouine Iflands has been looked upon as an object of fo much importance, that the Englifh, having been informed of the expedition we made there in 1764, thought it neceffary to eftablifh themfelves in thofe iflands, notwithftanding that we had already taken poffeffion of them in the name of the crown of France. In preparing for this voyage, which excited the attention of all Europe, they took extraordinary precautions. Commodore Byron was employed on this expedition with two fhips, the Dolphin and the Tamer frigate, under his command. The Florida was afterwards difpatched to carry them provifions of all kinds.

We had taken poffeffion of thefe iflands in the beginning of April, before the Dolphin was off the ftocks, and we quitted them the 8th of the fame month on our return to France, where we landed the 26th of June. The Englifh did not fail till fome days after. On the 4th of December they left Port Defire, and took their courfe towards the South of the fuppofed Pepys's Ifland, at 48 degrees South latitude, where they made feveral unfuccefsful attempts for the difcovery of that ifland. They were then obliged, as they obferve p. 69, of the Voyage round the world in 1764 and 1765 on board the Dolphin, to abandon that refearch, being well perfuaded of the impoffibility of finding this fuppofed ifland.

The 22d of the fame month (December) being in the Streights of Magellan, five leagues diftance from Terra del Fuego, they obferved a fmoke rifing in feveral places on the oppofite coaft, which is that of Patagonia. They fteered towards it, and cafting

B anchor

ii          PREFACE.

anchor at about a mile from shore, saw distinctly men on horseback, who beckoned to them.

On approaching the coast there appeared manifest signs of fear in the countenances of those, who were going on shore in the boat, when they perceived at the water side men of a prodigious stature. The Commodore, animated with the idea of making a discovery relative to these Patagonians, the question of whose existence had for a long time furnished matter of conversation in England, was the first who leaped on shore, and was followed by his officers and seamen well armed, whom he drew up in a posture of defence. The savages, to the number of about 200, immediately ran up to them, looking at them with an air of the greatest surprize, and smiling at the disproportion in size between the English and themselves.

The Commodore made signs to them to sit down, which they complied with; and he put about their necks collars of enamelled beads, and ribbands, giving to each of them some such trifling ornament. Their size is so extraordinary, that even sitting they were almost as high as the Commodore when he stood upright. (p. 77.)

Their middle stature seemed to be about eight feet, and the highest above nine [*]. The English did not use any measure to ascertain this; but we have reason, say they, to believe, the account we give rather falls short of, than exceeds, the truth. (p. 78.) The size of the women is as surprizing as that of the men, and the children are in the same proportions. The women wore necklaces and bracelets. (p. 79.) Their cloaths were made of the skins of Peruvian sheep, which covered their shoulders, and came down as far as their knees. The greatest part of them were on horseback, before we landed; but they alighted, and left their horses at some distance. The horses have the appearance of being

[*] The Commodore is said, in the preface to the same Account, (p. 61.) to be six feet high. It must be remembered, that the English foot is near an inch less than the French standard foot.

PREFACE. iii

ing very fwift, but their height is not in proportion to that of their riders, and they feemed befides to be in but indifferent condition. (p. 85.) They appeared to be of a mild and friendly difpofition. (p. 83.)

Among the Englifh was Lieutenant Cumnins, whom the Patagonians feemed to regard with particular fatisfaction, on account of his height, which was not lefs than fix feet ten inches. Some of them clapped him on the back; but though this was intended only as a mark of their kindnefs, their hands fell fo heavy upon him, that he ftaggered under the weight of them.

On the 23d of the fame month, the Englifh having advanced farther into the Streights difcovered feveral favages, on the Ifland of Saint Elizabeth, who made figns to them to come on fhore. Both the men and women were of middling ftature, and well fhaped. Their hair was black; their fkin, which is naturally of an olive colour, appeared red, becaufe they paint their bodies with a compofition of reddifh earth mixed with greafe. They are cloathed with the fkins of fea-calves, otters, or Peruvian fheep, fewed together, fo as to make one piece of about four feet and one half fquare. They wear caps made of the fkins of birds with the feathers, and have alfo fkins on their feet, which ferve them inftead of fhoes. Some of the women had girdles alfo made of fkins; but none of them wore caps; they were only diftinguifhed by a necklace of fhells. (p. 92.)

After having provided themfelves with wood and water at Port *Famine*, the Englifh failed from thence the 5th of January 1765, and fteering eaftward, cleared the Streights, and faw land the 13th of the fame month. The next day they entered a very commodious bay, within which were feveral fmall ones, and different harbours: to the third of thefe they gave the name of Port Egmont. The entrance to this bay is by the North; it is half a mile in width, and has from feven to thirteen fathom depth on a muddy bottom. (p. 121).

B 2 The

PREFACE.

The 23d of January, the Commodore took poſſeſſion of all theſe iſlands in the name of the King of Great Britain, and left them the 27th, without having eſtabliſhed any ſettlement there. Theſe iſlands are ſituated in 51 degrees 21 minutes South latitude, and 66 degrees ten minutes Weſt longitude. (p. 134). From hence they returned, coaſting along to the Streights of Magellan.

It will appear by the particulars of this Engliſh account, and by thoſe of my Journal, that we were acquainted with the Malouine Iſlands, and had formed a ſettlement there, near a twelvemonth before the two ſhips under the command of Mr. Byron had even diſcovered them. At the time even when theſe two veſſels arrived there, Monſ. de Bougainville was then returned; and having ſeen them from the port where he lay at anchor, ſet ſail for the Streights of Magellan, where he met with them, as will be ſeen at the end of my Journal.

I have entered into the detail of this Engliſh expedition to the Malouines in order to convince the public of the inconteſtable right of the crown of France to the poſſeſſion of them, in oppoſition to the injurious pretenſions of the Engliſh.

I have alſo given a ſketch of the account, which one of the officers of Mr. Byron's ſhip has printed concerning the giants of Patagonia, that the Reader might compare it with what is ſaid of them in the extracts from the journals of the French Captains, who have ſeen and made a longer ſtay with theſe Patagonians than the Engliſh have. Such a compariſon will prove to thoſe who are incredulous, or who have too much vanity to ſuffer themſelves to appear ignorant of what has never come to their knowledge, or, from the ſame principle, make a point of denying every thing they have not ſeen, that there exiſts, nevertheleſs, a race of men, the bulk and enormity of whoſe ſize may teach theſe unbelieving, vain, and ſelf-conceited perſons, to reduce their magnificent pretenſions, and be contented to conſider themſelves as not the ſmalleſt among the race of dwarfs.

The

# PREFACE.

The Streights of Magellan were little known. The accounts we had of it till this time, though many in number, were not to be depended upon; the obfervations were either deficient in exactnefs or in perfpicuity. This has determined me to give thofe of our two French Captains, and a chart of the Streights, corrected according to their obfervations.

It may be conjectured, and indeed with great appearance of probability, that the Malouine Iflands formerly made a part of Patagonia and Terra del Fuego, and that they were feparated from them by violent earthquakes, which opened a paffage for the fea through a cleft caufed by the eruption, and formed in time the channel, by which thofe iflands are divided from the continent. This conjecture is the more reafonable, as the Terra del Fuego took its name from the volcanos, which were fuppofed to have been feen there, and as at fome diftance from that part of the Malouine Iflands, where we have made our fettlement, the hills and vallies fhew clearly, by the diforder of the beds of free ftone, and the irregular heaps in which they lie, that this confufion is the effect of earthquakes. See what is faid on this fubject in my journal.

But what will aftonifh the Reader is, that a country fo extenfive as the Malouines fhould neither be inhabited by men, nor by any of thofe quadrupeds, which are commonly met with among the Patagonians; and that the fmall fpider with long legs, which is called in France *Faucheufe*, and the little brown cri-'-et called *Cri-cri*, which is alfo found in chimneys, are the only two infects we faw there. It is lefs wonderful, that we fhould not meet with any of the reptile fpecies, as travellers affure us, that there are none to be found in the territory of Chily, which lies to the Weft of Patagonia, in the fame parallel with the Malouine Iflands.

Another motive, which induces me to believe, that the Malouines were originally joined to Patagonia, is, that there are no trees on them, and that the whole coaft to the Eaft of the Patagonians, and of Terra del Fuego, is without trees, to about 25 leagues

## PREFACE.

leagues up the country. At that diftance fome trees begin to appear, but from thence to the fea fide there is nothing to be found but fhrubs and heath. It is the fame on the Malouines. The difcoveries which the Englifh, who have fettled more to the Weft, may make on that fide, will give us more light into thefe particulars. The Spaniards, who have fucceeded my countrymen in the Eaftern fettlement will inform us with regard to thofe parts.

The exactnefs of the plans and charts, as well as that of the figures of animals in the plates of my Journal, may be depended upon. The chart I give of the Rio de la Plata is the more interefting as it was taken with the utmoft accuracy, and as it is the only one of that river, the navigation of which is fo dangerous.

INTRO-

# INTRODUCTION.

AFTER the peace was concluded by a ceffion of all Canada on the part of France to England, M. de Bougainville, Knight of St. Louis, and Colonel of infantry, conceived the defign of indemnifying France for this lofs, if poffible, by a difcovery of the fouthern continent, and of thofe large iflands, which lie in the way to it. A perufal of admiral Anfon's voyage round the world fixed his ideas for finding the Malouine Iflands, and determined him to make them the firft object of his expedition, and to form a fettlement there. He communicated his project to the miniftry, who approved it. To carry it therefore into execution, M. de Bougainville caufed a frigate and a floop to be built at St. Malo at his own expence, under the directions of the Sieurs Guyot du Clos and Chenart de la Gyraudais, who were to have the command of them under him. But being defirous to make the execution of his defign as advantageous as poffible, and imagining that I might be of fervice to him in that refpect, he propofed to me, juft before he quitted Paris, to undertake the voyage with him. A few days after, I received the King's orders in a letter from the Duke de Choifeul, minifter for the marine department, to embark with M. de Bougainville. I made my difpofitions immediately for the voyage, and fet off with him for St. Malo.

Thofe, who are acquainted with the fituation of the Malouine Iflands, will applaud the project of M. de Bougainville; but few people have heard of thofe iflands, becaufe they were almoft unknown. Some navigators had feen them, but, I think, I may affert, that no one before ourfelves had ever landed there, at leaft in the part where we did. For this reafon it will be proper to give fome idea of the difcovery of them from the accounts given by authors of eftablifhed reputation.

Frezier,

## INTRODUCTION.

Frezier, in his relation *du Voyage* ... *la Mer du Sud*, printed in 4to, Paris 1716, p. 264, expresses himself thus: "If in this chart I have suppreft some suppofed countries, I have added others which are real, in the latitude of 51 degrees, and to which I have given the name of *new Iflands*; becaufe they have been difcovered fince the year 1700, the greateft part of them by the fhips of St. Malo. I have placed them according to the reports of the Maurepas and St. Louis, fhips belonging to the India Company, which had a near view of them, and the latter even took in frefh water there from a pond, which I have marked near Port St. Louis. The water here was reddifh and fomewhat infipid, in other refpects good for the fea. Both thefe veffels paffed them in different parts, but the one which kept clofeft along the coaft was the St. John Baptift, commanded by Doublet of Havre, who attempted to pafs through an opening he faw towards the middle of them; but perceiving feveral fmall iflands juft rifing to the furface of the water, he thought proper to tack about. This clufter of iflands is the fame which was difcovered by Fouquet of St. Malo, and to which he gave the name of Anican, his owner. The routs I have traced will fhew the bearing of thefe lands from the Streights of Le Maire, in her paffage from which the St. John Baptift faw them, and from Statenland, which the two other fhips had had a profpect of before they found it.

The northern part of thefe lands, which is here called the *the Coafts of the Affumption*, was difcovered the 16th of July 1708, by Poré of St. Malo\*, who named it after the fhip he failed in. It was thought to be a new land, at the diftance of about a hundred leagues eaft of the new iflands I am fpeaking of; but I have

---

\* It appears that Poré was not acquainted with the fituation of the coafts of the Patagonians, nor that of the new or Malouine Iflands, or that he was miftaken in his point. Thefe iflands are in fact no more than 90 or 100 leagues diftant from the Streights of Magellan; how then could they be at the diftance of 100 leagues Weft of the coaft of the Affumption, as it is called by Poré? If he had known the fituation of the Malouine Iflands, he would have feen clearly by the latitude and longitude of the coaft he ran along, that it could be no other than the coaft of thofe iflands.

INTRODUCTION.

have made no scruple of joining it with them, having convincing reasons to justify my opinion.

The first is, that the latitudes observed on the North and South of these islands, and the bearing of the known parts answer perfectly to the same point of reunion on the East side without leaving any space between them. The second, that there is no reason to imagine this coast lies eastward of the isles of Anican. For M. Gobien of the St. John, who was pleased to communicate to me an extract of his journal, supposes it to lie South of the river Plata *; which account, taken strictly, will not admit of its being at a greater distance than two or three degrees eastward, that is to say, five and twenty or thirty leagues †. But the difference of computations is always a mark of uncertainty. The first time they saw this coast on their passage from Saint Catherine's to the Brasils, they reckoned it at 329 degrees; the second, in passing from the river Plata, where contrary winds obliged them to put in, after having tried to pass Cape Horn: they supposed it at 322 degrees, and according to some 324; following the charts of Peter Goos, the errors of which we have taken notice of, so that little regard ought to be paid to them. However, as they relied upon them, they thought themselves at a great distance from the Continent, and reckoning that they were too far eastward, ran three hundred leagues too far to West in the South Sea, insomuch that they imagined themselves on the coast of Guinea, when they landed at Ylo. But the third and convincing

* The supposition of M. Gobien, of the St. John, is false, in placing this coast of Assumption South of the river Plata. We were on shore there, as he was, and in the same place, according to Frezier's chart, and found it by our computation about 64 degrees and a half W. longitude from the meridian of Paris, and the mouth of the river Plata 56° 30′; which carries that part of the coast where M. Gobien and we landed eight degrees farther S. W. and answers nearly to the mistake attributed by the author of Admiral Anson's Voyage (p. 78.) to Frezier's chart in regard to the situation of the coast of Patagonia.

† If we place the coast of the Assumption three degrees farther to the West, it will be more conformable to our estimation, which makes our landing place four degrees, or thereabouts, more to West than it would be according to Frezier's chart, which is formed on the extract M. Gobien furnished him with from his own journal.

C

## INTRODUCTION.

convincing argument is, that we ought to pafs to windward of this new land according to the longitude it was placed in, in the manufcript chart; and that it is morally impoffible any fhip could pafs without feeing it, it being about 50 leagues in length from E. S. E. to W. N. W. No doubt therefore remains, that this was the northern part of the new iflands, the weftern part of which will be difcovered in time, but is yet unknown.

Thefe iflands are certainly the fame, which were difcovered by Sir Richard Hawkins in 1593, to the eaft of the uninhabited coaft, and in 50 degrees latitude. He was thrown by a ftorm on an unknown land: he ran along the coaft about fixty leagues, and faw fires, from whence he concluded the place was inhabited *.

Hitherto thefe lands have been called Sebald's Iflands, it being fuppofed that the three which go under this name in the charts were fituated there at pleafure, for want of a proper knowledge of them. But the fhip *L'Incarnation*, commanded by the Sieur Brignon of St. Malo, took a near view of them in fine weather in the year 1711, on her departure from Rio Janeiro. They are in fact three fmall iflands † of about half a league in length, ranged

---

* I do not know whether the iflands, which Sir Richard Hawkins faw in 1593, to the Eaft of the defart coaft of Patagonia, in 50 degrees S. latitude, are the northern part of the new or Malouine Iflands. We ran fixty degrees at leaft along the coaft, as well as he, and faw no fire, or appearance of habitation, though we were very often at no greater diftance than that of half a league or a league.

† At our landing we difcovered three iflands about half a league in length, pretty high, and forming a kind of triangle, agreeable to the account of Sebald's Iflands. This refemblance in pofition and figure made us take them at firft for Sebald's Iflands; but we difcovered near them feveral fmall flat iflands, almoft even with the furface of the water, of which no mention is made in the Sieur Brignon's journals, nor in thofe of other people, who fpeak of Sebald's Iflands. A few hours after, having difcovered other eminences, one behind another, we judged that thefe three iflands were not Sebald's Iflands, but fome of the Malouines, which ftand out before the principal one, and we found reafon to confirm ourfelves in this opinion. If thefe three iflands were really Sebald's Iflands, they would be about two leagues diftance from land, or the principal ifland, and not feven or eight, as Frezier fays. See the chart of our route along the coaft. However in the two voyages of the Eagle and the Star Pink, which have taken a later view of thefe three iflands in their paffage from the Malouines to the Straits of Magellan, the Eagle in 1765, and the Eagle with the Star in 1766; thefe veffels found no more iflands than thofe three, and have fince looked upon them to be Sebald's Iflands.

ranged in a triangular form, as they are represented in the charts. They passed at the distance of three or four leagues from them, and saw no land, though the weather was very fine, which is a proof that they are separated from the new islands by at least seven or eight leagues.

In the memorial presented to the *Compagnie des Indes* by the Sieur de Lozier Bouvet in the year 1735, soliciting their assistance in furnishing him the means of observing the countries discovered by Gonneville, he reports, among other advantages of the establishment they might form there after that observation, the opportunities of fixing an immediate commerce with the Spaniards of the river Plata and the Portuguese of Brasil. He even asserts, that the ships, in putting into the southern coasts, would steer very little out of their ordinary course for India.

By the establishment we have made on the Malouine Islands * we have put the India Company, and all the French navigators in the most favourable situation for accomplishing these two objects. The Malouine Islands are not near so far to the South: the climate is much more temperate; they stand more convenient for the river Plata and the Brasils; more in the neighbourhood of Magellan's lands and Patagonia, with the inhabitants of which it would be so much the more easy to fix a commerce, as they are already acquainted with the Europeans by the traffic they carry on with the Spaniards.

Let us consider the situation of the southern lands discovered by Monsieur de Gonneville, a gentleman of Normandy. In 1503 he fitted out a vessel at Honfleur, and set sail in the month of June for the East Indies. After doubling the Cape of Good Hope, and meeting with a gust of wind, which was succeeded by calms, he thought of nothing but gaining some land, where he might recover the fatigues of the voyage. He had the good fortune to discover some, and called them the South Indies. He lay there six months, during which time he refitted, formed an

intercourse

---

* Since this journal was written, France has ceded the Malouine Islands to Spain.

## INTRODUCTION.

intercourse with the natives, and established himself so far in their confidence, that their King, Arosca, trusted his son Essomeric to him to make the voyage of France, on condition that he should bring him back in twenty months. Gonneville sailed from thence the third of July 1504 laden with the produce of the country. In the Channel he met with an English privateer, which took him, and carried him into Guernsey. This unlucky accident prevented his arriving in France till the year 1505, where he made his complaint and declaration to the admiralty at Honfleur. No advantage was made at that time of M. de Gonneville's discovery; who to make amends to Essomeric for not being able to keep his word with him, married him to one of his relations, and left him at his death half his fortune.

The Sieur Bouvet, who had some notion of this discovery, presented a memorial to the *Compagnie des Indes*, who fitted out two ships for him, the Eagle, and Mary, with which he sailed from l'Orient the 19th of July 1738. The 26th of November he got into 35 degrees South latitude and 344° longitude from the French meridian. Here he began to meet with fogs, which continued almost constantly while the two ships remained in company. They were often so thick, that the Eagle's crew could not discover the Mary at the distance of musquet shot; so that they had the greatest difficulty to keep together. The 3d of December, being in 39 degrees 20 minutes latitude, and 351 longitude, they began to discover some sea-weed, and more birds than ordinary, which made them imagine they were not far from land : they therefore took all the precautions necessary in such circumstances. The 5th, they found themselves in 42 degrees 40 minutes latitude, and 354° longitude. The 7th, in 44 latitude, and 355 longitude. The 10th, 44° latitude, and the first meridian, where several geographers place the nearest point of the Southern Continent. The 12th, they made 7 degrees longitude; the 15th, 48 degrees, 50 minutes latitude, which is equal to that of Paris, in 7° longitude. Here they saw ice, which they looked upon as a certain indication of land. They even observed a

change

change in the colour of the fea, and faw a great number of Puffins, and other birds, feveral of which flapped their wings, like land birds. They perceived Penguins alfo, an amphibious bird, a defcription of which is given in my journal. In proportion as they got farther to the South, the ice increafed. The 16th they faw Penguins again, and a fea wolf; the fogs and ice prevented their rifing to the 54th degree of latitude before the laft day of December. At length, on the firft of January, about three in the afternoon, they difcovered a high land, covered with fnow, and very foggy, which they took for a large head-land, and called it *Cape Circumcifion*. It lies, according to the account of the Sieur Bouvet, in 54 degrees South latitude, and from 27 to 28 degrees longitude from the French meridian. The 6th, they faw a prodigious quantity of birds, of a very fine white, and of the fize of pigeons: they thought they faw land at the diftance of one or two leagues. The next day they perceived a new land, nearly North North Eaft of Cape Circumcifion. They continued in fearch of it till the 9th, at four in the morning, when the weather being fair and the fog gone off, they found that the fuppofed land was nothing more than a mift.

From the time they came within fight of land, they had reaped no other benefit from it than that of concluding, that it extended from eight to ten leagues E. N. E. and from fix to feven leagues Eaft. They had not been able to difcover even, whether what they faw was an ifland, or whether it made part of the Continent. At length the bad weather came on, the feafon was advanced, and the crew were in a bad ftate of health. All thefe confiderations induced M. de Lozier Bouvet to take the refolution of going to fee for fome place to put in at, which might be more eafy and more convenient for their landing. He took his courfe with a view of finding the place where Gonneville had landed; which, according to the account of it, is fituated in a latitude equal to that of fome of the provinces of France. The moft northern lie in 51 degrees, which is the latitude of the Malouine Iflands. He made therefore for the parallel from 51 to 52, and

paffed

xiv        INTRODUCTION.

paffed it with the fame inconveniencies, without reaping any kind of advantage. They reckoned themfelves in 51° longitude, when they were really in 55°, as they found on landing at the Cape of Good Hope. They kept the Cape to the North of them, and continued that courfe till the 5th of February, when the two veffels feparated, the Mary fteering for the Cape with M. Bouvet, and the Eagle for the ifle of France with Mr. Hay.

M. Bouvet left the Cape of Good Hope the 31ft of March, on his return to France, and in his route faw Trinity Ifland in 351 degrees longitude from the meridian of Teneriff, and 348° 30' from the French meridian, 20 degrees 20 minutes latitude. He likewife faw the ifle of Afcenfion, which he places in 349 degrees longitude. He fays, that Trinity Ifland is, without that name, very well defcribed by the *Flambeau Anglois*. After we had got, fays M. Bouvet, within gun fhot of this ifland, we faw three-fourths of it diftinctly. It is properly fpeaking, nothing more than a rock inacceffible on all fides. There are four little iflands between 8 and 9 leagues Eaft of it. Oliver de Noort, who had the command of four Dutch fhips in 1599, followed this parallel of 20 degrees 20 minutes from this ifland as far as the coaft of Brazil, and found no other in his courfe. This has made it imagined, that what is called Martin de Vaz's Ifland, and the Ifland of Afcenfion are the fame with Trinity Ifland\*, which goes under thefe three different names. We have been more fortunate in our enterprize than M. Bouvet was in his. The fettlement we made at the Malouine Iflands would anfwer all the purpofes of that he defigned to make on the Southern Continent,

if

---

\* What M. Bouvet fays here of Trinity Ifland is very conformable to what we faw near the ifland of Afcenfion, which is recounted in this journal, on 27th April 1764. But though their fituation in refpect of latitude does not differ more than 12 minutes, the longitude is abfolutely different; fince, according to his eftimation, Trinity Ifland is at 348 degrees 30 minutes from the French meridian, which anfwers to about 10 degrees from the meridian of Paris. While we were reconnoitring the ifland of Afcenfion, I eftimated its fituation at 32 degrees 25 minutes from the latter meridian. It fhould follow from thence that Trinity Ifland and the Ifland of Afcenfion are really diftinct from each other; which is contrary to the opinion of feveral navigators.

## INTRODUCTION.

if the India Company's ships would take their route by the South Sea to China, the Philippine Iſlands, &c. and for the South Sea trade. The author of Anſon's Voyage expreſſes himſelf upon this point in the following manner page 54 & ſeq. 4to edition, printed for Charles Anthony Jombert. " I have proved above, that all our future expeditions to the South Seas muſt run a conſiderable riſque of proving abortive, whilſt we are under the neceſſity of touching at Brazil in our paſſage thither; an expedient therefore, that might relieve us from this difficulty, would ſurely be a ſubject worthy of the attention of the public." We may add, that this port is too far from the neareſt that can be found in the South Sea to be of ſufficient advantage. We put into St. Catherine's as well as Admiral Anſon: we had not indeed, like him, reaſon to complain of the reception we met with; on the contrary, we owe our acknowledgements to the Governor, as will be ſeen in this journal; but the other inconveniences of this harbour are ſuch as he has reported them. The unhealthy air and perpetual fogs, which are found there, are enough to create a diſguſt.

" The beſt method of effecting this, (ſays the ſame author) would without doubt be by a diſcovery of ſome place more to the ſouthward, where ſhips might refreſh, and ſupply themſelves with the neceſſary ſea ſtock for their voyage round Cape Horn. And we have in reality the imperfect knowledge of two places, which might perhaps, on examination, prove extremely convenient for this purpoſe: the firſt of them is Pepys's Iſland * in the latitude of 47 degrees South, and laid down by Dr. Halley about eighty leagues to the eaſtward of Cape Blanco, on the coaſt of Patagonia; the ſecond is Falkland's Iſles in the latitude of 51° † nearly South of Pepys's Iſland. The firſt of theſe was

diſcovered

---

* In the ſecond voyage to the Malouines M. de Bougainville endeavoured for ſeveral days, without ſucceſs, to find this ſuppoſed Pepys's Iſland: the ſame attempt was made in the third voyage, and proved equally unſucceſsful.

† *Note of the tranſlator.* The original Engliſh ſays 51° ½. The reſt, there being no very material difference, is copied verbatim from the original.

## INTRODUCTION.

discovered by Captain Cowley in his voyage round the World, in the year 1686, who represents it as a commodious place for ships to wood and water at; and says, it is provided with a very good and capacious harbour, where a thousand sail of ships might ride at anchor in great safety; that it abounds with fowls, and as the shore is either rocks or sand, it seems to promise great plenty of fish."

This reasoning appears to be merely conjectural, and very boldly advanced on the part of Captain Cowley. It is easy to convince one's self of this by reading his relation, since he says in so many words, that *the bad weather hindered his landing there, he not having been able to put his longboat to sea.* If then he really did see it, it was only in his passage, as many navigators have a multitude of other islands and continents, which are still unknown to us, as well in respect to the quality and productions of the soil, as to the real situation of their coasts. Since this captain did not go on shore there, how could he know, that it is a good place to water at? Perhaps there is no fresh water. As to wood, we have been deceived by appearances in running along the coast of the Malouines: we thought we saw some, and after landing, these appearances vanished into cornflags, a sort of rush or plant with long, flat, strait leaves, which grows on a hillock of three feet in heighth at least, and the leaves clustering together form, as they rise from the hillock, an eminence of six or seven feet. See the extract from the Sieur Alexander Guyot's journal at the end of this work.

" The second place, or Falkland's Isles, (proceeds the Admiral) have been seen by many ships both *French* and *English*, being the land laid down by Frezier in his chart of the extremity of South America under the title of the *new islands*. Woods Rogers, who ran along the N. E. coast of these isles in the year 1708, tells us, that they extended about two degrees in length, and appeared with gentle descents from hill to hill, and seemed to be good ground with woods and harbours (see what we have said in relation to this in the preceding paragraph). Either of these

these places, as they are islands at a considerable distance from the Continent, may be supposed from their latitude, to lie in a climate sufficiently temperate. It is true, they are too little known to be at present recommended for proper places of refreshment for ships bound to the southward: but if the admiralty should think it adviseable to order them to be surveyed, which may be done at a very small expence, by a vessel fitted out on purpose; and if, on this examination, one or both of these places should appear proper for the purpose intended, it is scarcely to be conceived of what prodigious import a convenient station might prove, situated so far to the southward, and so near Cape Horn. The Duke and Duchess of Bristol were but thirty-five days from their losing sight of Falkland's Isles to their arrival at Juan Fernandez in the South Seas: and as the returning back is much facilitated by the western winds I doubt not but a voyage might be made from Falkland's Isles to Juan Fernandez, and back again in little more than two months."

If Woods Rogers only ran along the North East coast of Falkland's or the Malouine Isles, how could he know, that they did not extend more than about two leagues? We ran along only one side of the coasts of the principal island and found that it extended more than three degrees from East to North East. It is true, we observed, that it is composed of eminences with gentle descents from one to another, but the ground did never appear to us to be covered with wood, although we steered close along the shore: we even doubted if there was any there, not having been able to find it during the stay we made in all the three voyages.

AN

# HISTORICAL JOURNAL

OF MY

# VOYAGE

TO THE

# MAlOUINE ISLANDS,

WITH THE

Obfervations made on the Inhabitants and on the Natural Hift ry of the Places I met with in my Way.

I LEFT Pari he 17th of Auguft 1763, at two o'clock in the afternoon. We ftopped at Pontchartrain, in expectation of M. d' rboulin, at that time Adminiftrator General of the pofts in France, who was returning from his eftate at Montigny to Paris. M. de Bougainville, his nephew, was defirous of confulting with him on the arrangements neceffary to be taken relative to the xpences attending the building the two frigates, and the voyage we were going to undertake: M. d'Arboulin had a large fhare in the undertaking. We waited for him till near feven o'clock; he came at laft, and after a conference of about an hour fet out for Paris, and we at the fame time for St. Malo. We travelled the two following nights and days, ftopping only at Rennes for a few hours in the middle of the

day

day to let the heat go off, which was exceffive, and to faften one of our wheels, the fpokes of which could not be kept in the nave. On Sunday, the 20th, about two in the morning, we arrived at Beaufejour. This is a very pretty country feat, fituated at one end of St. Servant. M. Bougainville de Nerville, coufin-german to M. de Bougainville, had arrived there five days before us, and waited our coming. We drank but one glafs of cyder and ran to bed, having more defire to fleep than eat.

M. Duclos Guyot, who had been pitched upon to command the Eagle frigate, under the orders of M. de Bougainville, came to meet us at Beaufejour, with fome of the officers who were to embark with us. I paffed my time in feeing the towns of St. Malo and St. Servant, and the environs, till the 25th, when we went to Port Solidor, for the ceremony of baptifing our two frigates, which was performed with the ufual folemnities. All the officers and failors, who were to embark in them, were on board. M. N. chaplain and director of the hofpital of St. Saviour, in the town of St. Malo, faid mafs on board the Eagle, and performed all the ceremonies cuftomary upon fuch occafions. The two frigates, anchored clofe by each other, gave a general falute at the beginning of the mafs, and another at the end during the prayer for the King.

The next day, Don Jamin, prior of the Benedictines of the convent of St. Benoit, with whom I had been much connected, while he was profeffor of divinity in the abbey of St. Germain des Prés at Paris, entertained M. de Bougainville, Meff. Duclos Guyot, Chénart de la Gyraudais, de Belcourt, Lieutenant of infantry, l' Huillier de la Serre, Engineer, and myfelf, at dinner.

We embarked our baggage, beds, and other neceffaries for the voyage, and the 29th we lay on board. It was the firft of September before every thing was embarked.

By five o'clock that morning we left Solidor, with a brifk wind to N. W. in the frigate *Eagle*, with a crew of 100 men, mounting 20 guns, pierced for 24, commanded by the Sieur Duclos Guyot of St. Malo, Captain of a firefhip, in company with the floop sloop Sphinx, crew 40 men, mounting 8 guns and 6 swivels, commanded by the Sieur Chênart de la Gyraudais of St. Malo, Lieutenant of a frigate, both under the command of M. de Bougainville, Knight of St. Louis, Colonel of infantry, and Captain of a ship: at ten in the morning we were in the road of Rance, or St. Malo.

We were only waiting for a favourable wind to set sail the next morning, the 2d of September, when three or four persons of St. Malo raised difficu ⸺ s at the Admiralty upon our departure. M. de Bougainville, having received notice of it, went on shore to St. Malo, appeared at the Admiralty, and answered every objection so fully, that judgment was given in his favour. Thinking, however, that it was proper to inform the ministry of this transaction, he sent off a courier with dispatches at two in the morning, Sunday the 4th. The courier, who was his own servant, made so much haste, that he returned to St. Malo, with an answer, in fifty-nine hours from his setting off.

On the 8th at night, being the nativity of the Virgin, the wind appearing at S. S. W. orders were given to unmoor, which was accordingly done by one in the morning, and at half past six we set sail, the gale continuing fresh.

We kept under sail the 9th, and after having cleared the harbour, the wind being got about to S. W. and veering more and more to Westward, as we approached Cape Frehel, we came to anchor about noon. The sloop Sphinx followed our example. Our two frigates were then in the same situation in which the English fleet was at the affair of St. Cas, where they were so roughly handled. This anchorage is by no means secure: many ships have been lost here.

While we remained here, I took the opportunity of putting into a small cask, which held about six gallons of water, a composition of M. Sequin's, to preserve water from spoiling in long voyages. A chymist had given another, for the same purpose, to M. de Bougainville. It was a paste of a greyish cast; which seemed to be made of clay, and the powder of crude antimony.

Some

Some said, there was a mixture of crude mercury in it. But, as M. de Bougainville did not shew it to me before we got on board, I did not analyse it; and he, under the uncertainty he was in with respect to the ingredients, was not very desirous of trying the effects of it. For myself, as I knew the compofition of M. Sequin's drug, which is nothing but spirit of falt, and that, at the same time, it preserves the water from corruption, and renders it more wholesome and useful in preventing or curing the scurvy, I made no scruple of trying it. What were the effects of it will be seen in the sequel.

The 15th we got again under sail, and the wind being still contrary, got sight of the light-house of Frehel the 17th, at the distance of about four leagues: on the 18th we resolved to come to anchor. Accordingly we stood in to shore: the Sphinx did the same; and, after much difficulty in weathering the castle of la Latte, we anchored about two in the afternoon.

As the sea was become very calm, and the wind tolerably quiet, by nine this morning, M. Bougainville, Mess. de Belcourt, l'Huillier, Donat, de la Gyraudais Captain of the Sphinx and myself, had been to the island *Agôt* to shoot rabbits; but we saw only two in the course of three hours. As I had no other game in view than the finding of plants, or other curiofities, that might happen to lye in my way, I amufed myself with picking up the seeds of radishes, or wild horse-radish, and some shells. Towards noon, we began to find ourselves hungry, we had killed nothing, and were at a lofs for our dinner. Upon this we called a council, and it was resolved to go and beg a dinner of the prior of St. Jacut. We went immediately into our boat, and got to the abbey about two o'clock. The prior, and the other Benedictines, my brethren, received us in the most obliging manner, and treated us with the same hofpitality, which we had met with the sixth of this month, when we dined five or six of us with the prior of Benedictines at St. Malo. The prior of St. Jacut had dined on board the Eagle the 13th, and M. de Bougainville had done the honours in the best manner.

As foon as dinner was over at St. Jacut, I put the prior in mind of the offer he had made us of greens from their garden. He, with great civility, gave us leave to take what we pleafed, and we loaded our boat with cabbages and leeks.

On the 20th, at one in the afternoon, we fhipped our boats, wind at S. S. W. brifk gale, inclinable to fqualls. By three we were under fail. After doubling the point of the caftle of la Latte, we found the wind at N. W. fo came to anchor again.

At nine in the evening we had a violent fquall of wind, which lafted above half an hour. During this, an Acadian, one of our paffengers, ftood on the forecaftle with his arms folded, and, while the crew were all employed, kept looking on with the utmoft compofure. M. de Bougainville, to whom a complaint had been made of this very man a few days before for the fame kind of behaviour, and who had fpoke to him about it, could not now refrain for giving him a reprimand. The Acadian, without returning an anfwer, went below deck, and there exclaimed loudly againft this treatment to his wife, his father, and two other Acadian families, which were likewife paffengers, advifing them to follow his example; for after all, fays he, we were not hired, nor taken on board to work our paffage, but as volunteers and paffengers; and, for my part, I would much rather have ftaid in France, than have embarked on fuch conditions.

All this difcourfe was reported to M. de Bougainville, who was piqued at it, and with reafon. Thefe Acadian families had lived at St. Servant, and St. Malo, ever fince the Englifh took Acadia from us. The King allowed them fo much a head, in the fame manner as his regular troops; and thefe families had fcarce any other refource than this fort of pay and their own labour. M. de Bougainville offered to take them on board with him, and to carry them to a country where he would give them a landed property, and many other advantages, which they could never expect in France. He had even furnifhed them with goods and money in advance. Upon the report that was made to him of the difcourfe of this Acadian, he faid, there was nothing more to be done than

to

to set them on shore, and send them back to St. Servant; since they were fond of misery, they might go there and enjoy it. As soon as this was told to the other families, it made so great an impression on them, that the women burst into tears, and the men upbraided the Acadian, who had been the cause of it, and a disagreement among them ensued. Of this M. de Bougainville was soon informed. The next day, the 21st, after prayers, he called them all before him; there are, said he, some discontented persons among you, who repent of having embarked with me. I do not require you to do the duty of common sailors: I did not take you on board with me upon that footing; but, at the same time, I did not mean that you should consider yourselves as mere passengers, and not lend a hand upon occasion. You are at liberty to go back to St. Malo, St. Servant, or whatever place you think fit; you have only to speak, and you will be set on shore immediately.

The Acadian and his father declared, they chose to return to St. Servant. The two other families desired to go the voyage. Early in the afternoon the father, the son and his wife were landed near St. Cast, with their effects; and M. de Bougainville, out of charity, left them the money he had obtained in advance for them from the King. The other two families were rejoiced at this separation and congratulated each other upon their departure. The wife was of a peevish temper, and her husband was so jealous of her, that he would scarce leave her an instant; he watched even her slightest motions, and would infallibly have disturbed the good understanding they were desirous of preserving among themselves. A perfect union prevailed between the two families, that made the voyage with us, and were landed and settled by us on the Malouine Islands. One of them consisted of a man, his wife, two children, one a boy of three years old, the other a girl of one year, and two sisters of the wife, one twenty, and the other seventeen. The other family was composed of a man, his wife, a boy of four years old, and the wife's

sister,

## TO THE MALOUINE ISLANDS.

fister, about sixteen. The wife was ready to lie in, when we left the island on our return to France.

In the morning of the 23d of September, the wind got to E. N. E. an easy gale. As it seemed steddy in that point, M. Duclos our Captain made a signal to bring in our long-boat, and yawl, which were on shore, the long boat to get water, and the yawl to fetch the sailors, and the women that washed the linen. M. de Bougainville, M. de Belcourt, M. l'Huillier, and M. Donat were out in pursuit of game, near two leagues up the country, and proposed to dine at the Castle of la Latte, where M. Mauclair and myself expected them till half past two. M. Duclos seeing that none of them came on board fired a gun, which hastened the return of our sportsmen; but as the time pressed, and they had dined in the country, they would not make any stay at the castle of la Latte. We sent the dinner on board again, where M. Mauclair, and I contented ourselves with a single glass till supper.

At three, signal was given to the Sphinx to weigh anchor. At six, our boats being embarked, we set sail from Cape Frehel; and after several tacks to double the castle of la Latte, at nine we were North and South of the point of the Cape.

On Monday, the 25th, about four in the afternoon, we threw out a line with a double hook. The hook was scarcely in the water, before a fish, in shape and colour resembling a mackrel, bit at it, and was taken. It weighed about thirty pounds, and had not two handfuls of entrails, liver, &c. All the rest was solid flesh, like that of the thunny, of which it had the colour and flavour. An excellent soup was made of it the next day. Several slices of it were brought up with different sauces, and we found it very good: it is somewhat dry, but not so much as the bonito. It is called by the French, *Grand-Oreille*.

The hook, with which it was caught, was not baited with flesh, fish, or any insect. It is composed of two stems of iron, about the thickness of the quill of a pen, fastened together. They cover this double shank with tow, so as to give it the form of a

spindle:

# JOURNAL OF MY VOYAGE

spindle: the tow is covered with a piece of strong white cloth and a plate of lead; to this they join two or four white feathers from the wing of a goose or fowl, placing them in such a manner as to resemble fins when extended. In this state, the hook has nearly the appearance of a flying fish. The end of the shank is turned in a ring, through which they put a brass wire of almost the same thickness, and about two feet and a half in length; the whole of this is thrown into the water, being fastened to a cord about the thickness of one's little finger, and of the length of twelve fathom. One end of this cord is fastened to the stern of the ship; the other, where the hook is, drags at a great distance in the track of the ship.

We continued our voyage for several days without any thing remarkable, wind varying, and weather generally stormy. We saw several ships at a distance, which we took to be on their return from the cod fishery on the banks of Newfoundland. One of them brought to, and spoke with us.

On the 2d of October, about nine in the morning, we descried a vessel without masts, and bore down upon her in order to give her what assistance we could. At ten we spoke with her. She proved to be a Dutch Merchantman of Amsterdam; she was coming from Curaſol, and meeting with a gust of wind at about a hundred leagues from Bermudas, they were obliged to cut away the mizzen and main mast. We inquired if they were in want of any thing; they answered, that they had five French ladies on board whom they were carrying to France, but that they could not put their boat to sea. We acquainted them, that we were just come from France, and should not return thither for several months, for which reason we could not take charge of the ladies; but if they were in want of any thing else, they might come and fetch it. They again told us, that they could not put their boat to sea. The sea indeed ran high, and we not caring to expose ours to it, wished them a better voyage and continued our course S. W. ¼ W.

The 5th, at break of day we difcovered a fail. We were in thofe latitudes, where the Sallee Rovers fometimes cruize; and we knew, they had a Frigate at fea, called the Bird, of 36 guns and 300 men, which the Englifh had fold to the Salletines, and they had given the command of it to a renegade captain of Provence, a good feaman and of approved courage. They had alfo a floop of 12 guns and a hundred men. In confequence of this, the commandant of our two frigates had iffued out orders, that they might be able to act in concert, in cafe of an attack. The plan of the engagement was fixed up; the guns and fmall arms were prepared; every man repaired to the poft allotted him, and we bore down. It was fettled, that if this was the Salletine frigate, the Sphinx fhould hoift Englifh colours, and feem to make all the fail fhe could to get under the fire of the frigate, to avoid falling into our hands. We in confequence were to hoift French colours, and make a fhew of purfuing the Sphinx, firing at her at the fame time as if to bring her to. As foon as the Salletine frigate fhould be got between the Sphinx and us, the Sphinx was to hoift French colours, and then make her a compliment of her whole broadfide, fo that fhe fhould find herfelf between two fires. It was hoped, that by this manœuvre, we might make up for our want of numbers, and fhatter her fo by a vigorous attack, that fhe fhould be obliged to ftrike.

Our men were brave fellows, and difplayed at this time an air of gaiety and refolution. They had indeed a great confidence in the fkill and courage of our captains, and other officers, with whom they had made cruizes in the laft war, and under whofe command they had taken many prizes, and had even made themfelves mafters of fome Englifh fhips at clofe quarters.

As we neared the fhip we had feen, we thought we could difcover that fhe was Englifh built. But as we knew, the Englifh had fold feveral fhips to the Salletines; and this, notwithftanding we bore down upon her, hoifted no colours, we took her for a Salletine fcout. On this we fired a gun, and advanced upon her. Still fhe hoifted no colours. We now fired a

loaded

loaded gun, and it is probable she felt the wind of the ball. She then lay to for a moment, and afterwards stood for us, without hoisting. When she was got pretty near, she hoisted English colours, and passed so close to us, that we discovered the captain to be the same Guernsey man, who served as pilot to the English in the last war, when they made their descents at Cancale and St. Cas. The usual questions were put to him in French, as, from what port, and whither he was bound, and what was the name of his ship. He made no answer. M. de Belcourt took the speaking trumpet, and put the same questions to him in English, with all the embellishments of the emphatic sea style, adding, that he deserved to have had his ship sunk for not hoisting, after having been twice fired at. To this he replied in English, and alledged, that his colours had been entangled among the goods. It proved to be a merchant ship with two masts, bound, as he told us, from Lisbon to St. Michael's, one of the Azores.

The 8th in the morning being calmed, we sent out our cutter for M. de la Gyraudais, captain of the Sphinx. He came on board us at seven. M. de Bougainville, and M. du Clos our captain, had a conference with him. He received orders for his rendezvous in case of separation, and exact drawings of the places we were to touch at, and of those we expected to find in our course. M. de la Gyraudais returned to his own ship about nine.

The 9th and 10th, the calms continued with fogs, and some storms of rain. The 11th the same. The currents here seem to run North; as may be conjectured from the difference we found between our reckonings and observation of yesterday and to-day, in which time we had made seven leagues and a half of way. The 13th in the morning, the sea being fallen after a storm which rose the evening before, we caught three fish called bonitos. There were not less than fifteen of them and two gold fish, playing about on the starboard of our stern. We saw at the same time some other fishes which go under the name of pilots. One of these was taken in a net; the bonitos were caught with a

line,

## TO THE MALOUINE ISLANDS.

line, baited with the figure of a flying fish. These weighed each of them about twenty pounds; the pilot was not more than eight inches long.

The 14th, being between 29° and 30° latitude, we expected to meet with the trade winds, of which we had hitherto had no signs. Some of our sailors, who had the most experience, had assured us they were commonly found under this parallel. M. de Bougainville was so impatient for them, that he never stirred out of his cabin without going to examine the compass. He was obliged however to put up with such winds as happened to blow.

At two in the afternoon, the Sphinx, which was to eastward of us, attracted our attention by hoisting a white flag at the foremast head, which was the signal agreed upon in case of seeing land. We answered her with the same signal, and found it to be Palm Island, the farthest to the North West of the Canary Islands. It bore E. S. E. of us by the compass, and appeared to us, at about 15 or 18 leagues distance, in the form it is represented in the plate.

We discovered another at the same time, more to the South West, which exhibited nearly the figure B.

The sight of these Islands was of use in correcting our reckonings and observations, and we found that we were about 20 leagues farther West than we had reckoned.

The 16th, at three in the afternoon, we made a signal to the Sphinx, that we were going to make all our sail; which we had not hitherto done since our departure, in order that she might be able to keep up with us. The Sphinx was not near so fast a sailer as our ship, and had kept us back at least a hundred leagues; but we did not choose to quit company sooner, for fear of meeting with the Sallee Rovers, which would have required our mutual assistance to extricate us from them. At this time that we had got out of the latitudes, in which they cruize, we resolved to stretch away for the place of rendezvous; that by arriving there as soon as possible, we might have all the refreshments,

ments, which the Sphinx might ſtand in need of, ready againſt her coming in, by which means our ſtay might be ſhortened.

As ſoon as the Sphinx had anſwered our ſignal, we ſet more ſails, the wind blowing freſh, and by ſix o'clock in the evening ſhe was at leaſt three leagues a ſtern of us; and before next morning we loſt ſight of her.

On the 18th and 19th, we ſaw a great number of flying fiſhes. They were purſued by thunnies and gold fiſh, which ſprang three or four feet out of the water to ſeize them. We threw out ſeveral hooks, but not one of them would bite.

During great part of both theſe days, our weather had been very ſtormy and the ſea ran high. On the morning of the 20th, a calm ſucceeded, with ſome rain at intervals.

Theſe calms and the winds which never blew freſh, and were continually changing, did not promiſe us a ſhort trip. We began all of us to be impatient at not meeting with the trade winds, which would have been ſo uſeful, and were ſo much the object of our wiſhes. M. de Bougainville particularly exclaimed againſt all former navigators, who have laid it down as a certainty, that thoſe winds never fail to blow in theſe latitudes. He told us, that, as we had experience of the contrary, he was reſolved on his return to Paris, to preſent a memorial to the Academy of Sciences, to prove the non-exiſtence of trade winds; at leaſt, the little dependence that navigators ought to have on what is related of their conſtant influence.

The 21ſt in the afternoon, we ſaw a great number of flying fiſhes, and of their enemies the bonitos, gold fiſh, and thunnies.

The morning of the 22d preſented us with about half a ſcore of flying fiſh, which attempting to fly over the frigate had fallen foul of the ſails, and dropped upon deck. They were dreſſed for dinner, and we found them extremely good and very delicate eating. I kept one in order to paint it from the life, the figure of it is to be found in the plate.

This fiſh in theſe latitudes is of a fine blue on the back, which fades or grows ſtronger inſenſibly towards the bottom of the belly,

belly, .. e the .lour is a blue with a silver caſt. Its wings are fi.. .f a gre..ter length, which in general extend as far as the ta.., but in ' me do not reach farther than to the middle of the body; though the fiſh is of the ſame ſhape, length and thickneſs. The one, whoſe figure is repreſented in the plate, was about ten inches from one extremity to the other.

On the 23d in the afternoon, ſome of the ſailors ſeeing a number of thunnies, got on the prow of the frigate with a harpoon, and caught one of them, which weighed 72 pounds. On a cloſe examination of it, I perceived ſome animals ſticking; and as it were glued upon its ears. See the figure of them in their natural ſize in the plate. The figure marked D is the upper part of the animal, which reſembled a compoſition of ſtrings of catgut almoſt tranſparent. Its eyes were two little black ſpots placed above the mouth B. They faſten themſelves on the thunny by means of two legs marked C, and two others conſiderably ſmaller marked D.

I took ſome ſea water and put it in a clean glaſs tumbler, that I might keep this animal alive and ſee its motions. I perceived in this water a black ſpot, which at firſt I took for a ſpeck of dirt; but when I attempted to take it out with the end of my finger, I obſerved the ſuppoſed atom to avoid my touch, and plunge under water. I attended to its motions, and found it to be a living creature of the ſtructure and ſize deſcribed in the plate. It was a ſpecies of cylinder formed by ten rings, ſo ſlight and tranſparent, that it was neceſſary to put the glaſs between the light and the eye of the obſerver in order to perceive it. It ſwam by means of two long fibres B B, and two others that are almoſt imperceptible C, which in gathering up and lengthening out again, gave the rings of the cylinder a motion perfectly cor- reſponding to that of a quail-pipe, or a powder-machine uſed by hair-dreſſers. The body A, was of a violet colour towards C, and of a light brown towards B B.

We ſaw likewiſe a great quantity of flying fiſh, and we caught with a hook a bonito and a pilot, which I have painted from the life.

This

The naturalists pretend, on the authority no doubt of some seamen, that the pilot always goes before the shark, and that it is for this reason that fish has obtained the name of the pilot, as being director of the other's course. For my own part, I have sometimes obferved one or two pilots before or after each shark we caught; but we have often seen pilots without sharks, as well as sharks without pilots.

Father Feuillée, p. 173, confounds the pilot with the sucking fish, and makes them both the same. "The sharks, says he, are accompanied by little fishes, which keep continually with them, and choose rather to share their fate than to abandon them; they swim always a head of them, at such a distance that the sharks cannot catch them, which has procured them the name of pilots. We did not catch a single shark without finding some of these small fishes sticking to his back, by means of a yellowish, cartilaginous membrane of a circular form, which they have on the top of their heads: this membrane has an infinite number of small holes filled with fibres, which, to all appearance, serve to draw from the skin of the shark some substance for their nourishment.

The same author allows the shark but three rows of teeth, one of which, he says, is composed of triangular teeth, and these are of a greater length than the others; I have counted seven rows of them in the mouths of all the sharks we took, all of them moveable and triangular. Nor were the suckers of these sucking fish of a circular, but of an elliptical form, such as is described in the figure I have given of them in the sequel.

The 24th the same winds continued, which we had had for some days. These were in fact, the trade winds we had so long looked out for, under which name are comprehended all those which blow from S. S. E. through the easterly point to N. N. E. inclusive. These are the most favourable winds that can blow, for ships bound from Europe to South America, the windward and leeward Islands, and the Gulph of Mexico.

About eight in the morning on the 25th, we had fight of land on our starboard side. At noon, we judged it to be the Island

Island of Bonavifta, one of the Cape de Verd Iflands, fituated North Eaft of St. Jago, the largeft and moft populous of thofe ifles. It bore North Weft of us, about nine leagues: the figure of it, in the moft extenfive view we had, appeared according to the reprefentation in the plate.

This ifland, like the reft, abounds in wild horfes, goats, and feveral other animals, notwithftanding the foil is rocky and barren. It is feen at a great diftance by means of its white cliffs, from which circumftance it derives its name.

We now found that we were near twenty leagues farther eaftward than our reckoning.

The wind blowing frefh from N. E. to N. N. E. accompanied with fine weather, afforded us a view of another of the Cape de Verd Iflands, about four o'clock in the afternoon, which goes by the name of Mayo's Ifland. The foil here likewife is rocky and barren. There are neverthelefs a great number of bulls, cows, goats and affes. A confiderable quantity of falt alfo is made here. The air is hot and unhealthy. The moft fouthern point of the ifland bore S. W. ¼ W. and the moft northern W. ¼ S. W. of us, and the whole appeared as exhibited in the plate.

The 27th, after having had fome lightning in the night, and in the morning a cloudy fky, with a high fea, and a fquall of wind at half paft ten, fucceeded by a ftorm at E. S. E. which was of fhort duration, the wind came about to the ufual points with an eafy gale; and about three in the afternoon, we caught a bonito, which weighed forty pounds.

The 28th and 29th, proved very ftormy, but notwithftanding this we were not driven out of our courfe.

On Sunday the 30th, in the morning, the fky cleared up and the wind came fair again.

At eight o'clock, Peter Lainez of St. Malo, a cabbin boy, about twelve years of age, going into the forecaftle fell overboard, without any one's knowing how the accident happened. The fecond mate, who was going a ftern, feeing him float along the ftarboard fide, cried out immediately, that there was one of the crew overboard. We ran at this time four knots an hour, with a quarter wind. They threw out a plank directly from the stern gallery, and whatever else was at hand either of board or any other buoyant materials, in hopes the poor fellow might be able to reach some one of them, and keep himself by that means above water, till the boat could be put out to take him up. The whole crew was in motion, and every possible means were used to stop the ship. Many ran up the main mast, others got on the quarter deck, all intent on looking for, and discovering the cabbin boy. After this, the boat was put to sea, though it was then very rough; it was manned with six stout sailors, under the command of the mate, who went in search of the cabbin boy to the right and left, wherever they thought they had a chance of finding him, to the distance of half a league from the ship, but without success. When they had been out about three quarters of an hour, a signal was made for the return of the boat, which was effected with much difficulty. We re-embarked her, and continued our route.

The names of the crew were then called over, in order to find out who was the person missing; for we did not yet know that it was the cabbin boy I have just now mentioned. He was the only one, that did not appear. They looked in his hammock and searched the whole ship over for him, and not finding him any where, it was easy to conclude, that this Peter Lainez was the hand we had lost.

At four in the afternoon, after vespers, the cloaths of the deceased cabbin boy, an inventory of which had been taken in the morning, were sold by auction. Our commandant, M. de Bougainville, bought almost every thing, and distributed them gratis among the cabbin boys, who were least in a condition to procure any for themselves. The sale amounted to fifty crowns.

The 31st, the weather was stormy at intervals, each storm being succeeded by an almost dead calm. During these calms we caught, in less than two hours, two sharks, which weighed about a hundred pounds each. They had both of them fishes

sticking

sticking to their bodies near the head. These fish are called sucking fish. I painted one after the life, in two figures; the first shews the side of the sucker, which is upon the head; the other figure represents the belly of the fish. It was seven inches in length.

A few hours before, some hundred porpoises, whose figure may be seen in the plate, made their appearance within pistol shot, and seemed as if they had come on purpose to amuse us. They sprang out of the water in an extraordinary manner. Several of them in cutting their capers, leaped at least three or four feet high, and turned round not less than three times in the air, as if they had been on a spit. One may judge from hence of the strength of this fish.

On the 2d of November, at three in the afternoon, a storm rose at South East attended with a heavy rain. During this storm one of the sailors brought me a flying fish, eight inches and a half long, which had just fallen on the forecastle. We had seen, before the storm came on, shoals of thunnies and bonitos. They leaped out of the water, and made the sea foam, as if they were fighting with each other.

On the 3d, a shark of a middling size, and about a hundred and fifty pound weight, came a stern of us. He bit at the bait, as soon as it was offered to him. When he was raised out of the water, he gave a sudden jirk, by which he disengaged himself from the hook, leaving part of his jaw behind him. Not dismayed or disheartened by this loss, the shark perceiving the same piece of bacon, which had been made use of as a bait for him the first time, thrown out again, returned to it with the same greediness, and swallowed at once not only the bacon, but the piece of his jaw, without however being caught by the hook. Another piece of bacon was immediately put on: the shark was without doubt very hungry, for he came again to seize that. But as at this time there was a dead calm, and besides, this fish is neither wholesome nor palatable food, instead of endeavouring to take him, we amused ourselves near an hour with only letting him smell the bait. When he attempted to swallow it, we drew it suddenly out of the water, and this was repeated at least a dozen times without producing the effect, which is said to be so common upon these occasions, of making the shark spring out of the water in order to seize it.

Another thing I must observe, is, that I did not see him turn upon his back to swallow the bait, but only a very little on one side. M. de Bougainville, while we were amusing ourselves in this manner, fired at him twice with musquet ball, but whether he missed him, though almost at the muzzle of his piece, or whether the skin was too tough for the ball to penetrate, the shark was not in the least disturbed in his motions by it; he kept swimming round and round the stern, and at last swallowed this second bait without being hooked. A squall of wind rising about this time, we left the shark to employ himself elsewhere.

The 4th and 5th, we had storms and calms at intervals. The 6th, about ten at night, we had a squall of wind, which cleared the sky. At this time we saw some stars; a sight we had not had for near a week, the sky having been always gloomy and covered.

The morning of the 7th, the sun rose fine, but with several clouds scattered round it. Before it appeared, the rays darting upon these clouds exhibited one of the most beautiful sights in the world for variety and brightness of colours. I was mortified more than can be imagined, not having it in my power to paint such a day-break, which would have made a most brilliant picture. I have only been able to preserve a very imperfect sketch of a setting sun, which we all of us admired for near half an hour. But it is not possible with water colours to execute a picture, upon which any exact idea of it might be formed. These colours are too faint to express the brilliancy and lustre, with which the borders of the clouds were illuminated by the rays of the sun. Oil colours would without doubt be less defective in the representation; but I had not any with me.

Besides,

Besides, it would require a skilful painter to execute such a picture properly; and I have not that qualification.

The weather continuing fine and very hot, we had all the hammocks between decks taken down, in order to dry the cloaths of the crew, which had been all wetted in the rainy days. This dampness of cloaths is a much more immediate cause of the scurvy, and many other disorders, than the salt provisions which are used at sea. A captain cannot pay too great an attention to the preserving of cleanliness among his crew, and to the airing of the hammocks, cotts, &c. if he would prevent disorders. Our captain assured me of the truth of this observation, from his own experience in the different voyages he has made to China, India, Peru, and Canada. He told me, he had always paid strict attention to this article, to which as well as to the choice of proper food, he attributed the general good health his crews had enjoyed during those voyages.

In the afternoon, we saw a large bird called by some *Goellan*, or *Gull*, and by others *Caignard*. At night a single swallow came and perched on the main mast yard, and the next morning continued flying round the ship.

During the night several flying fish dropped upon our deck. They were all of that species, which have the fins, that serve them for wings, reaching to their tail.

At five in the morning of the 9th, a bird pretty nearly of the size of a pigeon, but something longer, coming to perch on the foremast yard, one of the sailors caught him in his hand. This bird, which I have painted, and whose figure in half the natural size may be seen in the plate, is of a light brown inclining to red, almost the colour of a nut. The largest feathers of the wing and tail, are of a darker brown, or rather blackish. The bill is black, strait, and small, pierced through in the middle, with a small protuberance below, about the length of the bird's head. The upper part of the head near the bill is white; it then becomes of a pearl colour, growing deeper towards the neck, which is pretty long in proportion to its thickness. The feet are

of

of a dark grey, webbed like thofe of water fowl. After having made ufe of this bird in the manner I fhall mention hereafter, M. de Bougainville gave him to me to paint. I put him in a fmall prefs in my cabbin, where I found him the next day very lively, and fo little alarmed at having been taken, that when I fet him on my table, he put himfelf in the attitude, in which I have drawn him. I gave him fome food, and he eat of it, ftill keeping in the fame pofture, and continued fo for three days, by which means I had full time to paint him to the life. Some of our feamen faid, it was a fpecies of the *booby* bird, becaufe it fuffered itfelf to be caught in the hand, and grew tame, as foon as it was taken: but he had not however the crow bill, which belongs to the booby, and has procured it the name of the duck with the narrow bill. Our feamen gave the fame name to another bird alfo, very much refembling this, except that it has a crooked bill, like that of a parrot.

About ten o'clock in the forenoon the fea appearing of a light green caft, inftead of its ufual blue, and the colour continuing the fame at fix in the evening, we fufpected that this appearance was occafioned by our being in the neighbourhood of fome land, or fhoal. We therefore took the precaution of founding; but though we founded with a hundred and twenty fathom of line, we found no bottom. Thus we were freed from the apprehenfions we had entertained, and which arofe from an error of the charts; almoft all of them placing Brazil near fifty leagues farther Weft, than it is found to be by the obfervations of our feamen. We refolved however to found a fecond time, if the fea had continued of the fame colour; but as it appeared the next morning of its ufual blue caft, we continued our courfe without taking the trouble of founding.

Our mates, boatfwain, and thofe of the crew, who in former voyages had paffed the line, had for the laft week been making preparations for *the ceremony of Baptifm*, which is performed on the part and in the name of the *Bon-homme la ligne*, to all thofe, who

who have never before paſſed the line, without diſtinction of rank, or quality, or exception of perſon.

About ſeven o'clock, as we were at ſupper, we heard the ſmacking of a whip, which announced to us the arrival of a courier from the *Bon-homme la ligne*, according to cuſtom, the evening before the ceremony I juſt now mentioned is to be performed. This was the cockſwain properly equipped for a courier. He knocked at the cabbin door. We called out, who is there? A meſſenger, ſays he, from the *Bon-homme la ligne*, lord and governor of theſe latitudes. Let him in, ſays M. de Bougainville. The door was opened, the meſſenger alighted, and came in, leaving his equipage at the door. This equipage was formed by two ſailors tied back to back, and going upon all fours. One of them had on his head a ſwab, to repreſent the tail of the beaſt, the other had one for the mane, and a maſk of paſteboard in the ſhape of a horſe's head. The furniture conſiſted of the quarter cloths belonging to one of the boats; that is to ſay, of a carpet, or large piece of blue cloth, adorned with flowers de luce made of yellow ſtuff.

The meſſenger being introduced addreſſed our Commandant in the following terms: " *the Bon-homme la ligne, lord governor of theſe latitudes,* underſtanding, that the brave **Chevalier** de Bougainville, commander of the Eagle frigate, is arrived in his dominions, has ordered me to come and compliment him on his part, to let him know with how much joy he hath received the news of his arrival, to bring the beſt wiſhes for his health, and to deliver him a letter, in which my maſter hath expreſſed his own ſentiments.

M. de Bougainville read the letter, which was conceived in the following terms; *Brave Chevalier, your illuſtrious actions have rendered the French name highly celebrated in Canada: your renown has reached the latitudes over which I r ign, on the wings of fame, and the hearts of my ſubjects are ſo filled with veneration for you, that the gold fiſh and bonitos, the thunnies and porpoiſes as ſoon as they deſcried the frigate Eagle, which you command, came in ſhoals to me yeſterday*

## JOURNAL OF MY VOYAGE

*to announce your arrival. The joy, with which your presence had animated their hearts, they expressed by repeated bounds and leaps, which they continued for a long time as they passed by your ship. I send this ambassador to notify to you my own particular share in the general joy, at the same time that he delivers this letter into your hands, and I hope to-morrow to acquaint you in person, how much I am delighted with the visit you pay me.*

Signed BON-HOMME LA LIGNE."

Given at the 54th minute of the first degree of latitude, and in 29 degrees three minutes longitude, of my northern dominions, the 9th day of November in the year of my reign, 7763.

M. de Bougainville, when he had read the letter, told the envoy, that he expected to have the honour of presenting himself before the *Bon-homme* the next day, and of giving an answer to his letter in person. Let the courier drink, added he, and take care of his horse: it must be a fine one; lead it in, I have a great curiosity to see it. The horse was introduced curvetting, tossing his head, pawing, and neighing. As it was possible he might be tired with his journey, and might be thirsty, a glass of wine was offered him, which he drank. The courier informed us, that his horse had two heads, one at his stem and the other at his stern, upon which the head at his stern also was treated with a glass of wine.

The courier, before he retired, presented to the commandant a bird on the part of the *Bon-homme la ligne*, the illustrious president of these latitudes having requested his acceptance of it as a token of his goodwill and affection. This was the bird which they had just before caught in the hand, and which I have mentioned above. But as we knew nothing of this at the time, we were not a little surprised at the present. We took it at first for an artificial bird, till by pecking with his beak he convinced us, that he was not only a real bird, but also in full vigour. On examination, we found it to be a fresh water bird, which served only to increase our surprize.

After

After fupper, we affembled on the quarter-deck, and danced minuets, country dances, &c. to the tabor, and after that to two violins till near ten o'clock, when we retired to our cabbins.

Thurfday, the 10th of November, at five in the morning we paffed the line, at 29 degrees 3 minutes longitude according to our reckoning. At ten o'clock we faw a bird called the *Frigate*. This bird is frequently found at four hundred leagues diftance from land, though it is faid not to be able to fupport itfelf on the water without perifhing, which is the cafe with birds, that are not ufed to live in that element. Its legs are fhort, thick, and gathered up clofe to the body. Its feet are not webbed, but furnifhed with ftrong pointed claws. Some of them meafure nine feet from the tip of one wing to that of the other. By the extent of its wings when they are fpread, this bird eafily fupports itfelf in the air, the motion it gives them being almoft imperceptible. Sometimes it rifes to fo great a height, that the ftrongeft eye lofes fight of it. When it comes near any fhips, it flies round the vanes of the maft head, going and returning very frequently, but never perching on any part. The fize of it is nearly the fame as that of a fowl. Its look is fteady and piercing. It darts upon its prey with an incredible fwiftnefs and feizes it both with its talons and bill, the upper part of which is unciform. The males have a red granulated membrane defcending from their bill as far as the middle of their neck. The feathers on the belly are of a light grey, which at a diftance make it appear white. Thofe on the back and wings are brown. This bird faw fome flying fifh, which he caught very artfully, by fkimming along the furface of the fea, while they were flying to avoid becoming a prey to the bonitos, and other fifhes, which are enemies to them. It is faid, that he purfues the gull likewife and other fea birds, to make them difgorge the fifh they have fwallowed that he may feize upon them himfelf.

I do not well know for what reafon this bird is called the frigate, unlefs it be by way of comparifon between the fwiftnefs of his flight, and the lightnefs of thofe fhips, which go under that name, and are ufually better failers than any others.

Not having been able to get a nearer view of this bird than from the top of the mafts, I cannot pretend to gi.. a defcription of it otherwife than from thofe perfons, who have feen and handled them. Father Labat (Nouveaux Voyages, tom. 6. p. 395) in addition to what I have already obferved, fays, that this bird has large black eyes; that he feldom alights on the ground, and generally keeps himfelf perched, becaufe the fize of his wings, and the fpace which is necefary in order to put them in motion, would render it very difficult for him to rife from the ground. The feathers on his back and wings according to the fame author are black, thick and ftrong; and thofe which cover the ftomach and thighs, are more delicate and not fo black: perhaps that which I faw was the female, or at leaft a young one. I killed fome of them (continues the father) in the ifland where we were, for their greafe. It is faid to be an admirable fpecific in the fciatica, and in a numbnefs of the limbs, and other accidents arifing from a want of circulation. The greafe is to be heated, and while it is on the fire, the parts affected are to be well rubbed and chafed in order to open the pores; and fome good brandy, or fpirits of wine are to be mixed with the fat immediately before it is applied. A piece of blotting paper, fteeped in this mixture, may be laid on the part, with comprefles and a bandage to keep it in its place.

We now come to the baptifm of the line.

About two o'clock in the afternoon, they began by placing a bathing tub full of fea water and two buckets on the quarter-deck: athwart, from the ftarboard to the larboard fide, they ftretched a rope, which they called *the line*, the fame they ufed for founding; then the drum was beaten for every body to affemble. The weather proved very feafonable for the ceremony, for it was extremely hot. Near the gangway, which leads to the ftate room, was placed a bench covered with the quarter cloths, which had ferved the evening before to caparifon the

courier's

## TO THE MALOUINE ISLANDS. 25

courier's horfe; and this was to be the feat or throne for the lord governor of the line, his chancellor, and the vicar, who was to adminifter the baptifm.

When every body was affembled, a voice conveyed through a fpeaking trumpet called out from the main maft top; *what is the name of this ſhip I ſee below within my dominions? The Eagle*, anfwered the captain.—*Who commands her?*—M. le Chevalier de Bougainville.—*I am very glad of it; it will give me pleaſure to admit him into my ſociety, according to the eſtabliſhed forms and ceremonies. I received an account of him yeſterday, and as a teſtimony of my ſatisfaction, am coming down into his ſhip with all my court.*— *A la bonne heure*, replied M. de Bougainville, a fea phrafe to exprefs, that one underſtands what has been faid, and that one approves of and confents to it.

Upon this a failor, who had no other covering than a pair of tarred breeches, and on his fhoulders the fkin of a fheep with the wool on, ftained with red and yellow in large blotches, with a cap on his head made likewife of the fkin of a fheep painted, with a pair of bull's horns faftened on the top, and feveral pieces of wood blacked, and feathers of turkies and fowls upon it; his breaft, arms, legs and face, being ftained in the fame manner with red and yellow colours, diluted in oil, and large black whifkers; this failor, I fay, thus accoutred came down from the main maft top by the fhrouds on the larboard fide, with an iron chain round his middle by way of a girdle; in one hand he held the end of this chain, and in the other a pot-hook.

Six cabbin boys marched before him naked, painted from head to foot with red and yellow, fome of them in blotches, others in crofs bands after the manner of the favages.

As foon as they came on the quarter-deck, the failor drew them up in order, placed their thumbs on the rope, and made them dance for a quarter of an hou to the tabor. After this they approached the bathing tub, and the failor threw feveral buckets of water over them.

G 2  This

This ceremony being finished, the defcent of the lord governor of the line was announced by the throwing of white kidney beans, for fugar plumbs, from the main maft top on the quarter-deck. The Bon-homme la ligne, preceded by his whole court, took the fame route as the failor and the cabbin boys; he defcended flowly and majeftically. His court was compofed of the fecond mate, the boatfwain, the pilot, and the gunner. The firft mate reprefented the Bon-homme la ligne. He was covered with white fheep fkins fewed together fo as to make a garment of one piece. His cap, which was compofed of the fame materials came down over his eyes. A quantity of tow mixed with wool ferved him for a peruke and a beard. He had a falfe nofe made of painted wood. Inftead of a ribband, he wore acrofs his fhoulders a ftring of trucks of the parrels, as large as goofe eggs.

His attendants were dreffed up much in the fame manner, except that fome of them had their arms or their legs naked, and painted red and yellow, as likewife their faces ornamented with large black whifkers, and long wooden nofes. One carried a mace, or club fuch as the favages ufe, another a bow, a third an ax, and a fourth a calumet. Near the lord governor was his chancellor bearing the fcepter, which was a fort of mop, fuch as is ufed in fpunging a cannon, after it has been fired. The cockfwain dreffed like a woman, and painted with coarfe red paint mixed up in oil, flood clofe to the Bon-homme, who called him his daughter. As to the vicar, he was cloathed in a fort of linen robe, covered with pitch and tar; a cord about the thicknefs of one's thumb ferved him for a fafh. He wore a fquare cap of pafteboard blacked over, a mafk of the fame, and a linen gown painted red, and carried a book in his hand. One cabbin boy had a fquare cap painted red and black, another held a wooden cenfer, hanging by pack threads platted in the fhape of a chain, and in the other hand a chafing difh with fire to heat the perfumes, which were made of pitch and tar. A third cabbin

cabbin boy carried a bow and an arrow; and a fourth a bason and watering pot full of sea water for the baptism.

The whole proceſſion being come down upon the deck, and the crew aſſembled there, the lord governor deſired a conference with the commandant, who immediately advanced to receive him. *You are welcome hither, M. le Chevalier; I am happy to ſee you*, ſaid the Bon homme la ligne: *excuſe me if I do not make you a long compliment; my lungs are ſo feeble, I can ſcarcely ſpeak. You muſt not be ſurpriſed at this; for I am 7763 years old: it is even with difficulty that I can write. I have therefore ordered my ſecretary to do it for me; and here is a letter, which will acquaint you with every thing. I had to ſay to you, as well as my chancellor. I am come down from my palace on purpoſe to admit you into my ſociety. I hope you will make no ſcruple of ſubmitting to the ceremony of being baptized agreeable to the cuſtom on this occaſion.* M. de Bougainville received the letter, read it, and replied *à la bonne heure*. After this he ſaluted the daughter of the Bon-homme, and after congratulating him on his having ſo handſome a daughter, drew near the line, or rope, which was ſtretched acroſs. The officers of the Bon-homme accompanied him to it, and the lord governor ſeated himſelf on his throne with his daughter and his chancellor.

The officers tied M. de Bougainville's left thumb on the line with a red ribband. The reſt of us gathered round, viz. Meſſ. de Nerville, de Belcourt, l'Huillier and myſelf, and they tied our left thumbs with the ſame ribband.

The vicar with a ſolemn air, and with his book in his hand, approached M. de Bougainville. At the left hand of the vicar was the ſcepter-bearer of the lord governor; and at his left hand two cabbin boys dreſſed like ſavages; one of whom carried a plate covered with a napkin folded, to receive the tribute, which is called *ranſom*, becauſe they content themſelves with pouring a ſmall quantity of ſea water on the heads of thoſe, who ranſom themſelves, inſtead of plunging them in the ſea, as is done in the puniſhment of ducking: the other held a bow in one hand and

and a censer in the other. The censer was a piece of wood, hollowed in the shape of a porringer, with three handles, and suspended by three pieces of cord. The custom of dipping in the sea in performing this ceremony of baptism is abolished: it having been considered that that practice might be attended with much danger on account of the sharks, which are apt to lurk near the ships, and carry away a thigh at least from any unfortunate person, whom they happen to seize. In lieu of this, they have substituted the baptism of the bath, or bathing tub, on the edge of which they cause the person to sit, who has not ransomed himself, or whom they have a mind to plague, as will be seen in the progress of this account.

Things being thus settled, the vicar addressed himself to M. de Bougainville in the following manner: " In order to be admitted into the noble and puissant society of the lord governor of the line, it is necessary to enter into certain preliminary engagements, which you will promise to observe. These engagements have nothing for their object but what is entirely reasonable." " A la bonne heure," replied M. de Bougainville. " Do you then promise," pursued the vicar, " to be a good citizen, and to that end to labour at the work of population, and not to suffer young women to languish away their time, whenever a favourable opportunity shall offer itself?—I do promise.—Do you promise never to lye with a sailor's wife?—I do promise.—Do you promise to cause the same engagements to be taken, and the same, or similar ceremonies to be observed by all those who have not passed the line, when they happen to be with you?—I do promise.—Put your hand then upon this holy book in token of your obligation." M. de Bougainville laid his hand on a cut, which represents a genius or angel and a young girl tenderly embracing each other. It is the cut at the 47th page of a book intitled, *Sentimens d'un Chretien, touché de l'amour de Dieu.* At the bottom of the cut is this sentence: *quis mihi det te fratrem meum sugentem ubera matris meæ & inveniam te foris & deosculer te.* Cant. 8. The vicar went to the lord governor of the line, and

reported

reported to him that M. de Bougainville had taken the engagements: to which the Bon-homme answered: *dignus est intrare in nostro docto corpore: admittatur.* The vicar then returned to M. de Bougainville and said; the lord governor of the line is pleased to admit you into the society of which he is the head, and has ordered me to receive you therein by administration of his baptism. What is your name? Louis, said M. de Bougainville. Very well; *ego, nomine reverendissimi domini domini & serenissimi præsidentis æquatoris te, Ludovice, admitto in societate ejus.* In pronouncing these words, he sprinkled over his head some drops of sea water. Then they untied M. de Bougainville's thumb, who put some money in the plate under the napkin, and the vicar threw incense on him. After this the vicar proceeded to M. de Nerville, to whom he proposed the same questions, and after him to the other passengers and officers with all the same ceremonies.

It was now come to the turn of a midshipman, who was a sad dog, and hated by almost every body. The vicar told him, that the lord governor had given orders for his being admitted with all the ceremonies in form. In consequence of these orders, he threw one end of his robe over the fellow's head, muttered a few words, and afterwards gave him the robe, which had been fresh painted in oil, to kiss. He then took some blacking, mixed with oil, in a small pot born by one of the cabbin boys, and smeared his forehead and cheeks with it. This being performed they untied his thumb from the line, and conducted him to the bath, on the sides of which were two notches large enough to receive a stick, that was laid across, and was to serve as a seat for him. He had no sooner sat down, than they suddenly withdrew the stick from under him, and he fell with his posteriors into the water, the tub being about half full, to which there was a cord likewise adjusted in such a manner, that by pulling one end of it, at the instant the catechumen tumbles in, it fastens round his middle, and keeps him under, without his being able to disengage himself, till the by-standers are pleased to give him his liberty. As soon as the midshipman was noosed, they smeared his head and face all over with black and red: after that they threw at least five or six buckets of water over his head, and then suffered him to go about his business.

After this they came to the two Acadian girls. The vicar asked them, if they were virgins? they said, Yes. Do you promise then, said he, to preserve your marriage vow inviolable, in case you shall have a sailor for your husband? The promise being made, he just marked their foreheads, noses, cheeks, and chins with black, in the slightest manner possible, and then poured some water over their heads, after which they retired. The sister of one of these had hid herself in order to avoid this wetting. She was found however, and they were going to oblige her to submit to the ceremony; but the vicar being apprized, that there were reasons, why she should not be exposed to that part of it, which was to be performed with the water, told her, that he would content himself with making some patches upon her face. She submitted to this, and he kept his word. The two married women were not baptized, because their children, who were too young to be left by themselves, were so affrighted at the grotesque figures of the attendants on the Bon-homme la ligne, that they could not be pacified or brought out from the corners where they had hid themselves.

Several others were afterwards baptized and bedaubed with black and red, but none of them were seated on the tub; because when the others had begun to throw some buckets of water over them, they, to be even with them, returned the compliment. Those who had been wetted, chose to wet others: the struggle was who should throw most water, so that all those who remained on the deck were as wet, as if they had been dipped in the sea. But they were not satisfied with sluicing one another; those who had had their faces blacked rubbed them against others who had not undergone that ceremony, and by this means there was scarce a man in the whole ship's company who escaped a daubing; and they did not give over the sport, till

they

they were all tired. This proved an unlucky circumftance for the Bon-homme and his attendants, who loft part of the tribute they would have received from thofe, who were not baptized with the ordinary ceremonies. The reft of the day was paffed in dancing, and other kind of amufements.

This farce is performed in every European fhip on paffing the line. But there is no precife uniformity obferved in the ceremonies ufed upon this occafion. Each nation has invented fuch as are moft conformable to its genius and character; and every fhip is regulated according to the degrees of humour in thofe who happen to prefide. Sometimes the perfon, whofe office it is to adminifter the baptifm, gives each perfon a name taken from fome bay, fome cape, or fome remarkable promontory on an ifland or coaft; taking care at the fame time to apply them in fuch a manner as to exprefs the character, temper, figure or difpofition of the perfon fo named. The ceremony is in general called the *baptifm*, or the *ranfom*: the baptifm, becaufe of the water thrown over thofe, who are then paffing the line for the firft time: the ranfom, on account of the tribute, which is paid by thofe perfons who are not willing to be wetted. The tribute is ufually whatever the perfon, who pays it, thinks fit to give. Sometimes it is impofed by the actors themfelves: however they always take care to make their levy proportionable to the circumftances of the perfons, from whom the tribute is exacted. Thus it is not always required in money, but fometimes in wine, or brandy, or hams, or fuch like; as when the captain of the veffel, who is not exempt any more than his paffengers, paffes the line for the firft time.

When the fhip is not to pafs the line, but only the tropic, thofe of the crew, who have already paffed it, not being willing to lofe the tribute, which they look upon as their due, have taken it into their heads to call the tropic, the *eldeft fon of the Bon-homme la ligne, prefumptive heir of his poffeffions*. Upon the ftrength of this they play the fame farce at paffing the tropic, that others do on paffing the equator. They have even thought

I I                      fit

fit to perform this ceremony, when a ship for the first time doubles Cape St. Vincent to pass the Straits of Gibraltar. The ships which are employed on the cod fishery observe the same practice, when they come within sight of the great bank of Newfoundland.

From this time for several days we had nothing remarkable.

On the 14th, by our reckoning and observation we suspected, that the tides and currents set southward, agreeable to the remark made by the author of admiral Anson's voyage.

At eight o'clock in the evening of this day, a bird similar to that of which I have given a figure in the preceding plate, suffered himself to be caught in the hand over my cabbin. We shut him up in a hen-coop.

The next morning one of our boatswains having taken him out of his place of confinement to put him upon his hand, the bird took wing and flew away. A short time after we discovered a *frigate*: this bird kept wheeling round our weather flag, and seemed to peck at it more than once. We made the same observation on the currents this as the day before.

We found this clima ch the same as that of France in the month of May, the mornings and evenings being rather cold, though we were under the torrid zone; nor did we experience any of that burning heat, which is complained of in the relations of so many persons, who have sailed through these parts. It is true that since we had passed the line, we had always had some little wind at least, had never been surprised by calms, and had been secured by the clouds from the rays of the sun. Whether it were owing to our cleanliness, or to our frigate being new we were not troubled with those insects, which are mentioned in the same accounts; nor had we to this time one person sick on board. In order to contribute to the preservation of health, every evening after supper, the sailors were set to dancing on the stern-castle. And indeed they were so disposed to jollity, that they would play at hot cockles, hunt the flipper, or any other game; that promoted exercise and encouraged mirth.

mirth. Some of them, who were naturally of a comic turn, would drefs themfelves up in mafquerade, affuming very grotefque figures, and would pafs in proceffion, or make their appearance in groups on the ftern-caftle, where they would dance minuets, cotillons, allemandes, country dances, and hornpipes. Moft of them had learned thefe dances, while they were prifoners of war in the ports of Great Britain. The greateft part of them had made their efcape from thence at the rifque of their lives, in neutral veffels, fifhing-boats, and even fmall boats, which they found means to carry off. Several of them have affured me, that the Englifh connived at their efcape, and would even bargain with the neutral veffels for their paffage, or fell them boats; that fome lent them cloaths to difguife them, others advanced them money, others again gave them money out of charity, and others furnifhed them with letters of recommendation to their friends in London, or in fuch ports, where they thought the prifoners might embark with the leaft danger. They even went farther; and in order to give them the means of living comfortably in the prifons, where they were confined, made them prefents, and paid them very liberally for little toys, which fome of them employed themfelves in making, even to the buying of them little images of the Virgin Mary, of Saints, &c. made out of wood, and as ill fhaped as may be imagined, where the artifts had no other tools but their knives, and had never learned the trade. One of our crew, who had amufed himfelf in this way, has told me more than once, that they would give him to the value of half a crown for one of his figures, with this caution only, not to boaft of it among the Englifh. A fine leffon of humanity and charity!

Mirth and cleanlinefs are two points, to the promotion of which fea captains ought to pay great attention. They contribute in no fmall degree to prevent all thofe diforders to which feamen are ufually fubject. For the fame reafon they ought always to mix a little vinegar with their daily allowance of water, which they put in a cafk, called *charnier*. What was used for the chamber, or served up at the officers mess was put into great earthen vessels, which were filled to the height of half a foot or more with small pebbles. After the water has been drawn off from the casks into these large vessels, called *jarrs*, which are exposed to the open air on the stern-castle or thereabouts, it is left there to purify for three or four days before it is drunk. It is imagined that the pebbles serve to clear it from slime.

I must not omit to observe here, that the water we had taken on board at St. Malo, had not suffered the least change, as it usually happens between the tropics. Our biscuit was equally well preserved. There were only some pickled cabbage, and some small casks of veal, which were rather spoiled: and that probably was more owing to a fault in the seasoning of them, than to the heat of the climate we were in.

On the 20th of November at eight in the morning we took a porpoise of about a hundred weight. I painted him from the life, but without preserving any proportion to his bulk. For the figure of him see the plate annexed.

Several writers consider the porpoise, as a species of whale, and give it the name of *soufleur*. There are different kinds of them. Some of them have their backs of a dark grey, almost black, and their bellies much lighter. Others are of a grey approaching nearly to white, from whence they have the name of *white porpoises*. Those which we took, and whose figure is represented in the plate, had their heads formed, not like the snout of a hog, but almost in the shape of a bird's head, covered with a thick grey skin, and the beak armed throughout with sharp white teeth like those of a pike. They had an opening (A.) on the top of their head, through which they spouted water, and this was followed by a stream of air attended with a noise something like the grunting of a hog. Their tail is horizontal, contrary to what is usually found among other fish, who have it perpendicular, when they are lying upon their bellies. It is of great use, no doubt, in assisting the porpoise to spring out of the water,

water, and to turn round in the air with so much ease, as I have mentioned in a former article; to effect which they only incline a little more on one side of their tail than on the other. From this position of their tail probably it is, that they derive that peculiar method of swimming, as if they were alternately rising above the water and diving under it. The porpoise, which I am describing here (and all those we took were of the same kind) is, as I apprehend, of that species, which are called *moines de mer*. The fore part of the head terminates in a roll near the beginning of the snout or beak, answering to the border of the cowl. The back is blackish, and the belly of a grey, consisting of a pearl colour, somewhat inclining to yellow, interspersed with black and iron-grey spots. It has three fins, curved and very thick; one on the back, the other two under the belly. These, as well as the tail, are covered with a membrane, or thick coarse skin, which being removed, five white cartilages appear, disposed like fingers and articulated in phalanxes.

I dissected the head and fins with an intention of preserving them; but having hung them up over our cabbins near the flag staff, some of our crew, in working the ship, inadvertently threw them overboard.

Porpoises almost always are found in shoals, swimming in a line, as if they were drawn up for an engagement. They seem to go in search of the wind; for we remarked that in a short time after they had passed us, the wind would rise on that side, to which they directed their course. There is no fish perhaps, considering its size, that has so much strength as the porpoise. Among those, which we struck, two or three disengaged themselves from the harpoon, either by tearing their backs or breaking the harpoon itself; although the spike was as thick as a man's thumb. Those we took did always force the iron, and one of them twisted it like the end of a screw. There is a strong smell attending this fish, as well as the shark, and it is so permanent, that after the dissection I made, my hands were not free from it in three days, though I washed them very often with vinegar.

We

We had some of it served up at dinner the day it was taken, which several others at the table, besides myself, thought by no means so ill tasted, as it is generally said to be.

Perceiving a change in the colour of the sea, we thought proper to sound; a precaution the more necessary in the latitudes we were in at this time, as there is very little dependence on the charts. Those of Holland placing the coast of Brazil near 60 leagues more to the East than the French. Besides, according to our reckoning and our observations of the sun's altitude, we found ourselves among, or at least very near the shelves called Los Abrollhos, the extent and situation of which are not so exactly known and laid down in the charts, that they can safely be trusted to.

About half past seven in the evening, we sounded with a hundred and thirty-five fathom of line, but found no bottom. Immediately after, another of those birds, of which I have exhibited a figure, and which I take to be one of those they call *tropical birds*, came and settled on the larboard of the quarter-deck. Here we endeavoured to catch him but he escaped. He then flew to the other end of the ship, and settling on the larboard of the fore-castle, a sailor caught him in his hand. We put him in a hen coop, intending the next morning to fasten a ribband round his neck with this inscription: *I was taken on the French frigate, Eagle, the 20th of November 1763, in 16 deg. 44 min. lat. 35 deg. 10 min. long. and was set at liberty the 21st in the morning.* At midnight we sounded a second time without finding any bottom.

Tuesday the 21st, at half past six in the morning, one of the mates being desirous of examining the bird, which had been taken the evening before, and not holding him with sufficient caution, our prisoner escaped, and deprived us of the pleasure we proposed to ourselves in fastening about him the ribband I have mentioned. From the time we had suffered the second of these birds that we met with to fly away, we never failed to have one of them every evening about eight o'clock fluttering round our cabbins.

Having observed an alteration in the colour of the sea all this day, we sounded at eight in the evening. At the depth of 35 fathoms we found bottom, and brought up pieces of coral, shells, and rotten stone. At ten we sounded again, and found 30 fathom with the same bottom. At midnight, no soundings.

At two in the morning of the 22d, sounded again, 40 fathom, same bottom as before. At four, no soundings. The Abrollhos extend farther to the southward than is marked in the French chart.

It is to be observed, that the author of admiral Ahson's voyage, being in the same latitude and longitude according to our reckoning, found the same soundings, which served in some measure as a direction for us. This succesive difference, of soundings and no soundings, is the more remarkable, as by our reckoning we had not changed our course half a league; for from noon the day before we steered S. W. by the compass, till three quarters past seven, when we sounded: after that S. $\frac{1}{4}$ S. W. till ten, then S. till midnight, when we came about again to S. S. W. after having m— two leagues two thirds of way; at two we had soundings, and at four, steering the same course at the rate of five or five $\frac{1}{2}$ knots an hour, no soundings.

At noon we observed the sun in our zenith, and could not miss finding the altitude. Some minutes after we remarked that we had passed the sun, and that our shadow lay southward.

About three in the afternoon we made a signal to a sail, we had had in view for some hours, thinking it to be our sloop the Sphinx. She seemed to be making towards us, and was steering W. S. W. upon this we lay by for her; but finding that she did not answer our signal, and having discovered that she had but two masts, we concluded her to be a negro snow going to Rio Janeiro. We kept S. W. before the wind till nine at night, when we changed our course to S. W. $\frac{1}{4}$ S. At midnight we sounded without finding bottom.

At

At four the next morning, 23d of November, we steered S. W. ¼ W. and at six had sight of the coast of Brazil, bearing W. and W. N. W. about fifteen leagues distance. At seven we came about to the wind in order to make the land; but the weather grew so hazy, that by ten o'clock we had lost sight of it. The colour of the sea changing, we sounded, and found a bottom of fine sand at fifteen fathom depth. At eleven we sounded again, and found the same bottom.

In measuring our distance upon the chart, according to our corrected longitude, we found ourselves seventy leagues from the coast of Brazil, East and West of the southern point of the river Spirito Santo. At the same time we had sight of land, and found ourselves sixty leagues farther West than our reckoning; which confirms the remark of the author of admiral Anson's voyage, that the tides set South West. It is therefore very prudent not to trust to these tides, nor to the charts, especially the French ones, in the passage from the line to the river Plata.

Our first sounding might probably have been taken on a bank of sand in the open sea, not marked out in the French chart, which is to be found in the Dutch chart of Wan-Culen, marked *good bottom*, at 15 or 16 leagues off land. This is the same place where we sounded at ten and eleven o'clock. The chart of Peter Goos is more accurate; and one of M. Buache is still better.

After this the wind changing from N. N. E. to N. E. with a brisk gale, hazy weather, and a high sea, we sounded every quarter of an hour, and at three o'clock finding only nine fathom, we tacked, and put the Cape S. ¼ S. W. Our depth still decreasing, we came again to S. ¼ S. E. for half an hour; but finding that our water grew still more shallow, though we were standing out to sea, we put about again, and brought the Cape to bear E. S. W. From this time the depth began gradually to increase, insomuch, that at five o'clock we had twenty-five fathom water with the same sandy bottom of the colour of bran, but something more muddy than at the top of the bank. At eight we stood cross it, in 35 fathom, with a bottom of white shining sand. At ten

## TO THE MALOUINE ISLANDS. 39

ten we had forty fathom, with a bottom of rotten shells, and some coral.

Although this last sounding had almost removed the apprehensions we laboured under, through the error of the charts, in respect to the situation of the coast of Brazil, and the omission of this sand bank or shallow we had just met with, we thought it necessary to continue our soundings for the greater security. In consequence of this resolution, we found at midnight fifty fathom water, same bottom, but no coral: at four in the morning, being the 24th, sixty fathom, same bottom as the last. From half past five we steered S. W. till noon. These shallows are the flats of St. Thomas, which are very dangerous in stormy weather. They lie from sixteen to seventeen leagues out at sea, and the highest part of the shoal is not more than three or four fathoms below the surface of the water. Near the shore there is depth enough to pass. The Portuguese vessels, which are employed in coasting along these shores, and are well acquainted with them, keep between these flats and the land, but several of them have not been able to avoid running foul of the bank.

The ground between these flats and the shore is composed of sand, which resembles pounded glass, and that on the shoal itself is of rotten stone.

It is proper to observe, that the Dutch chart, of which I have spoken above, does not make the sand bank, marked *good bottom*, extend so far as it really does, which is not less than through the 24th degree of latitude. I am not acquainted with the extent of it from East to West. By our reckoning and observations of this day it appears, that the tides and the currents set southward and westward. At six o'clock the night before, Cape St. Thomas bore nearly North West of us by the compass, at the distance of fourteen or fifteen leagues.

The wind continued N. N. E. blowing hard, the sky gloomy and covered. We steered with the Cape S. W. till six in the morning of the 25th. After that W. S. W. At seven, the even-

I ing

ing before, we had founded, and found no bottom with fourscore fathom of line.

On the 26th, from four in the morning to six, we were becalmed. We took this opportunity to found, but found no bottom. At ten in the evening we founded again, with the same success. At midnight we found a bottom of grey sand at the depth of 90 fathom.

At two the next morning (27th) our soundings were 85 fathom, with a bottom of grey sand somewhat slimy.

At sun set, though the horizon was not very clear, we saw land a head of us. We kept on our course, sounding at seven in the evening, when we found thirty-five fathom, soft muddy ground, of a blackish grey colour, mixed with some small shells. At midnight we founded again, at which time we had thirty-one fathom, same bottom.

The 28th at sun rise the land began to open upon us. We made towards it in order to take a view. At eight o'clock I discovered a small island called in some charts *Aracari*. It bore N. W. 5 degrees W. of us by the compass, at the distance of about five or six leagues. The nearest point to us, as far as I could distinguish at this time, was that which runs out farthest to the East on this side, and forms a peninsula. It bore W. ¼ N. W. of us by the compass, at the distance of about three leagues.

On the 29th, after having with much difficulty weathered the point of the island of *Gal*, and that of St. Catherine's, we came about four in the afternoon to anchor in six fathom water, muddy ground and very soft.

*Marks of Anchorage.*
Moored South South East, and North North West.

In this bay, which forms a canal round the island of St. Catherine's, are three forts, and a battery of cannon near the entrance towards the town, on that side where we anchored. The first fort stands on the larboard side on coming into the bay. It is situated on a head-land in a small island, called Parrot Island, N. E. ¼ E. and E. N. E. The name of it is *the Grand-Point-Fort*.

s. We
k I dif-
It bore
ance of
far as I
farthest
N. ¼ N.
gues.
:red the
'e came
water,

St. Ca-
ntrance
he first
'. It is
: Island,
l-Point-
Fort.

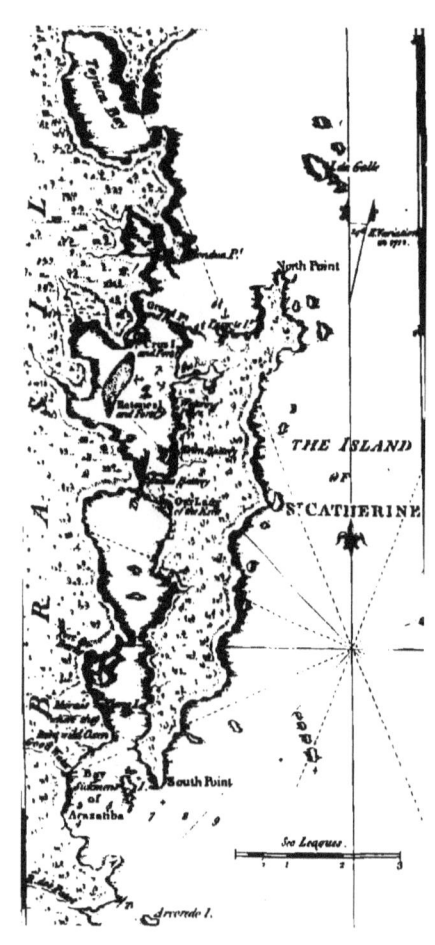

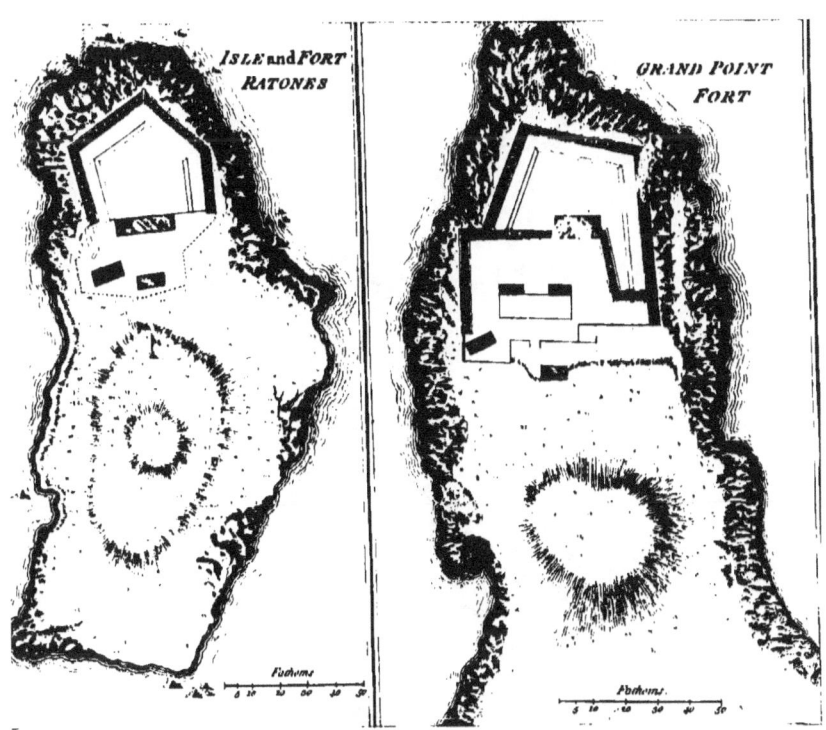

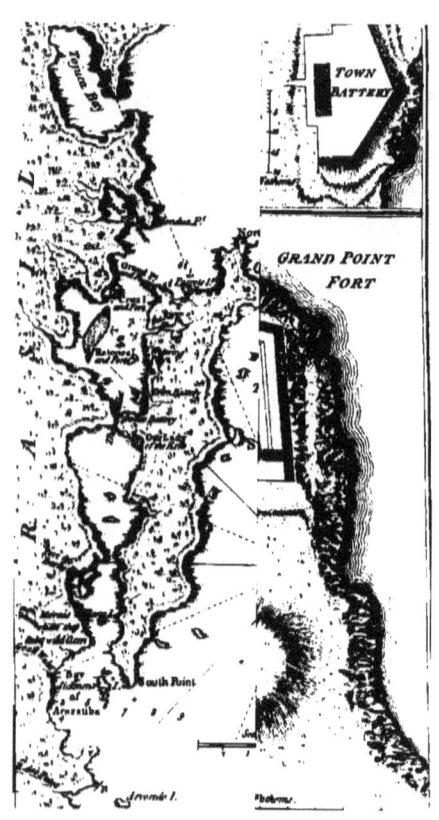

*Fort.* Almoſt oppoſite to this, but a little farther, is the ſecond fort, built likewiſe upon a little iſland near the main-land N. W. ¼ N. by the compaſs. This is called, *the fort of Santa-Cruz*. It makes a good appearance on entering the bay, being built on a terrace ſupported by arches. Here the commanding officer reſides. The third fort, which ſtands more in towards the town, is alſo ſituated on a ſmall iſland at almoſt an equal diſtance from the continent and the iſland, and goes by the name of *the fort of Ratonne*. Plans of all theſe forts are in the plate annexed. We lay at anchor in the middle of them, and the commanding officer gave us to underſtand by ſignals, that this was the beſt anchorage: but he had his reaſons for doing ſo, there being much more commodious anchorage farther in towards the main-land.

Upon our coming into the bay, we perceived the Portugueſe colours hoiſted at the top of ſome trees on an eminence in the iſland in the midſt of the woods, and placed ſo that it might be ſeen by the two advanced forts. They hoiſt this flag without doubt, as ſoon as they diſcover any ſhip at ſea, to give notice of it to the forts in the bay; for we ſaw it ſet up, and afterwards taken down again, as ſoon as we had come to an anchor and ſaluted the fort of Santa Cruz.

Before we moored, being over againſt this fort, which as well as the two others had hung out Portugueſe colours, we ſent our yawl with M. Alexander Guyot, our ſecond captain, who underſtands Portugueſe, to wait upon the commanding officer, and to aſk him, if upon our ſaluting the fort, he would return our ſalute, gun for gun. The Commandant ſent an officer of the garriſon back with M. Guyot to return the compliment, and to ſee who we were. As ſoon as they came on board, we caſt our anchors, and ſaluted the fort with nine guns, which was returned with the ſame number. The officer ſupped, and lay on board our ſhip that night, in order to conduct M. Guyot the next morning to wait upon the governor of this part of Brazil, who reſides at a little town, ſituated in the bottom of a creek in the

I 2       iſland

island of St. Catherine's, five leagues South of our moorings, and to defire his permiſſion, that we might wood and water. The fame evening, the commanding officer of the fort of Santa Cruz, fent us fome refreſhments, and the next morning M. Guyot went with the Portugueſe Officer in the longboat.

The governor, whoſe name is Don Antonio Franciſco de Cardofo y Menezes y Souza, colonel and knight of the order of Chriſt, and defcended from a very illuſtrious family in Portugal, gave a very polite reception to M. Guyot, and granted every thing we defired. Our longboat left the town about nine in the morning to return to us, but did not get back till feven in the evening, being detained by contrary winds.

As foon as the inhabitants on the coaſt perceived our frigate at anchor, three or four of them came along fide of us in canoes, and brought us lemons, oranges, and fome c hbages. But the commanding officer of the fort of Santa Cruz, obſerving this, fent orders to all the huts forbidding the people to carry any thing on board our frigate, or even to come near it; they were neither to fell us any thing or buy any thing of us. To inforce his orders more ſtrictly, he poſted foldiers in the neareſt huts, who were to watch the conduct of the inhabitants in this reſpect, and to prevent our ſtraggling about the parts adjacent. In the mean time he made us a thoufand proteſtations of his readineſs to oblige us, and was not at all ſparing of his civilities.

It is not to be doubted, that the Commandant immediately upon our arrival, difpatched a canoe to the governor to give him intelligence of it. The next morning, while M. Guyot was gone to wait upon the governor, the Oviodore, or chief judge came on board our frigate to make a verbal procefs of our an-chorage, our force, and the reafons which brought us hither. M. de Bougainville fatisfied him in all theſe points, and he returned about noon. At his leaving the ſhip we faluted him with feven guns, which were immediately returned by the fort of Santa Cruz.

After

TO THE MALOUINE ISLANDS. 43

After dinner M. de Bougainville, accompanied by Meff. de Nerville, de Belcourt, and l'Huillier de la Serre, went to vifit the Commandant of this fort. Here they found a general officer of Rio Janeiro, who had been confined prifoner in it for four years, the commanding officer having received orders, never to fuffer him to ftir out of the gates. The crime laid to his charge was, that he had not punctually executed the orders of the court of Lifbon, in refpect to the expulfion of the Jefuits of Brazil, and had extended fome favor to them. This gentleman had with him a Portuguefe, who acted as his fteward and fecretary; he was a man of good fenfe and had been page to one of the Portuguefe ambaffadors at Paris, where he had lived four years. The pleafure of feeing Frenchmen again delighted him, and he was happy in ferving as an interpreter to M. de Bougainville. His attachment to the imprifoned general had induced him to facrifice his liberty, and for the fake of bearing him company he voluntarily partook of his confinement. This fecretary accompanied M. de Bougainville, and the reft on their return. In the account he gave us of the caufes of the general's imprifonment, he exculpated him as much as he could, and told us even in the prefence of two officers, who had come on board with him, that he was indeed guilty of not having carried the orders of his court into execution as foon as he received them; but that the archbifhop, who favored the Jefuits had prevented it by giving him affurances that he had received counter orders; and that the other, as commanding officer, ought not to obey thofe he had received, till they fhould be confirmed. The execution therefore of them, whether out of refpect to the archbifhop or from other motives not known, was delayed too long, and the general was punifhed for it by the lofs of his liberty. After thi... ...on he begged of M. de Bougainville to take charge of a mem...... in juftification of the prifoner, and to deliver it to the Portuguefe ambaffador in France upon our return, that it might be tranfmitted to the court of Lifbon. But no fuch paper, I believe, ever came to the hands of M. de Bougainville.

When

'When M. Alexander Guyot paid his visit to the governor, he received an invitation from him, and was likewise defired to deliver one on his part to M. de Bougainville and the Officers as well as the principal paffengers on board our frigate to dine with the governor the next day, Thurfday the firft of December.

As foon as it was light we fet off, M. de Bougainville, de Nerville, de Belcourt, l' Huillier, Alex. Guyot and myfelf; and at half paft one we arrived at the town, the name of which tranflated into French is, *Notre Dame de l'Exil*, or *la Vierge Exilée, Our Lady in Exile*.

Almoft all the officers of the garrifon came down to the fhore to meet us. They received us at our landing with all the politenefs imaginable, and conducted us to the governor's houfe through a large concourfe of people.

The governor met us at the outer gate, and led us into a large falloon, where we found dinner ferved up. The governor, his fon, who talked pretty good French, the town major, who knew enough of it to make himfelf underftood, the Oviodore, two other officers and a friar of the Francifcan order dined with us. Many other officers of the garrifon were in the room, but did not fit down at table, and fome of them waited upon us. Thefe military *waiters*, according to the account of an officer of the garrifon of Fort Santa Cruz, take that method to pay their court to the governor, who invites them all in their turns to dinner, and they wait upon one another.

The difhes were dreffed after the manner of the country, which is not very agreeable to a French palate. In eating their foup, which is a kind of folid glue, they do not make ufe of fpoons, but eat it with the help of a fork. The bread was miferable, brown, heavy dough, or rather pafte made in the fhape of a roll, about three inches diameter, and an inch and a half in height. The outfide had fcarcely felt the fire, and was only a little drier than the reft. The infide was folid, and looked like that buck-wheat flummery, which is the chief food of the inhabitants of Limoges, and is by them called *Gallette*.

The

The second course was composed of a great number of dishes; all dressed with sugar, which is also an ingredient in most of their sauces, as well as Carthamum, or the flower of bastard saffron. The plates were pewter, not well scowered, and of an antique form: The covers were likewise very old fashioned, but they were ver, and very heavy; so were the dishes, and some drinking vessels, which were of an octogonal cylindrical form; and about seven or eight inches high. Our liquor was at first brought to us in very small glasses, such as were formerly used for *liqueurs*, having a long stem, and the bowl ending in a point. But as it would have been necessary to drink one of these glasses at least with every mouthful, I asked for a larger to mix wine and water in. Upon this they brought me one of the silver cylinders full. Another time I had a large goblet of crystal, the only one that appeared, and which held near a bottle, Paris measure. The other guests were served in the same manner. These great cups were handed from one to another, till they were empty. The wine we drank was port, and very good.

After dinner the cloth was removed, but we continued at table to drink coffee and to converse. At this time I perceived that the Franciscan had quitted the company. My design had been to address myself to him in order to obtain some knowledge of the country and inhabitants; for though he knew nothing of the French language, nor I of the Portuguese, I made myself sure of being able to converse with him in Latin. I acquainted the governor's son with my intention, and asked him why the Franciscan had retired. He told me, I might have perceived from the moment we came in, that the Friar had taken pains to avoid me, foreseeing my design; for not understanding Latin, he chose rather to keep at a distance from me, than be obliged to acknowledge his ignorance of that language. This want of learning, however, says he, is not peculiar to him; it is the case of almost all the ecclesiastics in the country.

The governor's son, from whom I received this intelligence is a captain in his father's regiment, and one of fifteen children as he informed us, that he had had, not by his lawful wife, for he never was married, but by one or feveral miftreffes. The reft of his children then alive were at Lifbon, where they enjoy according to the laws of that city the fame honours and prerogatives as the legitimate children of nobility; baftards being there, as I am informed, gentlemen by birth. One of the daughters of this governor is married to one of the minifters of State in that court, and another of his fons is in poffeffion of one of the firft employments.

While the coffee was pouring, a dozen of the officers of the garrifon came in, and entertained us with a little concert of inftrumental mufic; fome playing on the German flute, fome on the violin, one on the violoncello, and one on a fpecies of hautbois. The fame perfons played fucceffively on different inftruments. There were befides two blacks, who blew the French horn. The whole performance was very good. They had almoft all the pieces of our beft compofers. The treble ftring of their violins was made of filk.

After this we walked about the town, which appeared to me to contain about a hundred and fifty houfes, confifting of nothing but a ground floor with the roof over it. The garrifon occupies one part, and is compofed chiefly of white men. The reft of the inhabitants are almoft all negroes or mulattoes; they are to be found of all fhades from black to white. The greateft number of both fexes are mulattoes, and for the moft part ill-fhaped. They have befides an air of favagenefs, fuch as might be expected in a breed half Brazilian and half negro.

They go almoft all of them with their feet naked, their head bare and very ill combed, a fhirt, a pair of breeches, and fome with a cloke, which they throw over their fhoulder according to the Spanifh fafhion. It is common enough to fee their fhirts and breeches in holes, and torn in more places than one; which makes the cloke very neceffary. One meets with fome, but they are undoubtedly of the richer fort, who wear hats of a very large fize, the brims being about ten inches in breadth, and flapped down.

down. These have their feet covered; they have likewise a waistcoat, over which they throw an exceeding wide full cloak, which comes down to their shoes: they sometimes throw a corner of it over the opposite shoulder, and that in such a manner as even to cover their faces. Instead of a hat some of them have a hood of the same stuff as the cloak, to which it is fastened, and with this they are used to cover their heads so completely, that it is impossible to know any person in that garb, unless by their walk, or some other mark of distinction, such as the colour of the cloak or the manner of wearing it.

The governor, and the officers, as well as the whole garrison, wear cloth made up in the French fashion: and indeed I was very much surprised to see officers in so hot a country dressed in cloth at least as coarse as that of our soldiers.

The Oviodoré, and officers of justice are distinguished by a large cane or staff, or by a small stick, bent in form of a hoop, which the principal of them carry on their left arm above the elbow; the inferior ones have it fastened to the button hole of the left pocket of their coat.

The slaves go naked, except that the men have a pair of breeches or drawers, and sometimes a shirt, that is scarcely good for any thing: it often happens indeed that they have no other covering than a simple piece of cloth about their shoulders. It is very uncommon to see any of them with a shirt and waistcoat. But when they have obtained their liberty, they are permitted to wear the doublet and cloak made of stuff like the white people. The black female slaves are also naked, excepting a slip of linen which they tie round them by the two ends, and which reaches from their waist to the middle of their thighs at most. When they are made free, they are dressed like other women with a petticoat, and a shift, the upper part of which is open before, a good deal in the manner of our shirts: when they go out of doors, they put on a large piece of fine woollen, generally of a white colour, bordered with gold, silver, silk, or tape, according to the circumstances and condition of the wearer. It is about two ells in length, and one in breadth. It is put on fo that one of the corners hangs down to the middle of the back, and in this refpect bears a pretty near refemblance to the cowl worn by our Carmelites. The oppofite corner comes over the head, and the two others being drawn over the fhoulders and arms down to the elbows, are brought acrofs each other upon the breaft, like the mantlet of our French ladies. Sometimes too, inftead of croffing them upon the breaft, they bring thefe ends under their arms on the fame fide, by which means their neck is left expofed to view. This mode of drefs is very inconvenient, and requires a continual attention to re-adjuft it, fometimes on the head, and fometimes on the arms, the flighteft motion of the body putting it out of order.

The Portuguefe women, who are eftablifhed or born on the ifland of St. Catherine's, and on the coaft of the main land fo far as our excurfions led us, are of a very fair complexion, notwithftanding the heat of the climate. They have, generally fpeaking, fine large eyes; but little colour in their cheeks. Both men and women for the moft part lead a very lazy life, and truft to their flaves the management of their houfhold affairs, and what little work is to be done out of doors. The land produces almoft every kind of neceffary, without their taking the trouble to cultivate it.

There are fcarce any fhops to be feen in the town. I found only two; one a lockfmith's, and the other an apothecary's. The negro women, who have obtained their liberty, carry fruit about in great bafkets on their heads, or fquat down at the corners of ftreets with their bafkets before them.

While we were agreeably engaged in attending to the mufic, his excellency the governor ordered a parrot to be fetched, which was exceedingly remarkable for its beautiful and variegated plumage. As he faw that we all of us admired it, he begged M. de Bougainville to accept of the parrot. Its whole plumage, particularly on the head, neck, back, and belly was adorned with feathers, fome of a jonquil, others of a lemon colour, fome carmine,

mine, others crimson, and all intermixed with feathers of different shades of green, and of a lively blue, particularly at the ears. The governor told us, that this variety was partly owing to art, and partly to nature: for that when this bird is very young, and has scarcely more than the quills of the feathers rising after the down, these quills are pulled out in different parts, and a kind of poisonous liquid poured immediately into the place of them; that the feathers, which rise afterwards where the quills have been pulled out, are yellow or red instead of green, which they would naturally be: but of a hundred birds, on which this operation is performed, there are scarce five or six, that do not die of it.

The governor added to this present fifty skins of toucans, stripped from the beak to the thighs, and dried with the feathers, which are partly lemon colour, partly carnation, and partly black, in cross streaks from one wing to the other.

He carried his generosity so far, as to promise M. de Bougainville two guaras alive, a male and a female; and even offered to make him a present of those which he shewed us, if there were no others to be got before our departure from the island. He could not however accomplish his promise, a contrary wind preventing his return to the town the evening before we sailed.

The guara is a bird of the size of a large French magpye. It has a long beak, which is crooked at the end; its thighs and feet are also long. The first feathers, with which it is covered after it is hatched, are black. This goes off insensibly, and becomes an ash colour. When the bird begins to fly, all the feathers turn white; after which they become of a rose colour, and growing more and more red every day, at last attain to the brightest scarlet, which they preserve ever after. Though it is a bird of prey, feeding not only on fish but on all kinds of flesh, which it usually soaks first in water; yet it builds and lays its eggs

eggs on the roofs of houses, and in holes of walls, as our arrows do. It always flies in company. The feathers, with which the savages adorn their heads, are taken from these birds. The two which the governor had promised to M. de Bougainville were just beginning to redden.

On Friday the 2d of December the Acadians with their wives, children and sisters-in-law, were set on shore, and lodged in a cottage on the continent, which had been assigned them by the Commandant of the fort of Santa Cruz. Here they were employed in washing the linen of the vessel, and of several officers of the frigate.

The Commandant had pointed out to us a place near his fort to wood and water at. Some of the crew were sent there for these purposes; but after several trials, they found much difficulty in getting this water, which ran from a little torrent. Beside this, a small whale having run a ground near the place some time before infected the air with so horrible a stench, that it was resolved to ask leave of the governor to water on the island. Our request was granted with the greatest politeness, his excellency giving us at the same time permission to fish, sport, and to go wherever we pleased. One of the inhabitants shewed us a spring near his house which formed a little rivulet, where Admiral Anson had watered, and an oven built a few paces from it about seven or eight years before by some Frenchmen, who had put into the harbour. The water of this spring is very good; and we laid in a large stock of it. As to our wood, we got that from the place which had been mentioned to us on the continent, it being exceedingly commodious for that purpose: for after cutting down the wood on the brow of the hill, it was very easy to roll it down the side close to the water edge, and so load our boats with it. What we cut was mostly cedar, sassafras, cinnamon, and Brazil wood, which is used in dying. There was very little of any other kind in this place.

The

The next day (Saturday the 3d) we went on shore upon the continent, and walked along the coast with an intention of sporting. We found two or three soldiers posted by the Commandant in the next cottage to that of our Acadians, who endeavoured to prevent us from going forward, and told us they had orders from the governor to do so. We pretended not to understand what they said to us, as they spoke in Portuguese, and continued our route, upon which they made no resistance. In fact, it was not the governor, but the Commandant of the fort of Santa Cruz, who had given these orders. We proceeded above a league along the new road, which they are making to go by land to Rio Janeiro, and by the side of a chain of woods which cover all the eminences. These woods are so thick, that it is not possible for any thing but wild beasts and serpents to penetrate into them. We killed some toucans, parrots, tiepirangas, and one dove.

Sunday the 4th, M. de Bougainville accompanied by four or five officers went to dine with the governor, who had given us an invitation the Thursday before. I remained on board to say mass to the crew. The gentlemen who went were received and entertained splendidly as before. The wind and tide being against them hindered their returning to the ship that day, notwithstanding all their endeavours to accomplish it; they resolved therefore to go back again to the town. The governor had apprized them of the impossibility of their getting on board at that time, and had done every thing in his power to engage them to stay. He represented to them, the risque they must run by exposing themselves in such a manner to the dangers of a channel full of shallows, banks of sand, and rocks, which they would have the greatest difficulty in the world to avoid, if the night should come upon them before they reached the ship; that such an accident would put it entirely out of their power to discover the *sea marks*, and consequently to keep the channel. Besides, he had intended to give them the pleasure of a ball, and had already invited several ladies, wives to officers of the garrison.

The party being broke up by the departure of our gentlemen, he sent to all the persons who had been invited, to prevent their coming. But as soon as he understood that M. de Bougainville, and his companions were coming back to the town, he sent out to meet them, and without acquainting them of his intentions, dispatched fresh invitations for the supper and the ball, which was to follow.

After supper was over, at which the ladies were not present, the governor, without giving our gentlemen the least hint of what they were to expect, engaged them only to go and pass a few hours at the house of an officer of the garrison, where, as he said, they would find a very agreeable company. M. de Bougainville and the rest consented at first merely out of complaisance, but they were agreeably surprised to find there several ladies, by whom they were perfectly well received. They had never imagined from the reputation the Portuguese have of being extremely susceptible of jealousy, that they would have permitted their women to appear in such assemblies. They struck up however a kind of dance, in which the ladies figured as well as the gentlemen, and about two or three in the morning they retired very well satisfied with each other.

At this interview, M. de Bougainville took an opportunity of complaining to the governor of the behaviour of the Commandant of Santa Cruz, and obtained a general permission to take whatever measures he should judge proper for sporting, fishing, wooding, and watering wherever we pleased. At parting M. de Bougainville invited the governor, with the Oviodore, and such officers as he should think fit to bring with him, to dine on board our ship.

In consequence of this permission we sent our yawl out to fish almost every day, and she constantly came back loaded with fish of many kinds, and in such abundance as to serve the whole crew. The figures of them may be seen in the plates.

We went also every day a shooting either on the continent or in the island; though we soon left off going to the former, as

we

we found scarce any thing there but parrots, toucans, and some doves. In the island, beside these birds, which I have mentioned, there were sea larks, plovers, snipes, and some others in good number. The officers of the garrison, and the people of the country, whether from want of courage, or from indolence, or from the danger of meeting with wild beasts and serpents, which are in great plenty among the woods and morasses, never go out a sporting, and advised us to follow their example. It must be confessed indeed, that the cottagers are not provided with arms; and the few which one meets with are old, the greatest part made after the old fashion, with wheels for the trigger, and very bad. They had scarcely even powder or ball.

Less timid than they, and to say the truth better armed, we more than once penetrated into the accessible parts of the island. By the assistance of our light boots we surmounted the obstacles which presented themselves to us among the woods and thickets, from a species of thorny aloes, of which they are full. We never went alone, but always two or three in a company in order to assist each other in case of an attack from any overgrown serpent, or wild beast, particularly ounces; some claws of which we had seen here in the hands of some of the inhabitants mounted in silver, and which, as we were informed by them, were very common, and were more ravenous than even tygers.

One day when we were out in search of game upon the island, and had separated into different parties, I, with M. de Belcourt and his servant, kept along the side of a creek, which runs a considerable way within the land, and was called by us *the river*. M. de Belcourt amused himself with shooting at water-fowl. As we advanced along the border of this creek I perceived on the sand recent traces of some four-footed animal, which, to judge by the marks, must be very large, and seemed to be a tyger. We followed these traces till we came to a very marshy spot, where we did not dare to venture ourselves, not knowing either the bottom or the extent of it. Returning by the same way

way that we came, I perceived M. de Belcourt advancing towards us, and shewed him the traces.

These, said he to me, must certainly be the traces of a beast I saw hereabouts but just now, at the very instant he was darting into the thickets. He is about the heighth of the largest sized Danish dog, and of a greyish colour. He went in at that place, let us pursue him. With all my heart, replied I. We made our way as well as we could among these marshy thickets, which were so choaked up with a sharp species of aloes, whose leaves are sometimes not less than five feet in height, that we had all the trouble in the world to disengage ourselves from them. We beat about in vain for near two hours without seeing any thing of the beast we were in pursuit of: we only got sight of the hind part of another, the hair of which seemed to be of a greenish grey: his height about that of the largest kind of spaniel: his tail seemed to be as green as the leaves of the plants, which surrounded it, and to resemble that of a fox in thickness and in length. He hid himself among the bushes at the instant M. de Belcourt was going to fire at him.

The heat was now suffocating. We stopped and sat down on the ends of some branches, leaning our backs against a tree. We had with us some oranges and some sea-biscuit. While we were regaling ourselves in this posture, we were stunned with the incessant hissings of serpents, which surrounded us, and reduced us to the necessity of keeping constantly upon our guard with drawn sabres. After this breakfast, of which we had stood in great need, we continued our sport, drawing towards an eminence, at the top of which we discovered a cottage. Being arrived here, we found M. de Bougainville and his servant. Two Portuguese women, whose figures were not very inviting, received us, and displayed for near two hours, that we continued with them, the utmost freedom in their air and conversation. They had a tame parrot, which was tolerably pretty, and talked well. We proposed to purchase this bird; but the women refused to part with it. They longed for every thing we had,

handkerchiefs,

handkerchiefs, knives, hats, and even our fuzils and fabres: they
aſked us for all theſe without ceremony, and if we had been
willing to give into their way of thinking, neither our cloaths
nor even our ſhirts would have incommoded us on our return.
We contented ourſelves with a few oranges, and ſet out to dine
on board. On entering the wood we ſeparated again from
M. de Bougainville and his ſervant without intending it. The
path which M. de Belcourt and I took led us to a moraſs, where
the trees were luckily at a ſufficient diſtance from each other:
Here we ſaw ſeveral ſerpents about the thickneſs of the ſmall of
a man's leg, and others leſs, ſome of a reddiſh colour, others
red and yellow, and others grey, which laſt a good deal reſembled adders of the largeſt ſize; but inſtead of attacking, they fled
before us. When we were almoſt got to our boat, M. de Belcourt fired at a bird, called *the ſpoon-bill*, and broke only one of
his wings. He took it up and brought it on board. It was a
young one, and all its plumage was of a faint roſe colour; the
proceſs of the quill from which the beards of the wing feathers
riſe, was of a bright roſe colour. Its legs were a foot long including the thighs, and of a light grey as well as the feet, which
were webbed, like thoſe of geeſe. Its beak was ſix inches in
length, and both the upper and under part flat grey towards
the root, and white towards the extremity: it began to ſpread at
about two thirds of its length, and ended ' a ſpatula, of two
inches and a half diameter in its grea' .t breadth. We carried
it to the ſhip, where it lived three days on ſome ſmall fiſhes,
and bits of freſh meat, which were forced down its throat; for it
would not eat of itſelf. When any one came near it, it made
a noiſe with its bill as loud as that of two wooden battle-
dores ſtruck one againſt the other.

Some of our ſailors gave it the name of flamingo, but that
of *ſpoon-bill*, or *palette (battledore)* is more ſuitable, on account of
the ſhape of its bill, very unlike to that of the flamingo, which
is made almoſt in the commoneſt form of a bird-bill.

L                                           The

The next day we went again on the ifland in purfuit of the animal we had not been able to meet with the evening before. There were feveral that made their way into the fame wood. M. l'Huillier found there another beaft of the fame fize as that I have mentioned, but of the yellow colour, and nearly of the fhape, of a lion. He fired three times at him loaded with bullet, two of which wounded without ftopping him, and without making him go one ftep either fafter or flower. We followed him by the traces of the blood, but he rufhed in among the thickets, and we faw no more of him. The heat being very intenfe, and we having fcarcely more than time fufficient to get on board for dinner, contented ourfelves with killing parrots, plovers, fnipes and fome other birds. As I was curious to have a humming bird, of which I faw many flying round our heads, and could not, or at leaft did not know how to take them alive, I ventured to fire at one, which was fluttering about like a butterfly, and hovered in the fame manner over a fmall branch of a tree. The little bird, whether through fear or the violent concuffion of the air, dropped inftantly. After having looked for it a long time, I found it at laft dead on a leaf of the fame branch. The figure of it in its natural fize is to be feen in the plate.

Some call this bird, *Lifongere or Beequefleurs*, becaufe it is continually fluttering about flowers, like the butterfly, and fucks the moifture of them in the fame manner. The whole compafs of its body with the feathers is not larger than a common nut. It has a tail near three times as long as its body; its neck is rather fmall, its head in proportion, and its eyes are very fharp. The bill is fomewhat whitifh at the root, the reft of it is black; it is as long as the body of the bird, is fmall and very fharp. The wings are long, thin, and very extenfive in proportion; the extremity of the feathers reaches to two-thirds or thereabouts of the tail, which as well as the wings is of a purpleifh brown. The reft of the plumage is green with a gold caft, as if one had fpread a layer of green almoft tranfparent over a leaf of gold.

The

## TO THE MALOUINE ISLANDS.

The neck and head are of a deep blue, gilt in the same manner. These colours vary according as the light strikes more or less forcibly on the different parts. Sometimes the whole plumage of this bird resembles a pigeon's neck, or the green feathers on the wings of wild ducks; sometimes it is of a fine blue, sometimes of a fine green, sometimes of a purple, and all these mixed with the splendor of a lively gold colour, bright and burnished. The tongue of this bird in miniature is forked, and has the appearance of two twists of red silk. Its feet are short, black, and furnished with very long claws.

There are several species of them, which differ both in size and colour. One of the small kind, which I have preserved in brandy, has white feathers from the breast to the tail. The colour of the rest of its plumage is like that of the others.

The female lays but two eggs, of the size of a small pea. They build their nests in orange trees with the smallest straws they can find. The Portuguese, who lived in the cottage near which we watered, gave us one of these nests with two young ones in it, which were not yet covered with the first down. He had just taken it with the father and mother, close by his habitation; we put it down on a stone bench at the door of the house, while we were eating an orange, and had scarcely turned our backs, when a cat came and carried off both nest and young ones. These nests are of an admirable construction, and about the size of a half crown. The Brazilians call this bird by the names of *Guainumbi, Guinambi, Aratica, Aretarataguacu.* The Portuguese call it *Pegafrol.*

We had beside these a third kind, somewhat larger than those I have been describing, but much less than the smallest wrens we have in Europe. The feathers of their head begin towards the middle of their upper bill. They are exceedingly small at their rise, are disposed in scales, and grow larger as they are nearer to the head, at the top of which they form a little tuft of uncommon beauty for the brilliancy of the gold, and the variety of colours, which change according to the direction of the rays of light, or the position of the spectator's eye. Sometimes the plumage of this bird is of a black equal to that of the finest black velvet, sometimes of a pea green, sometimes yellow. At other times it resembles cloth of gold shaded with all these colours. The back is of a dark green shot with gold. The large feathers of the wing are of a deep violet, approaching sometimes to purple. The tail is composed of nine feathers as long as the whole body, and of a black mixed with brown, purple, and violet, which form a most agreeable assemblage of colours, and have the same changeable property as above. The whole lower part of the belly likewise exhibits a mixture of black, violet, green, and yellow, which always strike the eye of the observer differently, according to the difference of his own situation or of that of the bird. Its eyes are of a lively, brilliant black, not inferior to the finest polished jet; its legs are short, and black, as well as its feet; which are composed of four claws, three of them in front, all furnished with black, crooked, sharp talons, very long in proportion to the rest of the body. When it flies, it makes a buzzing with its wings, very much like that of certain large flies which we see in France fluttering about among the flowers. It builds its nest upon shrubs, among high branches of orange, or other low trees. In our French islands it goes by the name of *Colibris*, and sometimes *Quinde*. The Spaniards call them *Tomineios*, because the nest and bird together do not weigh more than the Spanish *Tomin*.

When we came on board, we found a Spaniard there, who was settled in the country, and to whose care we had, the day we came to anchor, committed a sheep that was distempered and very lean: the sheep was to graze about the man's cottage, by which means we hoped to restore him. This Spaniard had brought us some hundreds of oysters. They were much larger than the white oysters of Saintonge; for the shells were at least five inches in diameter. We do not eat fatter or better oysters in France. They were a perfect cream, both in taste and whiteness. We did every thing in our power to induce the Spaniard to discover the place where he found them, but we could not succeed,

succeed. All we could obtain from him was a promise of bringing us some more, and this was not performed till a day or two before our departure. We endeavoured to find out his cottage, but in vain; he had not given us a proper direction; and as for our sheep we saw no more of it: he made us ample amends, however, when we were on the point of quitting the harbour, by a present he brought us of some thousands of oranges and lemons, and of seven or eight hundred of the same kind of oysters.

There was a Portuguese too on board, who had brought a large handsome canoe, which our captain M. Duclos Guyot had bought for M. de Bougainville, who imagined at that time, that it might be very useful to us at the Malouine islands, to which we were bound. She was fitted out with her \* *Pagaies*, or PAGALLES, as father Labat calls them in his *Nouveaux Voyages*. This canoe was made of a single trunk of a cinnamon tree hollowed, nineteen feet, odd inches in length, and three feet in breadth on the inside, and about the same depth. Some of our officers, as well land as sea, who had been in Canada, understood the working of her. She was used on our fishing expeditions. But when we put into Montevideo, M. de Bougainville parted with her to a Spanish officer for eight piastres; she had cost him about eighteen French livres.

About four o'clock in the afternoon we went over to the main land, and visited several cottages on the coast, where we made provision of lemons, oranges, and some pine-apples, which we found ripe. This fruit, and the plant which bears it are known at present in Europe, as they bear the voyage very well, but there is a very great difference both in flavour and smell between the specimens of this fruit produced in France, even in Provence and Languedoc, and what is found in Brazil. It grows there of itself without cultivation, and in great abundance. It turns the knives, with which it is cut, black, and spoils them; which pro-

\* Paddles.

bably

bably has given occasion to some authors to say, that the rind of it is so hard, that it blunts the edge of a knife. It is true, that if, after cutting the pine-apple in slices, you neglect to wash and wipe your knife very well, you will find it after a few hours spoiled and rusty, as if you had put *aqua fortis* somewhat lowered upon it. The juice of this fruit is of great efficacy in taking spots out of cloaths. That of Brazil, they will tell you, is a preservative against sea-sickness.

In my walk I gathered some seeds of plants, and some grenadillas, with a small red fruit of the colour of cinnabar, which bears a pretty near resemblance to the love-apple. A Portuguese, who was with us, told me, they call it *Maracuja*, the figure of it is in the plate annexed.

The plant which bears this fruit is prickly, the leaf is very like that of the *Stramonium furiosum*, but not so large. Under the rind of the fruit is a pulp, of one sixth part of an inch in depth, white, and of the consistence of that of the Calville apple, of a sweetish but insipid flavour. The inside is intirely filled with flat seeds, of the same form as those of the large Pimento or long pepper. The Portuguese informed me, that the fruit, Maracuja, was never eaten, altho' he did not know that it had any dangerous qualities.

The Grenadilla of Brazil is round, yet rather flat at the ends, and of the size of a pullet's egg. Its bark is very smooth, glittering on the outside, and of a carnation colour, when the fruit is ripe. On the inside it is white and soft, its thickness about the eighth part of an inch. The substance which it incloses is viscous, it is of a refreshing and cordial nature, the taste of it is between sweet and sour. It may be eaten in quantities without any inconvenience. There are to be found in it a number of small seeds or kernels much resembling linseed in shape, and not so hard as those of the common pomegranate. This whole substance is separated from the bark by a very thin skin. The plant which bears this fruit twines about the trees, and resembles as to its leaves and flower, what we call the passion flower. It diffuses a very sweet scent. To eat the Grenadilla in perfection, it should not be suffered

fered to ripen entirely upon the plant. It would decay and dry up. It muft be gathered a little before it is ripe, and kept a few days.

Since our arrival at Brazil we were conftantly in fearch of parrots, but could not find any tame ones to be bought. In the tour that we made, we had the good luck to meet with fome complaifant Portuguefe, who parted with one to Mr. l' Huillier; this officer found means alfo to get one for Mr. de Belcourt. Upon our returning on board, a Spaniard who talked a little French, and whom we had commiffioned to procure us fome, offered us four, two of which were already reared, and talked the Portuguefe language, as did the two of which I have already fpoken. The other two were but juft taken from their neft, and could not feed themfelves. I gave a ftriped ribband for one of thefe laft; and I preferred it with an idea that it would learn the French language with greater facility. I kept him till the beginning of May, when he died of a catarrh in the head. This catarrh had caufed his eyes to fwell. It fell upon his lungs, and having rendered him aftmatic, it was impoffible for me to fave him.

Among thefe parrots there were three kinds, which differed in their plumage and fize. One of M. l' Huillier's had the feathers of his neck and ftomach of a tawny and changeable red, mixed with a little grey; the top of the fore part of the head of a vermilion colour, rather faded and extinguifhed, the tips of the wings of a brighter red than that of the rofe, and feveral of the feathers in the wings and tail of a fine carmine; others of a very fine azure blue, and fome black: all the reft of the body was green. He fpoke Portuguefe extremely well, and learned French very eafily. He died juft upon our arrival at the Malouine iflands. The fecond was bigger than any we had: the top of his head was of a vermilion red, the two fides of a light blue towards the ears, and which grew fainter even fo much as to become grey in proportion as the feathers were at a greater diftance from them. The wings and tail were like thofe of the firft. The others

others were scarce above half that size; they resembled them however as to their plumage, except that the red upon their heads was much more lively, which might perhaps be owing to their being younger. Monf. de Bougainville's parrot died of the same disorder as mine, during our stay at the Malouine iflands; M. de Belcourt's fell into the sea and was drowned, so that out of seven, we brought no more than two to France, Mr. l' Huillier's large one, which I delivered to him safe and sound at Versailles, and one of the smaller kind which had no tail, for he plucked out the feathers of it as fast as they grew. The sailor to whom it belonged, had not taken near the same care of him as we had done of ours, and yet preserved him. It was impossible to speak better than he did; and he imitated the cries of the children we had on board, and those of the cabbin boys when they were whipt for any fault they had committed, the cackling of the hens, and the noise of all the other animals we had in the frigate, so well, as to deceive every body that heard him.

Paffing by the habitation in which we had lodged our Acadian families, we heard a noise like that of a wood-cutter felling of wood. We asked a freed negro, what it was? It is, answered he, a monkey that ranges about the garden to eat the fruit and the corn, and is giving notice to his comrades to come and affift him; but if I had a good gun like yours, I would soon dislodge him. He has been two or three days making this racket. One of our boatswains lent him his gun; the negro loaded it with large shot, followed the noise, and shot at the monkey twice without making him run away: at the third shot he fell dead at the foot of the tree. The boatswain brought the monkey on board the frigate where we had opportunity to examine him at our leisure. He was near two feet eight inches high, when standing upon his hind legs; his hair was long, and of a fawn coloured brown all over his body except under the belly, which approached the clear fawn colour. His brown beard began from his ears and fell near five inches upon his breast; his feet and hands were black; his ears, destitute of hair, were well detached from each

each other and his face covered with a tawny down, fo clofe as to be hardly diftinguifhable from the fkin. His eye brows were of a darker hue and prominent. His tail was as long as his body including his head.

I know not at what fport he had loft his left eye : this, however, was not to be perceived without a clofe examination ; for in the focket he had fubftituted a ball, compofed of a gum which was unknown to us, of rotten wood and fome very fine mofs, the whole mixed up together. The eye-lid covered this ball as if it had been really the globe of the eye. Whether he had contrived this falfe eye to appear lefs deformed, or to cure his wounded eye, or to defend it from the infults of flies and other infects, I leave to conjecture. We obferved alfo, that this monkey appeared old, for the fkin of his face was greatly wrinkled, and he had fome white hairs in his beard. We faw but this one during our ftay at the ifland of St. Catherine's, though we were told that there were a great number, and that the inhabitants eat the young ones, which are very good. They endeavoured even to perfuade me that one of the ragouts of which I ate at the Governor's, and which I took to be an excellent rabbit, was really a monkey. Be this as it would, many others ate of it as well as myfelf, and appeared well pleafed with it.

The mafter of the habitation near which we got our water, having perceived that Mr. le Roy, lieutenant of our fhip, had a great inclination for a pretty little bird that he had in a cage, and which fang very well, made him a prefent of it. This bird is called in the Brazils, *Guranbé Engera*. It is of the fize of a Canary bird. Its wings, back, neck and tail are blue, with fome white fpots about the middle of the large feathers of the wings and tail, difpofed in the fame manner as thefe fpots are in the wings and tail of the gold-finch. From the under part of the bill along the breaft to the under part of the tail, all the feathers are of a golden yellow, bright and glittering; its warbling varies like that of the Canary, and it imitates the finging of other

M     birds.

birds. There are several forts of them. The Brazilians call them alfo *Teitei*. For its Figure, fee the Plate.

As I was walking in the fields with our captain, I perceived him gathering a large quantity of a plant with yellow flowers, which I took at the first glance for the yellow amaranth, which abounds on the rifing grounds on the coaft of Terra Firma. Curiofity led me to afk him the ufe which he meant to put it to. He told me, that it was the *Doradilla*; that when he was at Valparafo, he had heard it called by that name; and that in that town, as well as in all the others in er where he had been, they ufed a great deal of it in infufion a the cure of pains in the ftomach. Our captain was fubjec them at times. I gathered a pretty large quantity of it, and drank it fometimes by way of tea. The tafte of it is agreeable enough. Others call it *Vira-verda*; this is the name that is given to it at Montevideo alfo. Frezier, in his account of his voyage to the South feas, fays, that a French furgeon made ufe of it with great fuccefs in the cure of the tertian ague. But the *Doradilla* which the Spaniards have, is a kind of fpleen-wort, the leaf of which is curled. They attribute great virtues to it. The ftalk and leaves of the vira-verda, which we fpeak of at prefent, are fpongy, and like the yellow amaranth, its flower is an affemblage of fmall yellow buds, the leaves of which are pointed. The flowers of the amaranth are in form of a rofe, and the leaves of it are difpofed in the fame manner.

At our return from fifhing, abundantly fupplied as ufual, we examined the different forts of fifh, and among them found that which is called in the Brazils *Panapana*. The one that I give the figure of was two feet and a half long from the head to the beginning of the tail, the diftance between the eyes was ten inches. Its fkin was rough and hard like that of a fhark, but confiderably finer, nearly the fame as that of the fkin of a kind of fhark, commonly flim and of a middling fize, which our failors call *Demoifelle*; we catched three or four of them during

our

our stay at the island of St. Catherine's, and two at the Maldonades at the mouth of Rio de la Plata.

The head of the Panapana is flat, ill-formed, and in the shape of a hammer. Its eyes are at a great distance from each other; being placed at the opposite extremities of the head. Its mouth and tail are like those of the shark, its teeth are very sharp; but I did not find seven rows of them. Our sailors gave it the name of *marteau* or hammer, which is very applicable to its shape.

Among the number of plants which I gathered, was a sort of pepper, or piment, very common in the fields along the skirts of the woods. It is infinitely sharper than that of the pimento or long pepper, which we are accustomed to in France. On this account our sailors called it *piment enragé*. This fruit is of the same length form and colour, but at least twice as thick as that of the Barberry tree. It is at first green, and grows red as it becomes ripe. The flower which precedes it, is like that of the pimento. The plant which bears it, grows to the height of about two feet. It is full of branches and joints; its stem is round, green, and rather slender. The leaves of it are in shape like those of the *solanum hortense*, or garden nightshade; but as small as those of the *chenopodium fœtidum* or *vulvaria*, which they resemble much. One of the small fruits of the *piment enragé* put into sauce, heightens the flavour as much as an entire one of the larger sort. This induced our sailors to lay in a large provision of them.

I had also furnished myself with all the ripe seeds of the plants which I found, and having met with some Portuguese women in a hut, who were picking cotton to separate it from its seeds, they gave me a handful of them. They did me the greater pleasure, as I was very desirous of having some, and as I could not gather any from the plant, the shrub being just then in flower. The wood of it is tender and spongy; the bark thin and grey. Its leaves are of a bright green when young, but grow of a deeper colour as they approach to maturity, or as the shrub grows old. They are large, and divided into five parts, which terminate

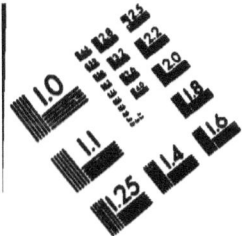 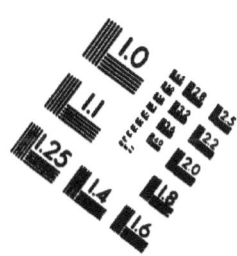

**IMAGE EVALUATION
TEST TARGET (MT-3)**

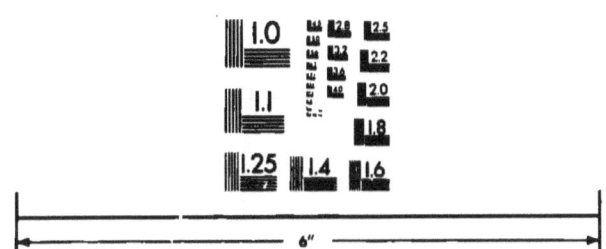

Photographic
Sciences
Corporation

23 WEST MAIN STREET
WEBSTER, N.Y. 14580
(716) 872-4503

terminate in a point. Thofe which are nearest the flower are only in three parts, and refemble much thofe of the *Ricinus*. Its flowers are almoft like thofe of a fmall fhrub, which is now in fafhion for the decoration of our parterres, called *althea*; They are not however quite fo open. They are yellow towards the end, and fpotted with red at the bottom. It is a pentapetalous plant, fupported by a calix of fmall green leaves, which are hard and pointed. To the piftil fucceeds a bud, or oval fruit, which in its ftate of maturity is of the bignefs of a duck's egg. This fruit is divided into three or four different cells, filled with a white ftringy fubftance, which inclofes ten or twelve feeds of a dark brown colour fticking together two by two, like wheat in the ear. Thefe feeds are of the fize of a pea, and about three or four lines in length.

- This ftringy fubftance is that which we know by the name of cotton. It fwells and fprings in the fhell, which contains it, in fuch a manner as to force it open when the fruit is ripe. At that time the feeds, full of an oily fubftance, feparate themfelves, with the locks of cotton which inclofe them, and fall from the fruit, unlefs care is taken to gather them in time.

The Portuguefe muft certainly be unacquainted with the machines which are made ufe of in our Antilles, for feparating the cotton from the feeds which it inclofes, and to which it fticks; or elfe the Portuguefe women I have feen employed at this work, did it merely by way of amufement; for they feparated it bit by bit, only by pinching the cotton between their fingers. They fpin it afterwards to make cloth of it; but I do not know with what machine, as I never faw them at that work.

This is the only kind of cotton tree which I found cultivated in the ifland of St. Catherine's, and upon the coafts of the Continent in its neighbourhood. It is very different from the cotton tree in the Brazils, of which Dampier fpeaks in the following terms: " Its flower is compofed of fmall filaments al-
" moft as loofe as hair, three or four inches long, and of a dark
" red except the tips, which are of an afh colour. At the bot-
" tom

"tom of the ftalk there are five narrow ftiff leaves about fix inches long." The kind which Frezier fpeaks of, refembles in every refpect that which I have defcribed, except that the feeds of the latter are not feparated from each other, and difperfed in the cotton, as that author fays, and as he has reprefented them in the figure which he has given of the fruit. It feems as if father Labat had copied from this figure of the cotton tree the one which he has inferted in the fecond volume of his new voyage to the American iflands, or perhaps Frezier may have taken it from him. The figures given by each of them are exactly alike.

In a hut a little farther on, where we went to beg fome water to drink, the woman who gave us fome was employed in ftripping leaves, with long thin thorns on the ftalk, from a kind of reed very common along the fides of the woods and roads. She drew from them a fort of green thread extremely fine, much like raw-filk, and of a light green colour. She told us, that fhe afterwards fpun this ftringy fubftance to make lines and fifhing nets of it, which fhe faid lafted a long time. Perhaps it might be made ufe of for other purpofes.

Not far from thence, I faw for the firft time, a kind of aloes called *pitbe*, the leaf of which when fteeped like hemp affords a fubftance fit for fpinning, and of which they make linen cloth in the Eaft. From the midft of a fcore of leaves, about five feet high, and at leaft three inches thick at the bottom, their edges thorny, ending in a point, hollowed out, and of a fine green, fprang up a green ftalk of about eight inches diameter at the bottom, which diminifhed gradually to the top, and grew to the heighth of at leaft thirty feet. From the heighth of about twenty feet of this ftalk quite to its fummit, there fprang branches to the number of twelve or fifteen, adorned with a number of fprigs, almoft like the growing ftalk of the lilly plant, when rifing about two inches from the earth. Thefe tufts of fprigs grow irregularly along the branches, which are deftitute of any other foliage, and fpread themfelves almoft horizontally. Without doubt, thefe fprigs when arrived to a certain pitch of maturity, break of themselves, and take root in the earth where they happen to fall. I picked up about fifteen with their roots, which I carried on board, where we planted them in boxes placed over our cabbins. They did very well there, and we should in all probability have preserved the greatest part of them, if, notwithstanding all our care, two cats which we had on board had not scratched up the earth of these boxes, and poisoned it with their urine and excrement. We resolved at last, though rather late, to cover them with fishing nets, supported by hoops, and we preserved two plants of them, as well as some cotton trees, raised from the seeds which we had sown. They were all transplanted at our arrival at St. Malo's, into the garden of Beau Sejour at St. Servant, which was occupied by M. Duclos Guyot our captain.

The Portuguese have perhaps remarked that the sprigs of the *pitbe*, which have thus taken root of themselves, do not thrive so well as those, which have been carefully put into ground well tilled. This is probably what induces them to make holes of about a foot square in the earth beneath the branches, and about the plant itself, where I found five or six of these sprigs planted; and which, in reality, seemed to have thriven better than those which had been wholly abandoned to nature. I cannot say, whether the *pitbe* bears any other fruit, or whether it multiplies by any other means.

Besides lemons and oranges, there is in the isle of St. Catherine's a sort of refreshy for sportsmen. This fruit, which is very common, is called the American Indian fig. It is in shape much like our figs. Its first skin is green; it then grows rather yellow, and afterwards assumes the colour of red lacker on the side which has been exposed to the rays of the sun. This skin is stuck full of very small prickles. Those who gather this fruit and peal it must be very dextrous, not to fill their fingers with these prickles, which are almost imperceptible. Happily they cause more uneasiness than mischief, till one has found the method of getting rid of them.

Under

TO THE MALOUINE ISLANDS. 69

Under the skin, which is about as thick as that of a fig is found a white covering, thin and tenderer than the other. It inclofes a foft fubftance, of a bright red, mixed with fmall grains like thofe of the fig. This fubftance has an acid tafte, a little fweet, and extremely grateful. When people eat a confiderable quantity of it their urine becomes red, but without any harm refulting from it. This fruit is even cooling. Our captain, his two fons and myfelf, were almoft the only people who eat of it: the others did not dare to follow our example through apprehenfion of fuffering fome inconvenience from it.

In order to avoid running any of the rifques which I have mentioned in gathering thefe prickly figs, get a fmall piece of wood fhaped like a bodkin, and ftick it into the fig near the ftalk; cut off this ftalk with a knife, and holding the fruit in this manner at the end of the bit of wood, peal it lightly all round, without touching it with your fingers.

On Saturday the tenth of December we fent out fome people to fhoot in the ifland, in order to procure fome game to treat the Governor, whom M. de Bougainville had invited to dine on board our frigate the next day. They brought nothing but parrots, fnipes, and fome other birds.

We found in a wet marfhy foil a prodigious quantity of a fort of crab which live on fhore, and make their retreat in holes which they dig. They give them the name of *tourlouroux*; the biggeft are not above two inches wide. The fhape of their fhell is almoft fquare, of a brownifh red, growing lighter by degrees towards the belly, which is of a clear red. This fhell or helmet is pretty ftrong though thin. Their eyes are of a fhining black and as hard as horn. They fhoot out and drawn in again like thofe of lobfters.

Thefe crabs have four legs on each fide, each of them compofed of four joints, the laft of which is flat and terminates in a point. They make ufe of them to walk fideways, like common crabs, and to dig up the earth. Befide thefe, they have two

other

other legs or claws bigger than the former, but especially the right, which is at least double the size of the other. These claws or pincers are of a bright red, shaped like those of sea-crabs; they make use of them for cutting leaves, and the roots of plants on which they feed. When they see any thing which frightens them they strike these two claws against each other, as it were to frighten their enemy, and lift up the biggest of them perpendicularly, marching thus in a state of defence; but retiring at the same time into their holes. These claws as well as their legs, are so slightly fixed to their body that they come off in the hands of those who endeavour to take them, and the tourlonrou escapes.

Both sexes have their tails bent under their bellies, where it enters so exactly into a cavity which is in the shell of the belly that it can hardly be distinguished. That of the male diminishes in size quite to the end. The female's is equally large to its extremity. As fast as the female lays her eggs, they attach themselves to the long rough hairs with which the under part of the tail is furnished. These support, cover, and prevent them from falling, or from being detached by the sand, herbs, or other unequal surfaces which fall in her way.

These animals were so numerous in this marshy ground, that it was impossible to set down one's foot without crushing several of them. I cannot say whether the inhabitants of the coasts eat these animals, as they do in the Antilles, where they are of great service to the Carribbees and negroes. The Creoles themselves, according to father Labat, regale themselves with them.

About ten o'clock in the morning, on Sunday the eleventh of December, we received the Governor on board. He left the town by two in the morning, in his canoe, with his son, accompanied by a minister from the King of Portugal, who was first president of the sovereign council of Rio Janeiro, by the Oviodore, the major, and some other officers of the garrison. The tide and a contrary wind had prevented their arriving sooner.

The

The tent was pitched upon the quarter-deck, which was set out in form for the company; the ship was spread with the quarter-cloths, and the French flag displayed. When every body was seated, I said mass with the usual solemnities; and at noon a dinner was served up as elegant as possible in our present situation. The King of Portugal's health was drunk, under a discharge of eleven pieces of cannon, which were all answered regularly from the fort of Santa Cruz.

After dinner some inferior officers, the same who had played on different instruments at the Governor's, played again, and made a kind of concert, which lasted about two hours. During this amusement, a wind arose unfavourable to the Governor's return, the weather became overcast, and so heavy a rain fell that it was scarce possible to think of going back to the town, or even to one of the forts. M. de Bougainville proposed a party of play to amuse these gentlemen, which was accepted. The wind and rain continuing, M. de Bougainville persuaded the governor and his company to lie on board. While we were waiting for supper, which consisted only of the remains of the dinner, and at which the Governor, as well as most of the rest of the company, drank only a glass of water, I conversed all the time with the Portuguese minister, who wanted nothing but practice to speak the French language well, and who made use of very expressive Latin words, whenever he was at a loss for a French term. This minister, who was well acquainted with Brazil, and was at that time upon his tour through the country, according to custom, was so obliging as to answer all my questions, and gave me all the information I could wish relative to the country and its inhabitants, of which I shall give an account hereafter.

Messieurs de Bougainville, and de Nerville, gave up their beds to the governor, and the Portuguese minister; the Oviodore lay in the cabbin of M. Duclos Guyot our captain, and the other officers would absolutely lie upon the table under the tent, where matrasses were spread for them. We all passed the night as well as we could. At four o'clock in the morning, the governor and his

his company set off in his boat for Fort Santa Cruz, to give orders that we might be supplied with oxen, &c. and every thing we wanted. At his going away, we saluted him with nine pieces of cannon, which were immediately returned by the fort.

Before we sat down to supper, M. de Bougainville had begged the favour of the Governor, to get the letters we had written to give our friends some intelligence about us, conveyed to Portugal, and from thence to France. A few days after, a Portuguese snow, which then lay at anchor before the town of *Our Lady in Exile*, intended to set sail for Rio de Janeiro, and had promised us to deliver our packets to some one of the captains of the fleet, which was to set out from thence towards the end of the month. The Governor very readily took this commission upon himself, and M. de Bougainville sent him our parcels. But whether the Rio de Janeiro fleet was gone, before our letters reached that place, or whether from any other accident, it is certain that our parcels never came to hand.

Five or six hours after the Governor's landing at Fort Santa Cruz, a present came to us from him of two oxen, as many cows, a heifer, two turkeys, twenty-six Brazil ducks and drakes with large red tufts, and other refreshments. M. de Bougainville had in the evening presented him with a box full of snuff-boxes, painted and varnished by Martin, and with some very handsome fans.

The two following days were employed in compleating our provision of wood for firing; it was composed of sassafras, cedar, and of yellow wood of Brazil. Having been told by a free negro, that the tree which bears the balsam of *copaiba*, known under the name of copahu, is not rare in this country, I did my utmost to get some of it, but could not succeed. The Portuguese who had promised to procure me some, assured me that this balsam only flows during the full moon.

As our destination was for a country, where our sailors had never yet been, and whose seas and weather were reputed tempestuous,

pestuous, before we set sail from Saint Catherine's, our captain, with his usual prudence and foresight, took care to provide himself with small top-masts and top-gallant sails, to serve in case of bad weather.

For this purpose he applied to the free negro, of whom I have made mention more than once; he rendered us all the service in his power with the greatest readiness, and even made a proposal to M. de Bougainville of going with him; adding, that he was ready to go to any place where we pleased to take him. He was a stout fellow, and worked hard; M. de Bougainville would willingly have acquiesced in his demand, if he had not been apprehensive that the Portuguese might have complained we had put in to decoy away the negroes of the country; and that such a report or suspicion might be of disservice to those French vessels which might afterwards put in at St. Catherine's.

This negro went himself into the forest, to look out for such trees as he thought might best suit our captain's purpose. When he had found them he informed him of it, and conducted us there through thickets and bushes, in the midst of which we were obliged to climb up the mountain to get at these trees, which were in the thick of the forest. We went thither well armed, and in a pretty large body, as well for the convenience of cutting down these trees, as to be able to convey them to the sea side. We met with no wild beasts in the forest, but only two or three large serpents which we killed. As we were going along I cut seven or eight bamboo canes; they are a kind of knotty reed, the joints of which are very close, and the closer they are the more beautiful are the canes. These bamboos were of a good size, from five feet and a half to six feet long; but unfortunately were not come to their maturity. In drying them they shrivelled up, and became as it were fluted. I left them at St. Malo's.

In order to convey our wood to the water side, we were obliged to tie them with cords, and to drag them, sometimes even to lift them, over branches which stopped up our way. We were often forced

forced to make a road, which we did with hatchets. I obferved palm trees there of a prodigious heighth, of about a foot diameter, and as ftraight as bulrufhes; this is a kind of tree whofe trunk and branches are quite covered with fmall thorny excrefsences, of about fix or eight lines in diameter, or fometimes more at their bafe, projecting about half an inch, and the thorn, which grows in the center, being about four lines long. The bark of this tree is grey, and refembles that of the beach tree. May not this be the fame, which is in our Antilles called *bois epineux?*

On Tuefday morning a failor, after having cut fome grafs for our cattle, fitting down by it with his legs bare, was bit near the ancle by a ferpent, as he told us, about a foot and a half long, of a reddifh yellow colour in ftreaks. He paid no attention to the bite, and as foon as he came on board he dined heartily without uneafinefs, faying he was hungry. In about half an hour after he found himfelf fick; and perceiving his leg very much fwelled and painful, he came and acquainted me with it. I began by endeavouring to keep up his fpirits, and to eafe him of the fear which had feized upon him. Whilft I was giving notice of this to the two furgeons of our frigate, he vomited, and did the fame once or twice in the fpace of an hour. We made him take two drams of theriaca mixed in a glafs of wine, with ten drops of volatile fpirit of fal ammoniac, and after having fcarified the wound, which was already become black, applied to it a plaifter of theriaca pounded with garlick. Notwithftanding this his ficknefs continued, and he vomited two or three times more. The fame remedy was repeated. In the meanwhile, a Portuguefe officer from Fort Santa Cruz came on board, to whom we related what had happened. The failor's account, with the defcription of the reptile, gave the officer reafon to judge, that this ferpent was of one of thofe kinds which the people of the country call *Jararaca*. " Its venom, faid he, is fo dangerous, that it caufes inevitable death to thofe, who are not excited by it to vomit within the four and twenty hours. But

fince

since your sailor has vomited, you may make yourselves easy upon his account. Continue however to give him the same medicine, with the addition of an emetic. There are several other kinds of *Jararaca*, which are equally to be dreaded; especially one, which is of an earth or cinder colour, with some streaks on the head which are rather darker." The next day, neither the blackness of the wound, nor the inflammation of the leg being increased, the emetic was given to the patient, and a fresh plaister of the same kind as the former was applied. After this no other accident happened to him, and the wound was treated as a common one. He was purged twice afterwards, and from that time was very well. In going into the woods and fields, you are almost always liable to be bit by these dangerous reptiles, which are very numerous there. We very frequently saw in the sand on the sea side, winding furrows formed by the traces of serpents which had passed there. If any one who has the misfortune to be bit by one of them, does not immediately meet with proper assistance, he must expect to die in the most cruel tortures. Some sorts, especially those of the Juraracas, exhale a very strong smell of musk. This smell is of great service to those who know it, to prevent their being surprised by them.

The only lizard which I saw in the isle of St. Catherine's, might be about two feet long, and three or four inches broad. Its skin was black, spotted with white from the head to the end of the tail. The belly was much the same, but the white was rather prevalent; all over the rest of the body, the black and white was almost equally disposed in spots of a regular figure; its shape in other respects was like that of the green lizards in France. M. de Nerville, who was with me, was preparing his gun to fire at him, when I perceived that the animal was dead. We went towards it; but as it already stank very much, we did not think proper to examine it with greater attention. Might not this be what is called by the people of the country the *Maboya*, or *Tejuguacu*, and *Iguana* by Pison and Margraff?

The

The rattle snake is very common there: its length extends as far as three feet, but very seldom exceeds above half a foot more. Its colour is of an iron grey, regularly streaked. At the extremity of its tail is fastened what the Spaniards call its *cascabelle*, and for the same reason the serpent *cascabella*. This cascabelle, which we have chose to call the rattle, on account of the noise it makes, resembles the husks of peas dried upon the plant. It is divided in the same manner into several joints, which contain small round little bones, whose friction produces a sound much like that of two or three rattles, or small bells which make but a dull noise. The day that M. de Belcourt and I were in the woods looking for the animal whose traces we had seen in the sand, we thought we heard this sound mixed with a kind of hissing; which also was much like the noise usually made by grasshoppers. The bite of this serpent is so dangerous, that it is happy for the inhabitants of the countries where it is found, that nature has given to this reptile a sign to warn them of its approach; without which, its colour differing very little from that of the earth, it would be very difficult for them not to be surprised by it, and to avoid it. This animal is also called *boicininga*.

To feed the cattle which we were taking with us from the island of St. Catherine, we laid in a provision of the stalks of the *banana tree*, with which we covered our quarter-deck, both within and without. This forrage is the most convenient for transportation; as it takes up very little room, and was therefore less cumbersome than any other. Besides, meadows are very scarce in this island, as well as along the coast of the Continent, and the little grass which grows there is marshy. It would have been difficult to have procured a sufficient quantity of it; and that even, not being come to a state of maturity fit for keeping, would have heated, and afforded a very bad subsistence for these cattle. The stalks of the banana were a very good substitute, as much on account of their keeping very well, as because they are very nourishing. We had only to cut them in pieces with a knife,

TO THE MALOUINE ISLANDS. 77

a knife, after which our oxen and sheep ate them with great eagerness.

The banana is a plant, the stem of which is compofed only of leaves rolled one upon the other, of a reddifh white colour in fome places, and a greenifh yellow in others. When the root fhoots out a fprig, there are only two leaves rolled one within the other, which appear coming out at the edge of the ground. Thefe leaves unfold and expand themfelves, to give way to two others, arifing from the fame center. Thefe being rolled up as the former, expand themfelves in the fame manner, and are followed by feveral others, which growing higher and broader as they fucceed each other, and being always rolled up in the fame manner, form at length the ftem of this arboreous plant, which rifes to eight, ten, and even twelve feet; but not any higher. Then the leaves grow out from the top, and the middle of the ftem, to which they are connected merely by a foot ftalk about an inch in diameter, a foot long, round on one fide, and hollowed on the other by a groove in the middle. This foot ftalk being continued, forms the vein or band which runs along the middle of the leaf, which is fometimes fifteen or eighteen inches wide, and fix or feven feet long. The fupine difk of this leaf is of a fine green colour, the prone difk of a green inclining to grey, which makes it appear filvered. It is nearly of the fubftance of very thick parchment; yet it is fo delicate, and its fize expofes it fo much to the action of the wind, that it is divided into feveral flips. Thefe flips extend from the vein running in the middle towards the edges of the leaf, by the fide of the fmaller veins running in the fame direction, and appearing, fome like narrow filver ribbands, others like flips of the fame colour, fixed to the vein in the middle, and rolled upon themfelves.

When the banana is grown up to its natural height, it is from nine to ten inches in diameter, and the ftem of it is fo tender, that, though the leaves of which it is compofed, are joined very clofe to each other, it may eafily be cut with a knife, or even with a fingle ftroke of a hedging bill, taken a little aflant; for

the

the leaves are pulpy and full of juice, and this is the reason why it always thrives best in a rich and moist soil.

When it is come to such maturity as to be capable of bearing fruit, it pushes out, from the middle of the top of its stem, another stem of about an inch and half in diameter, and three or four feet in length, which is covered with circular rows of buds of a yellow colour bordering on green. A large bud in the shape of a heart, from six to seven inches in length and three in diameter, terminates this stem. It is composed of several pellicles laid one over another, the outside of which is red, and has a second covering which is compact, smooth, and of the colour of the lilack. This bud rises from an aperture made by the division of the stem into four parts. At first the stem is strait, but in proportion as the blossoms disappear, and give way to the fruit, which succeeds them, the increase of weight bends it insensibly, and draws it more and more towards the ground.

In our Antilles, this stalk laden with fruit is called a *régime*. I know not by what name the Portuguese call it. One of these stalks is sometimes furnished with as many bananas, as one man can carry. The fruit is fastened to the part which before supported the flower. It is customary to cut off the stalk, as soon as the fruit upon it begins to change from green to yellow. It is then suspended in an airy part of the house, and the fruit is eaten as it grows ripe, which is discovered, by its giving way to the finger, and becoming yellow. We hung up about a score of these stalks round the quarter deck; and some of our officers were so fond of this fruit, and eat it so eagerly, that they would not give it time to ripen. The banana is about two inches in diameter, and the longest I have seen of them did not exceed six inches in length. The two ends terminate in a rounded point: the figure of it is angular, but the angles are very obtuse. The skin is smooth, pliable, rather thicker than that of a fig, and much more firm. The pulp is of a yellowish white, and of the consistence of very fat new cheese, blended with its cream; or of butter recently churned, which the banana resembles very much,

especially

especially when roasted. It tastes indeed much like this kind of butter, supposing it to have been mixed with the pulp of quinces rather too ripe. It is esteemed an excellent kind of food; for my part, I found nothing extraordinary in it; though I eat the fruit both raw and roasted, ripe and unripe, in order to judge of the difference of the taste.

We had been very desirous of providing ourselves with a quantity of *batatas* and *yams*, but they were not yet in a state fit to be taken out of the ground. The *batata* is a species of potatoe, or topinambou, but much more delicate.

The *yam* is a creeping plant, furnished with branches which take root, and spring up again without cultivation; so that if care is not taken to root out a number of them, they will soon spread all over the soil, though there should not have been more than one or two roots planted at first. The stem is square, of the size of one's little finger, or thereabouts. Its leaves are cordiform, having apex a little lengthened out and pointed. They are of a dark green colour, as large as those of the *lappa major* or greater bardana. They grow less in size as they are placed farther from the root; but they are still smooth, thick, and pulpy, fixed to the stem in pairs, by short petioles, square, and rather curvated. From the stem arise some clusters of small campanulate flowers, the pistil of which becomes a siliqua or pod, filled with small black seeds. These seeds are seldom sown, because the plant thrives better and faster from slips. For this purpose, the head of the fruit, with part of the stem supporting it, is put into the ground.

The root is more or less thick in proportion to the goodness of the soil in which it grows. The rind is unequal, rough, thick, of a deep violet colour, and very hairy. The inside is of the consistence of beet-root, of a greyish white, bordering sometimes upon a flesh colour. It is eaten prepared in the same manner as the beet-root, boiled in water, or roasted on the embers, sometimes with the meat. It is well tasted, very nourishing, and eafy of digeftion. The negroes and Portuguefe are remarkably fond of it.

One of the two married Acadians, who were lodged in a hut on fhore, was afflicted with a violent diarrhœa, which baffled all the fkill of the two furgeons of our frigate. The freed negro offered to cure him with a ptifan, and might probably have fucceeded, if he had had more time for the application, for the man found himfelf much better after having taken it only for two days. What this negro called a ptifan, was no more than a fimple decoction of the ends of the buds and infant fruit of the guaiava. If this fruit had been a little farther advanced, perhaps it might have been ftill more ferviceable. The Acadian not having laid in a ftock of thefe buds, before we failed, had it not in his power to continue the medicine: his diforder returned upon him with greater force, and did not leave him till about a fortnight before our departure from the Malouine iflands, where he began to find himfelf better a few days after our landing. The wholefomenefs of the air, added to the exercife he took, made him ftronger every day, and at the time we fet fail from thence, he thought himfelf perfectly cured.

The fame negro had cured the Acadian's wife's fifter, whofe name is *Benoit*, in a few days of an inflammation in her legs, which had got to fuch a height, that fhe could fcarcely ftand. This inflammation was attributed to a fcorbutic habit. However this was, fhe complained of great pains in her ancle-bones, which went off after the negro had applied a fomentation made of fome herbs of the country boiled in clear water. In fix or feven days fhe was cured; and they affured me, that the negro had ufed nothing but the guaiava.

The guaiava is a tree well known in our American iflands. Thofe which were called by that name on the ifland of St. Catherine's, were not more than eight feet high, and the trunk between feven and eight inches in diameter. None of thofe I faw were of a larger fize. The bark of it was fomething whiter than that of the apple tree, its branches extended in the fame

manner,

manner, and the fruit, which was very young, refembled apples of about a month's growth. By the leaves and the fhape of the tree, I took it at firft for a quince-tree. I was told, that the fruit when ripe is excellent, and it was reprefented to me as of the fame kind as our guaiavas of the Antilles; although the defcription, which father Labat gives of this tree and its leaves, does not anfwer to the guaiava tree of Brazil. In other refpects, the Portuguefe afcribe the fame properties to their guaiava tree, as father Labat does to that of Martinico.

The fame Acadian, when he came on board again found himfelf very much incommoded with a fmall tumor, which had come a few days before on the great toe of his left foot. This tumor increafed, and the pain it occafioned, increafed in proportion. He fhewed it to the doctor (for fo we call the two principal furgeons on board) who immediately difcovered it to be *anigua* or *nigue*, or the *pique*, as it is called at Peru. This is an infect fo exceedingly fmall, that it is fcarcely vifible. A particular defcription of it may be found in M. Ulloa's voyage to Peru, which exactly agrees with what we faw at the ifland of St. Catherines. Our Acadian was cured by extracting the neft, and applying tobacco afhes to the part. The legs of this infect, fays the author I have juft referred to, are not formed for fpringing like thofe of fleas, which is a very providential circumftance, for if it had the power of leaping, there is no living creature in the parts where thefe infects are found, but what would be full of them. Such a breed would deftroy three fourths of mankind, by the different accidents it might bring upon them.

The nigua always harbours in the duft, and particularly in dirty places. It faftens upon one's feet, even upon the foles of them, and upon one's fingers, and pierces the skin fo fubtilely, that it makes its way almoft without being felt. It is feldom perceived, till it begins to extend itfelf. At firft, there is no great difficulty in pulling it out; but if it has once got in only its head, it fixes itfelf fo firmly, that it cannot be got rid of without the lofs of fome of the parts adjacent. If it happens not to be difcovered foon enough, it pierces through the firſt ſkin without reſiſtance, and lodges itſelf there, where it continues, ſucking the blood, and makes itſelf a neſt of a fine white membrane reſembling in ſhape a flat pearl. Within this ſpace it lies ſo that its head and feet are turned towards the outſide for the convenience of nouriſhment, and the reſt of its body towards the inſide of the membrane in order to depoſit its eggs there. As the eggs are laid, the membrane grows larger, and in four or five days time, becomes one fixth of an inch in diameter. It is of the utmoſt conſequence to remove this, otherwiſe, it will burſt, and ſpread about an infinite number of ſpawns, like nits; that is to ſay, ſo many niguas, which will inſinuate themſelves preſently into the parts about, and create a great deal of pain, not to mention the difficulty of diſlodging them. Sometimes they will penetrate even to the bone; and after one has ſucceeded ſo far as to get rid of them, the pain continues till the fleſh and ſkin are entirely healed.

The operation is tedious and painful. It confiſts in ſeparating with the point of a needle the fleſh which touches the membrane, wherein the eggs are contained; and this is not eaſy to be done without cracking the membrane, a circumſtance abſolutely neceſſary to be guarded againſt. After having detached every ligament even to the ſmalleſt, the pearl is next to be removed, which is larger or ſmaller in proportion to the time the infect has been lodged there. If unfortunately the neſt ſhould be broken, double care muſt be taken in ſeparating all the roots, and particularly in ſecuring the principal nigua; who, if ſhe eſcapes, will begin again to lay her eggs before the wound is cloſed, and burying herſelf in the fleſh would make it much more difficult to remove her. In the cavity made by the tumor, they put ſome hot aſhes of chewed tobacco.

Although this inſect is not felt at the time of its penetrating through the ſkin, by the next day it cauſes a violent and very painful itching, particularly in ſome parts, ſuch as under the nails.

The

The pain is not so great at the bottom of the foot, the skin there being thicker.

It is observed that the nigua has a mortal antipathy to certain animals, particularly the *Cerda*, which it devours by degrees, and whose fore and hind feet are found after its death full of holes.

Notwithstanding the smallness of this insect, it has been observed to be distinguished into two species, the one venomous, the other not. The latter is of the colour of fleas, and makes the membrane white, in which it deposits its eggs. The other sort is yellowish, and its nest is of the colour of ashes. One of the properties of this species is, when it has insinuated itself into the extremity of the great toe, to cause a very high inflammation in the glands of the groin, accompanied with sharp pains, which do not go off till the eggs are extirpated. It is to M. de Jussieu that we owe this distinction of the niguas into two species. That gentleman, as well as the other French Academicians, who accompanied him in his voyage to Peru, having had the mortification of repeatedly experiencing these pains, which they knew not how to account for.

During the great heats, the utmost care is necessary to avoid wetting one's feet. Without this precaution as appears by experience a man is liable to a disorder of so dangerous a nature, that it is generally mortal.

On Wednesday, the 14th of December, having got our provisions on board, and the wind being southerly, at ten in the morning we unmoored and sent our longboat on shore for the rest of our things, and the Acadians. Before they were taken into the boat, their baggage was examined with great care to see if no *Cancrelas* had got in amongst it, some of them having been seen in their hut. These are insects of the size of a May bug, and something of the same form, though rather flatter and longer, having a coat of a very dark green, but neither so hard nor so solid. They do an incredible deal of mischief in ships, as they multiply very fast, and lodge themselves every where,

where, eating through paper, books, cloaths, bifcuits and even wood itfelf. They fpoil every thing with their excrements and the difagreeablenefs of their fmell. As fome of them had been feen in the hut, where the Acadians lived, it had been recommended to them to clean their cloaths thoroughly : and we had the good fortune to be as free from them as from other infects ufually met with at fea. At the Antilles, thefe infects are known by the name of *Ravett*.

At the fame time we difpatched M. Alexander Guyot to Fort Santa Cruz, to make our apology to the Commandant for not faluting him at our departure, which we could not do on account of the live ftock we had on board.

At eleven we fet fail, and after doubling the point of *Bon-port* anchored in fix fathom water, muddy ground, about two thirds of the diftance of one fhore from the other towards the north fide; here we waited for our longboat and yawl, and to take in ten oxen, which was finifhed by five in the afternoon. We lay to after this with one anchor all night, the weather being dull and hazy.

Thus we took leave of the ifland of St. Catherine's, where, as has been feen, we did not meet with the fame caufe of complaint as admiral Anfon had done. It might be made an excellent habitation, if they would take the pains to clear it. Befides the little town I have fpoken of, there are only a few huts or plantations on the coaft of the ifland and continent adjacent. All the reft is a foreft covered with lofty trees, and, as it were, choaked up with underwood. On the ifland particularly, the fpecies of thorny aloe grows fo thick, as to render it in many parts almoft impenetrable. On the fkirts of the woods towards the coaft, there are many different forts of trees of the height and thicknefs of apple-trees, but whofe leaves are for the moft part fmooth, of a beautiful green, and fhaped like thofe of the wild laurel. There is fcarce any other difference between them than in their height or thicknefs. I obferved one amongft them, which at firft fight might have been taken for an almond tree :

tree: but the leaves were a little too large: the fruit had the appearance of a green almond, but on a close examination was found to be made somewhat in the shape of a heart. Another bore a flower or fruit, resembling the vesicles or membranes which encompass the fruit of the plant called *Alkakengas*. This Brazilian fruit is of the size of a small nut, and the outside is of a whitish yellow. It opens itself into four parts, and is composed of several similar coats, whose internal surface is of the colour of the finest carmine. These barks, or parts of the fruit or flower are so ranged, that the middle of the upper coat forms a covering to the edges, by which the four internal divisions are connected. These coats are eight in number, four external, and four internal, each of them about the thickness of the twentieth part of an inch: on the inside is fastened to the center, a small white ball, which is undoubtedly the pistillum; if it is a flower I am describing. I shewed it to a Portuguese, who could not inform me either of its name or properties.

The *caraguata* is a plant very common in these woods, and most of the rocks upon the coast are covered with it. It is likewise found in great plenty upon the branches of large trees, like the misletoe upon our apple-trees and oaks. It has a long, sharp, prickly leaf, almost like that of the flags, which plant it resembles both in the shape of its leaves and their situation, as they all come out from the root: but this produces a round stem furnished with some leaves that are of the colour of the finest carnation, as is likewise the tip of some of the internal leaves of the tuft, which are nearest to the stem. At the top of this stem are produced spikes of flowers of a lively red, which are succeeded by a kind of fruit half an inch long, of the thickness of a large quill, and of a violet colour. It contains a white viscous substance full of seeds, which are flattish, reddish, and very small. I should imagine, that the caraguata is a species of the algæ or flags. In a narrow path traced out near the border of the woods, we found some plants called by the Brazilians *juquiri*, and *cuaco*, and by us *sensitive*. Of these we saw

two

two forts; that which I am going to speak of, produces stems about two feet high, full of branches, and striated, nearly quadrangular, of a green colour, and pretty well defended with small yellowish prickles. The leaves are stationed oppositely upon the pliant branches: the prone disk is of a whitish green, the supine disk of a pale green. From the length of the stem several branches push out, whose extremities are ornamented with a small round head, which is hairy, and of a whitish purple. This is the flower, which is succeeded by a husk or small pod, crooked, and of a chesnut colour; when ripe, it is covered with small white hairs.

The second sort does not rise to any great height from the ground; I have only seen it in the sandy lands along the coast: it seems to creep as it were, and does not differ from the former. Both of them shut their leaves and let their branches fall, as if they were blasted, almost at the instant they are touched with the hand. The next moment they appear again in their full vigour. It is from this circumstance, no doubt, that they have obtained the names of *the chaste herb, berba casta, mimosa.* The leaves when eaten are a deadly poison, which can only be counteracted by eating the root itself. The same leaves, when applied as a cataplasm, are a cure for scrophulous humours.

The soil of St. Catherine's island, and the coasts of the continent are so prodigiously fertile, that the best fruit grows there in abundance almost without culture. The forests abound with odoriferous shrubs. The road affords a very great variety of excellent fish. The figures of those, to which our seamen have given the names of *Balaou, Lune, Brune, Lame d'épée, Crapaux de mer,* &c. may be seen in the plates. The long beak by which the *Balaou* is distinguished induced me to name it the *Beccaffine de mer,* or snipe-fish. The extremity of this beak which is very solid, and as hard as that of a bird, is about a quarter of an inch in length, and of the colour of the finest vermilion. Its body is almost transparent: a fillet or stripe of greenish blue runs from the gill, to the tail: its scales are so fine that they are hardly discernable.

discernable. Its flesh is firm, and has an excellent flavour. This Lune, or moon-fish, appears to be covered with a sheet of silver.

The *Lome d'épée*, or sword-blade, could hardly have a name better adapted to its figure. The *Crapauv de mer*, or porcupine fish, might have been called sea-urchins their body being covered with prickles about two lines in length. In the species which approached the nearest to the ordinary shape of fishes, the jaw, was armed with teeth, which were pretty large and flat like the canine-teeth in the human species, and was not unlike the human mouth even in the lips.

We did not catch any beautiful shell-fish here; the only one deserving notice was a helmet shell, which was at least eight inches in diameter. We met with a soldier-fish, and some small sea-horses. Our fishing was always accompanied with fear, on account of the sharks which very much infest this road.

The sharks taken by us, a specimen of which is exhibited in the plates, were not of an extraordinary size; they were of that species called the dog-fish. On an attentive examination of their rows of teeth, we thought they amounted to seven in number, instead of six, which are generally attributed to them. They were flat, triangular, sharp, and their edges were serrated. They did not appear to be firmly fixed in the jaw like those of other animals. They were moveable, opening and shutting like the fingers, in such a manner that each row in recovering its situation lay over the next to it, so that the upper row, bending towards the inner part of the gullet, filled up the vacuity or interval between the lower row of teeth. They are disposed like the slates of a roof, or, perhaps, like the leaves of an artichoke.

It is said that the shark is constantly preceded by another fish called the *Pilot*: we can affirm the contrary; at least we have several times seen sharks without this harbinger.

The pilot is among the number of beautiful and good sea fish. It is of a blue colour disposed in stripes; some of them to the number of six are of a fine blue, which upon the back is of a deep cast, but becomes gradually lighter as they verge towards

P                                         the

the belly. Four other stripes, together with the head and tail, are of a very clear blue, or of a white dashed with blue. The eyeball is of a fine gold colour, except the pupil which is black; the two forks of the tail are white.

I did not recollect this fish by the description given of it in M. Valmont de Bomare's dictionary of natural history. It seems rather to belong to some species of the *Remora*. Is he mistaken in this article, as he is in several others? Or have I been imposed upon by being told that a fish was called the *Pilot*, which has no title to that name? See the figure of it in the plate.

As we did not see any sharks preceded by pilots; so neither did we catch any one that had not upon it several sucking fishes fastened close to it about the head. The Brazilians call the sucking fish *Iperuquiba*, and *Piraquiba*, the Portuguese, *Piexepogador*. The largest that we caught was about eight inches long, and two and a half over in the broadest part. The upper part of the head, which is two inches long, is flat, resembling an ox's palate, furrowed across, and fastened to it in such a manner that the edges should not adhere. These furrows are armed with prickles so hard and solid, that when rubbed upon wood, they act as a fine file. By means of these, the sucking fish fastens himself so strongly about the gills and belly of the shark, that he suffers himself to be taken along with him. He cannot even be separated without a knife or some other instrument. The under jaw is longer than the upper. This fish has small eyes of a gold-coloured yellow, and the pupil is black. An infinite number of small tubercles, that are pretty solid, supply the place of teeth. Near each of the gills is a triangular fin about an inch long: there are two others near the belly, which unite at the place of insertion, and one under the belly and another upon the back, which extend from the middle of the body to the tail. Its skin is smooth and slippery like that of an eel, and of the colour of brown slate.

Many have mistaken the back of the sucking fish for the belly, on account of the part by which it fastens itself to the

shark.

shark. I have observed it with all the attention I was master of, and am convinced of the mistakes of authors as to this particular, as appears by the plates.

One of our officers had a present made him of two young *Tucans*, called by some *Tulcan*, and by the Spaniards in the isthmus of America, *Preacher*, because this bird, it is said, perching on the top of a tree while others are asleep below, makes a noise with his tongue resembling words ill articulated, and spreads the sound on every side, lest the birds of prey should seize the opportunity of devouring the others while they are asleep.

The Toucan is pretty nearly of the size of a wood-pigeon; but stands higher on its legs, which are of a blueish grey as well as its feet, which are armed with pretty long claws; its tail is about four inches long, sometimes black, and rounded at the end; but usually variegated with blue, purple, and yellow upon a dark brown. The back and wings are of this last colour, except some black feathers in the wings. Its head, though very large, is very small in proportion to its bill, which is between seven and eight inches long from the place of insertion to the end. The upper part near the head is about two inches at the base, and as it lengthens forms a figure pretty nearly triangular, and at the same time convex at the upper part, the two lateral surfaces being a little raised and rounded. The upper one which forms the inside of the bill is hollow, having serrated edges or lips. The lower one is shaped like the upper, only it is rather concave underneath. These two are of an equal length, are inserted into each other, and grow gradually less towards the extremity, which is rather crooked and sharp underneath. The tongue is a whitish membrane almost as long as the bill, but very narrow and flat, and has the appearance of the point of a pen; its eyes are round, beautiful, lively, and sparkling, and are inserted into two bare cheeks, which are covered with a sky-coloured membrane. In some the iris is of a clear blue encircled with white, in others it is quite black. There are

are different species of them, at least they differ from each other in the colour of their bill, and their feathers. The bill of some is green, having a black circle and two white spots near the root. That of others is black, the inside red, with a greenish yellow circle near the head. They are very common in this country. We were likewise assured that great numbers of pheasants were found here, but we saw none. The green parrots fly here in flocks like the sparrows in France. We killed great numbers of them, and found them to be as good as the pigeons in our dove-cotes. Lions, panthers, leopards, ounces, and tygers, infest the woods and make travelling dangerous. It is happily very seldom that they come near inhabited places. The water of the rivers is of an excellent quality. But all these advantages are defeated by the inconvenience arising from a very unwholesome air, which is probably the cause of the pale complexion of the white people who inhabit this country. From these woods, which the sun never penetrates, gross vapours arise without intermission, which form continually thick fogs on the tops of the mountains surrounding the island. The low grounds which are very marshy, are equally misty from between six and seven in the evening, till the sun disperses the vapours at eight the next morning. These vapours frequently smell like mud, and as there is no free circulation of air, they seem to disperse only to make room for others which succeed. This unwholesome atmosphere is undoubtedly corrected, at least in some measure, by the multitude of aromatic plants, whose sweet smell is perceived three or four leagues at sea when the wind sets off the shore. Our dogs informed us of our approach to land at this distance at least, by smelling towards that side for near half an hour. We were likewise regaled with the perfume. It is observable, that dogs are of great use on board a ship in discovering its approach to land. Ours never failed to go upon the fore-castle, where they turned their noses to smell on that side nearest the land, though at the different times between five or six leagues, when the wind set towards us from the shore. They

would

## TO THE MALOUINE ISLANDS. 91

would even give us notice of a fail, at the same distance, if to windward of us. They stayed there about half a quarter of an hour, and returned more than once to the place after they had quitted it.

Besides the birds already mentioned, we frequently met with *Criards*. The Portuguese give this name to a kind of crow, whose plumage is of a fine pale blue. These, they say, are the ravens of the country. Their shape is the same, and they are almost as unpalatable. The *Tiéperangas* are of the size of the thrush; their wings, tail, and part of their bill are of a deep brown; the rest of their plumage is of a beautiful vermilion tinctured with carmine, and inclining to scarlet. They are called by some of our seamen Lorys, by others *Cardinals*; but this last name belongs to a bird of nearly the same shape, whose plumage is intirely red without any mixture of brown.

On the morning of our departure from St. Catherine's as we cast anchor when it was almost dark, we perceived all along the shrouds, haliards, and the rest of the tackling, a number of small moving lights, or rather small moveable lamp-glasses. Though we concluded that they were fire flies our surprize was the greater as we had not seen any of them before. They had four wings, two of which were transparent like those of our common flies, and two opaque, smooth, brown and solid like the outer ones of the May-bug, and like those, serving as a case to inclose the under ones. The head is black, shaped like the trefoil, and furnished with two antennæ which are likewise black, four lines long, and seem to be composed of small horns inserted into each other by their points. The eyes which are placed near these antennæ, are round, black and firm as horn; they are sparkling and prominent, and of the size of the smallest poppyseed. The body and legs which are six in number, are of a darkish brown. With the naked eye one may easily perceive six rings gradually decreasing in size from the neck to the extremity of the body, which terminates in a rounded point. These rings are as solid as those of which the body of the May-fly is composed. The largest ring which forms all the fore part of the

body,

body, to which the legs are articulated, is something more than two lines broad, and two in length, and is covered with a down or light dust like the wings of butterflies. From this part, and from the head proceed rays of light, resembling that of the glow-worms which are seen in France during the summer season, and at the beginning of autumn.

I put one of these flies into a piece of paper when I went to bed, intending the next day to make a drawing of it. But when I was going to set about it, the fly was not to be found. It had gnawed its way through the paper, and made its escape. The day following, when I was laid down, I perceived a light in one of the places where I had put my books. I thought no more of the fire-flies, and imagined at first that this light proceeded from the lamp in the binnacle, which was near the window of my cabbin; but perceiving the light change its place, I recollected that it must be the fly which had got away the preceding night. Having caught and inclosed it in a glass vessel, the next day I observed it at my leisure, and drew a sketch of it.

When we left Montevideo, we saw the same appearance upon the river of Plata, or *Rio de la Plata*, during the unexpected calm that happened on the day of our departure. As these diffused, a more brilliant and sparkling light than those of the island of St. Catherine, I put some of them with fresh grass into a glass vessel which I inclosed in another, and having placed it upon my table, fetched a book which I read with great ease without the assistance of any other light, though the print was very small.

The next morning I took one out of the vessel, and transfixing it with a pin, which I stuck into the table, I made a drawing of it.

It was four lines broad, and eleven and an half long including the cap of three lines which covered the head.

The body was furnished with four wings. The two upper ones were of a fine black velvet lace, having a streak of gold coloured yellow near the outward edge. This reached from the neck to two thirds of the length of the wing. The hood was
intirely

## TO THE MALOUINE ISLANDS.

intirely of the fame colour, except a large black fpot in the middle near the neck. This hood had the fame motions as the head, which was round, and ferved it for an helmet: extending the breadth of a line beyond it, quite round. On the fore-part of the head, two black antennæ, as flender as a fine hair, and three lines in length, were placed above the eyes, which were black, not very prominent, and refembled the feed of the amaranth. Three fmall legs, equally black, came out from each fide of the body; quite covered at the place of infertion, with very fhort. fmall, fine hair of a yellow orange colour. The hind part was compofed of five rings, the two neareft the body, were black and covered with a fhort velvet fhag; the two next were invefted with golden hair, and the fifth, which was as broad as either of the other two taken together, and which alfo completed the termination of the body in a rounded point, was likewife befet with a black velvet fhag, but rather longer than that of the other rings. Thefe rings were not fo firm as thofe which formed the body of the preceding fly; they bent under the flighteft preffure of the finger. The firft fly emitted fcarce any rays of light but from the head; this diffufed them from every part of its body, the head alone excepted. Thofe which I had kept clofe in frefh grafs, lived four days, and preferved the fplendor of their light with almoft as much brilliancy as at firft, even to the time of their death.

Before we quit the road of St. Catherine's, I fhall mention a few circumftances relative to the Brazilians, which I learned from the firft prefident of the fupreme council of Rio Janeiro, whom I have fpoken of above.

I did not fee any bread made of corn, except at the Governor's of St. Catherine's. In every other houfe the Caffavi bread was fubftituted in its room. This is a kind of a baked pafte made of the flower of the root of the Manioc, which is looked upon as a ftrong poifon, when it is eaten raw. I have however feen children, who were employed in taking off the rind of it to make the Caffavi, eat it raw without finding any ill confequence.

Some

Some of the inhabitants used to roast it on the coals, then strip off the outside and eat it.

There was but one sort of Manioc, which I met with on the island of St. Catherine's, and about the houses on the continent. Laët, who is quoted in the collection of voyages published by the Abbé Prevot, affirms that there are several sorts of it, one in particular at Brazil, which is there called *Aypi*, and may be eaten raw without any danger. *Some nations,* adds he, *of the race of the Tapouyas eat likewise the common Manioc raw, which has the effect of poison on all other people: but these are not hurt by it, being accustomed to eat it from their infancy.* Those however, whom we saw eating it raw, were not of the race of the Tapouyas. They were white children born of Portuguese parents. The leaves of this Manioc come very near in shape to those of the Piony.

The roots are dried before the fire on hurdles, and then being scraped with sharp stones, are made into a kind of meal, the smell of which resembles that of starch. This meal is put into large pots, where it is stirred till it grows thick, as is done in France with the black wheat. When it is cold and become of the consistence of a stiff jelly, its taste differs little from that of white bread. What they provide for their cruizes and land expeditions is thoroughly baked, and is therefore firmer and harder for the convenience of carriage. It is sometimes boiled in broth, and makes a very nourishing dish, much like our rice-soup. These roots pounded or grated fresh, and before they have been exposed to the fire, yield a juice as white as milk, which, if it is but set in the sun, curdles like cheese, and becomes very good food with the least assistance of the fire. The method of scraping the Manioc roots with sharp stones, is an invention of the Brazilians, who are not at all acquainted with the mechanic arts of Europe. The Portuguese, who were born or merely settled on the island of St. Catherine's, and on the coast of the main-land, which encompasses it, use for this purpose a large wooden wheel, the points of which have on the outer surface a groove. This groove is covered with an iron grater, upon which

the

the roots are placed, one perfon preffing them a little down, while another turns the wheel, which has the fame effect as a tobacco grater. By this contrivance much time and labour is faved. But they did not preferve the white juice, which dropped from thefe roots as faft as they grated them, and falling into a fmall hole, ran off upon the ground. After this operation the roots are dried in order to be reduced to meal, and to make the Caffavi. But this is not their only ufe. The Brazilians make a drink of them. The procefs in making of which is very difgufting, as well as the liquor itfelf, to thofe who know how it is made. The females are employed in this bufinefs, efpecially the old women. Laët gives a particular defcription of the whole.

The laws of every country form the manners of its inhabitants; hence it is, the manners of different nations have fo little refemblance to each other. The climate likewife contributes very much to produce this effect, it being evident that a law highly falutary in Norway may be equally pernicious in Guinea. The improvements introduced among thofe, which we call *civilized* nations, have alfo given rife to many laws unknown among, what we are pleafed to call, *barbarous* nations.

Among the Brazilians, the girls before marriage not only give themfelves up freely, and without any fenfe of fhame, to unmarried men, but even their parents offer them to the firft comer, and carefs their lovers exceedingly; infomuch that perhaps there is not one girl who is a virgin at the time of her marriage. On the other hand, when they have once given their promife, which is the only ceremony on that occafion, they are no longer folicited, neither do they liften to any other addreffes.

The only education they give their children is to make them expert in hunting, fifhing, and war. They live peaceably notwithftanding among themfelves, and very feldom have any private quarrels. If by chance any of them fall out and fight, they let them go on till they are fatisfied; but as the law of retaliation

taliation is strictly observed among them, the man, who has wounded another, is wounded in the same manner by his relations, or if he has killed him, is killed in his turn by them. All this is done by consent of the relations on both sides, and without appeal. This law is probably the source of that implacable hatred they bear to their avowed enemies. If this rule was introduced among us, we should scarcely see so many quarrels ending in the effusion of human blood; our only weapons then would be our tongues and our pens.

It is an injustice to the Brazilians to consider them as the most cruel of all men against every other nation: they are only so to their avowed enemies: and excepting some few of certain nations whose ferocity approaches to that of wild beasts, perhaps from the continued insults of their neighbours, the Brazilians are very humane, particularly to strangers, whom they receive with great kindness, and in the manner related by Lery; the particulars of which are as follow.

If one has occasion to go oftener than once to the same habitation or village, one must take up one's lodging with the *Moussacat*, or head of the Family; because the person to whom one goes first would be extremely offended at one's leaving him him to go to another. One must always lodge with the same person.

As soon as the traveller appears at the door, the Moussacat, or whoever is master of the house, presses him to sit down on a hammock or bed of cotton, slung in the air, on which they leave him for some time without saying a word. They take this opportunity to assemble the women, who come and sit on the ground round the bed, with their hands over their eyes. They melt with joy; they weep, and in the midst of their tears address a thousand flattering compliments to their guest: "How good! How valiant you are! What obligations we have to you! What trouble you have undergone in coming hither! How beautiful you are! How happy you have made us by coming hither;" and

others

others to the same effect. If the stranger wishes to impress on them a good opinion of himself, he must appear to be affected in his turn. Lery affirms, that he has seen Frenchmen really affected and crying, as he expresses it, *like calves*. But he advises those, whose hearts do not happen to be susceptible of such tender emotions (that is to say, to the shame of us, Europeans, who pique ourselves, but with so little reason, on having more humanity than the Brazilians) to sigh, or at least pretend to sigh. Is not this reproaching us in few words, with having only the outside of politeness and hospitality, while the Brazilians are really polite and hospitable?

After the first salutation, the Moussacat, who has retired into a corner on pretence of making an arrow, or some other business, as if he was not taking any notice of what passed, comes near the bed, asks the guest how he does, receives his answer, and enquires the reason of his coming. If the guest understands the language, he must answer all these questions. After this, if the *Mair* (for that is the name they give to Europeans) came on foot, they bring him water, and the women wash his feet and legs. They then inquire if he is hungry or thirsty. If he answers, that he is both, they immediately set upon the table as much fish, fowl, venison, and other provisions as they have in the house, with the liquors of the country.

Should the guest choose to pass the night there, the Moussacat not only causes a fine white *inis* (or hammock) to be prepared for him; but, notwithstanding the continual heat of the climate at Brazil, makes a pretence of the dampness of the night to kindle three or four small fires round the hammock, which are kept up all the time the *Mair* is asleep with a sort of small fan, called *Tatapecoun*, which resembles very much our fire-screens.

In the evening, says Lery, who had been in this situation himself, they remove their children out of the way; so careful are they to get rid of every thing that may interrupt the stranger's repose.

As foon as he wakes in the morning, the Mouffacat comes to inquire if he has flept well, and how he finds his health; and though the ftranger by his anfwer appear ever fo well fatisfied, he cries, "Go to fleep again, my child, you have occafion for it: I am fure you were very much fatigued yefterday." It is cuftomary with Europeans to make them fome prefents upon thefe occafions, and no man ought to ftir abroad without carrying fomething for that purpofe about him. For this reafon travellers provide themfelves with fome trifling commodities, fuch as knives, fciffars, tweezers (which laft are in great requeft, both men and women being accuftomed to pull out the hair from all parts of their bodies, except their eyebrows) combs, little looking-glaffes, bracelets, glafs beads and buttons, and even fifhhooks.

Some doubts perhaps may be entertained in refpect to the conduct of the Brazilians as reprefented in this account; but thefe will ceafe, when it is known, that thefe men, whom we look upon as barbarians on account of their cruelty towards their enemies, never eat any other men but fuch as are their declared enemies: that they bear a ftrong affection to their friends, and allies; and that they would fuffer themfelves to be cut in pieces, to defend thofe with whom they live in amity from the fmalleft inconvenience.

It is not to ftrangers alone that the Brazilians fhew themfelves tender and affectionate. When they happen to be afflicted with diforders, they treat each other with the moft humane attention and regard. If any one is wounded, his neighbour immediately offers himfelf to fuck the wound, and performs every other office of kindnefs with the fame zeal.

Yet religion has no fhare in regulating the conduct of the Brazilians. They have no notion of a Deity: they do not adore any thing, and their language has not even any word to exprefs the name or idea of a God. In their fabulous hiftories, there is nothing to be found that has any relation to their origin or to

the

the creation of the world. They have only a kind of ftory, that feems to refer to the general idea of a deluge, which deftroyed the whole race of mankind except one brother and fifter, who peopled the earth again. They unite fome idea of power to thunder, which they call *Tupan*, for they are afraid of it, and believe, that they derive from it the knowledge of agriculture. They have not the moft diftant conception that this life is to be followed by another, and they have no terms to exprefs heaven or hell. It feems, however, that they have a notion of fomething remaining of them after their death; for they have a tradition, that feveral of their people have been changed into genii, and dæmons, and that they rejoice and dance continually in charming fields planted with all forts of trees.

The Indians of Brazil are paffionately fond of dogs of the European breed; and they bring them up for fporting. Thofe of the country, though they refemble ours, are never broke of their favage and carnivorous appetite. A Portuguefe made us a prefent of two, one grown up, the other fo young that he could fcarcely walk. We were obliged to get rid of them both in time, for it was found that no correction could keep them from the fheep and fowls. But the Governor had given M. de Bougainville a brace of pointers out of the fame bitch, about four months old, and of the beft breed in Portugal. When we were landed at the Malouines, and went out a fhooting, they pointed naturally without any teaching. M. de Bougainville carried them to France, and made a prefent of them to a nobleman at court.

The 15th we failed out of the road, and continued our route the 16th and 17th, without meeting any thing remarkable.

The 18th, in the morning, we faw a great number of birds, which our feamen called *Dadins*, and fome *Quebranta-kueffos* or Ofpreys. One of the latter flying too near our veffel was fhot, and taken up out of the fea.

It is an opinion which prevails in the South Sea, that the Quebranta-huellos never appear but a day or two before a ftorm or very bad weather. But we saw many of them in fine weather, when it was what the sailors call *a long sea*, and no storm followed. The same thing is said of the Halcyons or King-fishers, or as they are otherwise called *Puants*. Whether it is that they really have a bad smell, or whether it is, that mariners have an aversion to seeing them, as they look upon them to be birds of ill omen, it is true we never saw any King-fishers but we had hard weather afterwards.

The Quebranta-huessos are frequently seen to stoop and hover on the surface of the water, skimming the waves, and following the direction of them, without appearing to move their wings, which they constantly keep open and spread out. When they do not float on the waves, they fly round the ship at a small distance.

The body of this bird is about the size of a large capon, but its long close feathers give it the appearance of being as big as a Turkey. Its neck is short, and somewhat bent: its head large, and its beak very singular, such as I have sketched it out in the plate.

The beak is divided as it were into four or five pieces. The tail of the bird is short, its back high, legs low, feet black and webbed, with three claws before, and a fourth very short behind, each of which are furnished with black talons, which are blunt, and not very long.

There are several kinds of Quebranta-huessos. Some of them have a whitish plumage, spotted with a dark brown, or red; in others, the breast, the under part of the wings, the lower part of the neck, and the whole head, are all extremely white; but the back, the outside of the wings, and the upper part of the neck, are of a dark red, speckled with a few spots of a blueish grey colour. The one we shot was of this kind. They may perhaps be all of one species, and the differences may serve only to distinguish the male from the female. Their wings are very long. Seven feet two inches and a half was the length of our bird's wings, measuring from the extreme points

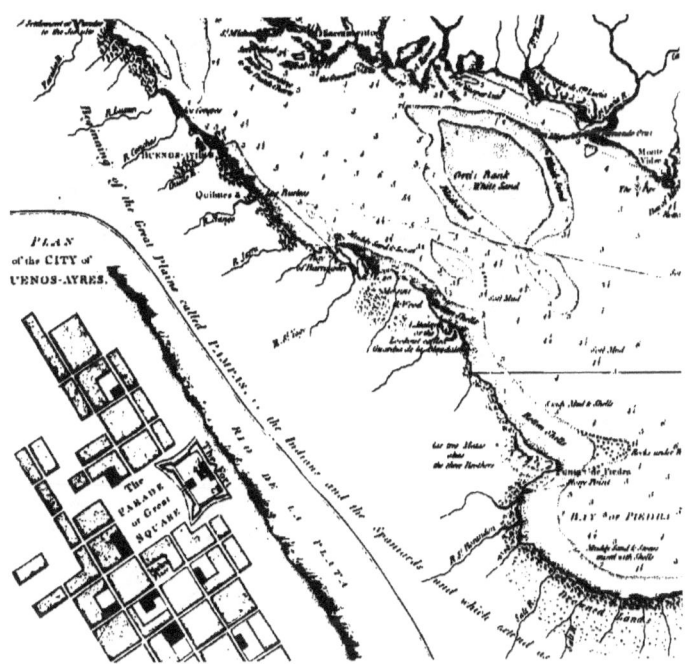

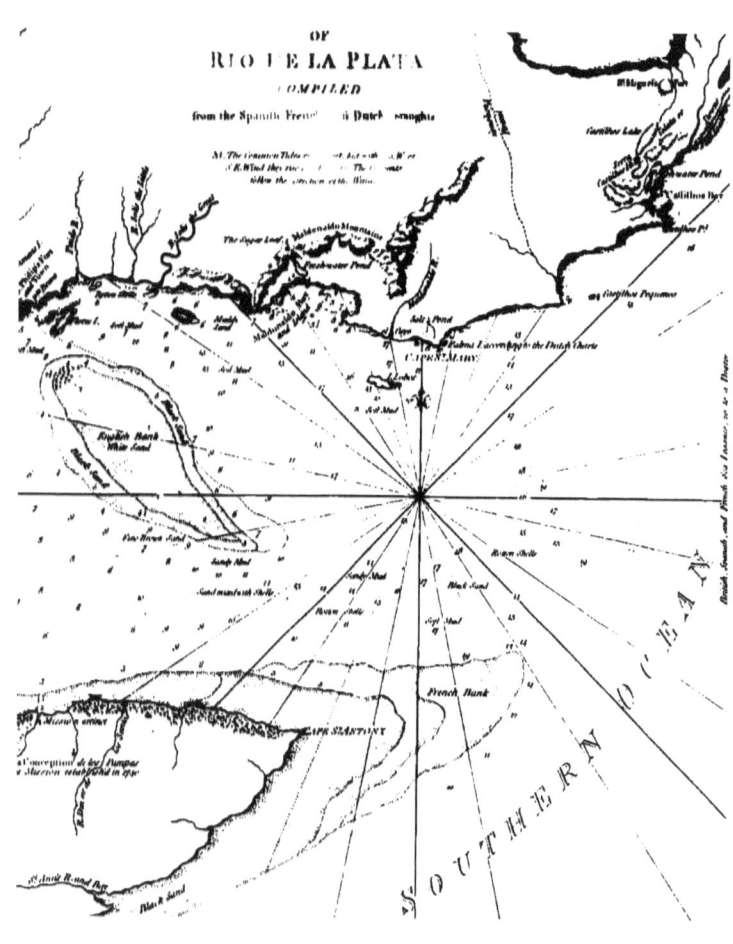

of the feathers of one wing to those of the other. These birds are found at the distance of more than 300 leagues from any land, neither is it known from whence they come, or in what places they build their nests.

On the 21st in the morning, the colour of the sea appearing different, we resolved to sound, and found bottom at the depth of fifteen fathoms. The end of the bank, which is at St. Mary's Point, may possibly make this bottom.

According to our observations, the currents from the line tend to the South when the sun is in the Southern point.

On the 22d, about two o'clock, we saw land pretty clearly. We steered immediately towards it, in order to discover it well; the tides carried us S. S. E. from 14 to 15 minutes. This circumstance must be attended to, in making the entrance of Rio de la Plata. The course should be to the North.

As we came near the land, we judged it to be the most Eastern point of St. Mary's cape. Perceiving then some lands more to the South, we turned the head of the ship South West ¼ W.: and at fix o'clock discovered the island of *Lobos*: so called from its being inhabited only by sea wolves, which are here met with in great abundance. As we came nearer to it we steered South ¼ South West, in order to keep a league and a half out to sea, that we might avoid a ridge of rocks Eastward of this island. This ridge extends near a league out at sea. As it was dark, we did not perceive the mouth of the canal, which forms the island and port of the Maldonnados; so that we advanced nearly two leagues too far up the *Rio de la Plata*, or river Plata, in which we cast anchor at eight o'clock in the evening.

On the morning of the 23d, our yawl went on shore with Messrs. de Bougainville, de Nerville, de Belcourt, l' Huillier, and Alexander Guyot, our second Captain, to acquaint the Commander of the fort of the island of Maldonnado of our anchorage. They asked leave to supply themselves with fresh water and provisions, which the Commandant gave them in the politest

politeſt manner. He was even ſo kind as to tell us, that we had not anchored ſo well as we might have done at the mouth of the canal leading to the port: that the anchorage at the port was by no means ſafe, and that we ſhould do very well to quit it; which we accordingly reſolved to do, as ſoon as the weather ſhould permit, and the Commandant ſhould ſend us a coaſting pilot.

The whole coaſt diſcovers nothing to the eye but low banks of ſand, ſome few remote eminences only appearing, which are called the mountains of Maldonnado, and are at the diſtance of ſome leagues from the coaſt. There are no trees to be ſeen, but a great quantity of cattle, very large oxen, and horſes. All the trade indeed of the country of Plata conſiſts in ſilver, and the hides of oxen.

On coming from the Eaſt, to enter into the Rio de la Plata, the iſland of Lobos is ſeen W. S. W. of the compaſs.

The weather had been calm, very fine, and very hot ever ſince the morning. Many of the crew employed themſelves in angling; and no ſooner was the line thrown into the ſea, than it was brought up again with a fiſh. Sometimes there were as many fiſh caught as there were hooks to the line. The fiſh were only of four or five different kinds. Some of them were what the Spaniards call *Viagrios*, and our ſailors *Machoirans*. The others were Carangues or *Guarencas*, dog and cat-fiſh of different ſizes, and ſome ſharks. We caught one cat-fiſh, one dog-fiſh, and two young ſharks.

The Machoiran, or beard-fiſh, has its belly flat, and ſome beards, as the little barbel; the head large, the ſkin covered with ſmall brown and almoſt imperceptible ſcales, nearly reſembling thoſe of the tench; at the root of the fins neareſt the head, there is a ſmall ſerrated bony proceſs, the teeth of which are inclined towards the body. This proceſs is as long as the fin, and has the ſame motions. When the fiſh wants to defend himſelf againſt other fiſh, or againſt the fiſherman, he puſhes out theſe proceſſes, and
thruſts

thrufts them into the bodies of other fifh, into the fifherman's hand, or, into any thing that is near him, even into wood if he can, to which he fometimes faftens himfelf by the ftroke. His punƈture is venomous, fo that fifhermen take care to guard againft it. I know not whether there are any larger than thofe we caught. The biggeft of thefe was one foot and a half long, and four inches broad. It is a very well tafted fifh.

The Guarenca is an excellent flat fifh. We caught fuch a quantity of a kind of barbel fifh, that after the whole crew had been fupplied with it for this day and the next, the remainder of it was falted and dried, in the fame manner as the dried cod is prepared at Newfoundland. The largeft of thefe barbels, was of the fame fize in every way as the beard-fifh, defcribed above. The cat-fifh, and the dog-fifh, are kinds of fharks or fea dogs; they refemble them fo much in their figure that they are not eafily diftinguifhed: they were about two feet and a half long.

About three o'clock in the morning of the 24th, there arofe a violent South wind. At five o'clock the wind being fomewhat abated, we put ourfelves in readinefs to fet fail for Montevideo. The wind rifing again at feven o'clock, we caft our beft bower, by ten fathoms, on a muddy bottom of fine fand, and remained part of the day in this ftate.

M. de Bougainville, trufting to the mildnefs of the weather, had been gone ever fince the morning, to the Fort Maldonnado, with the fame perfons who had accompanied him the preceding evening; with a defign to view the country, as well as to procure frefh provifions. Fortunately for them they returned, between fix and feven in the evening. We had juft hoifted our anchor on the cat-head, on the profpeƈt of a calm: no fooner was this done than a moft violent ftorm arofe, blowing from the South Weft part of the horizon. It is not poffible to behold a more beautiful fight, than that we enjoyed, from the continual numberlefs flafhes of lightning, which fhot from between the clouds as they rofe upon the horizon, which was all on fire; fo that

that fireworks the most elegantly contrived, the best kept up, and the most diversified, could not possibly exhibit any thing to be compared to what we now saw in the Heavens for the space of an hour. We did not then suspect, that this prospect would soon give way to one of a much less pleasing kind; from which, our captain, who was better acquainted with the danger and the consequences, was all this time endeavouring to shelter us, by taking all the necessary precautions against a storm.

We thought the storm would pass off along side of us, as it appeared to be going that way; but in an instant a most violent wind arose, and the thunder and lightning came upon us at the same time. We passed the whole night striving against the impetuosity of the wind, and the roarings of an extremely boisterous and angry sea, which broke in upon us.

This wind is called in the country *Pamperos*, because it comes from the plains of Pampas, beyond Buenos Ayres. These plains extend as far as the Cordeleirias mountains, which divide them from Chili. They are at least three hundred leagues in length, without the intervention of any wood, or eminence, to check the violence of this wind; which swells the river Plata, raising its waves as high as mountains, so as often to destroy the vessels in that river, breaking them upon the coast opposite the wind. The anchorage where we were was extremely unsafe, from the vicinity of the island of Maldonnado, and the circumjacent coasts, all bordered with rocks and sands. Thirty years ago, an English vessel laden with piasters, or pieces of eight, was lost in this place. The inhabitants of the island, in the neighbourhood of the spot where the wreck happened, are still endeavouring to this day, to recover part of the cargo. On the evening before our arrival, they had taken up with the drag, two thousand four hundred of these piasters.

The wind Pamperos is much more frequent in winter than in summer, and always blows strong, which makes the Rio de la Plata a dangerous road. This river is fit only for the trade

of

## TO THE MALOUINE ISLANDS. 105

of piafters and oxen, the largeft of which are fold here for five pieces of eight, or five and twenty livres of French coin. In general, they are fold for three piafters, or fifteen livres. It is very difficult to get wood here; not only becaufe it is very fcarce, but alfo becaufe the little there is of it, is found a long fide the rivers, the only places of fhelter for tigers, leopards, and other wild beafts, which are here found in great number, much more fierce and larger than thofe of Africa and the Eaft Indies. Figs and peaches are to be found all the way from Maldonnade and Montevideo to Buenos Ayres.

The Pamperos blew with equal violence the whole night; and the fea was terrible. Notwithftanding the continual rolling and pitching of the fhip, I was fallen into a pretty found fleep, when I was fuddenly awakened by a violent fhake the veffel received, which made it crack in all its parts, as if it was breaking againft the rocks. It was then near five o'clock in the morning. I jumped out of bed, opened my window, and afked the helms-man if we had ftruck againft any rock. He anfwered, that we had not yet ftruck, but that the fhip dragged her anchors, and that we were in a fair way for it. He told me that the cable of our beft bower had failed; and that the other anchor was loofened from the ground. This was the reafon of the violent fhake we had felt; our only hope was now in the fheet anchor, which we had juft dropped.

I dreffed myfelf, and went upon deck, and I perceived indeed we had dragged fo much, that the coafts towards which the wind and the waves were driving us, did not feem to be more than half a league diftant. But our fheet anchor luckily keeping her hold, we continued in the fame manner, labouring very hard for our prefervation, till about fix in the evening, when the wind and ftorm began to ceafe.

As they were working the fhip yefterday evening, a pully broke. A failor received a ftroke on the forehead from one of the fplinters, and prefently after fainted away. The furgeons gave it as their opinion, that the ftroke had only grazed the

part,

part, from the small quantity of blood loft, and the little apparent contusion. The man was pretty quiet to-day, complaining of nothing more than a great head-ach, which was looked upon as the effect of the shock. He was blooded twice and very carefully attended, having even had a bed made for him in the cabbin.

During the tempeft, the sea was agitated quite to its bottom: two or three hours after the storm began, the sea formed such deep cavities, that one would have thought we were going to touch the bottom; and the billows followed so close that they did not allow us time to breathe. I saw more than once the end of the main maft yard, which indeed was brought very low, dip three feet or thereabouts into the wave, part of which often broke upon the deck. Our situation was more dangerous from our being so near the coaft. Our sea officers, who were all able men, having had the command of ships, and privateers, were so sensible of the danger that threatened us, that most of them were considering how they should save themselves from the shipwreck. The danger appeared even so urgent to them, that the guns were already disposed so as to serve instead of anchors, in case the cables should happen to break.

The night of the 26th was fine, and the wind having shifted to the North, blowing a gentle gale, about four o'clock we began to prepare; and we set sail about seven.

On the 27th at sun rise, the land neareft to us bore N. N. E. about four leagues diftant: and the land moft to the South Weft, bore N. W. five degrees North of us. We sounded the whole night from hour to hour, and even more frequently, and found sometimes at twelve, sometimes at thirteen fathoms, a muddy bottom. Those who sail along this road, will do well to sound as often as they can, especially if it is the first time of their going to Montevideo or Buenos Ayres. The river Plata is extremely dangerous, from the number and extent of its sand banks, which leave but a very narrow channel, for the passage of ships, and that very serpentine. The bank called the Bank of the Englifh advances near five leagues from the coaft; and the iflands we meet with, form flats, projecting confiderably.

All this coaft is flat, except the part where the Maldonnado mountains are, which are of a moderate height, and at a fmall diftance.

On the 28th we tacked about towards the ifland of Flora, till we came within about a league and a half from it, and till we were two leagues clear of the coaft. One muft, take care not to go too near either of thefe places, on account of the ridges of rocks, which extend pretty near a league out at fea. At nine o'clock we were about two leagues diftant from Montevideo. Half an hour afterwards we difpatched M. Alexander Guyot in our yawl, to give notice of our arrival to the Governor.

About half an hour after four, as we were going to fail into the bay, the captain of a Spanifh veffel, named Saint Barbe, came on board of us with offers of fervice from the Governor, and in order to pilot us. About five o'clock we caft anchor in this road a little beyond the Spanifh veffel, in three fathoms depth of water, on a muddy bottom; after which we faluted the citadel with twelve fhots, which were returned fhot for fhot.

The firft days we lay at anchor, were taken up in fettling with the Governor of Montevideo, what we had to do during our ftay. He feemed firft to ftart feveral difficulties, not only with regard to allowing us the liberty of fifhing along the coaft, but alfo to the fuffering our longboat and yawl to come on fhore. He required that we fhould give him previous notice every time we wanted to land, that he might poft guards at the place where we fhould put to fhore, with orders to wait till our longboat or yawl went back, to prevent us from carrying on any kind of trade whatever.

Not forefeeing any of thefe difficulties, we had fent our fmall boat a fifhing at the foot of the mount, the very next day, after we had caft anchor. The Governor who received intelligence of this, fent two dragoons of the garrifon, to take the men into cuftody, together with the boat and goods, in cafe they fhould have

have brought any on shore. Meff. de Bougainville, de Nerville, Guyot, and myfelf, came into the palace, immediately after this order had been given, which the Governor communicated to M. de Bougainville. The Governor, apprehending certainly that he could not exprefs himfelf properly in French, fpoke in Spanifh, and had a provincial, feitled in this city for fifteen years paft, for his interpreter. This provincial explained the Governor's intentions to us in fuch a manner, as induced us to believe, that he was not inclined to do us all the fervices he had offered, and we had reafon to expect from him. This however, was far from being his way of thinking; of which we were thoroughly convinced by the fequel of our conference.

The order given, which feemed to agree with the provincial's interpretation, was far from being agreeable to M. de Bougainville, who expreffed his refentment of it to the Governor, nearly in the following terms: It is very furprizing, Sir, and at the fame time very mortifying for us, to meet with difficulties among our friends the Spaniards, which we have not experienced among the Portuguefe, with whom we have juft been at war. I will fet fail immediately, and give notice of this to the King my mafter. The Governor replied; that he did not intend to difoblige us, but on the contrary, to do us all the fervice in his power; that he was not the mafter: that the laws and orders of his court were, not to allow any kind of trade to be carried on by fhips which were not Spanifh, or privileged for that purpofe by the court of Spain; and even to put a ftop to any trade carried on by the Spaniards themfelves for other nations; that a frigate belonging to the Eaft India Company, which had anchored in the fame port three years before, had made no fcruple of fubmitting to what he had juft propofed. M. de Bougainville anfwered, there is a wide difference, between a trading frigate, and a King's frigate of war. We have no trading commodities on board; and are come here only with intent to take in fome refreshments, and to wait for the Sphinx, which we have parted from, and which we have appointed to meet in the Rio de la Plata.

Plata. As soon as you give me your word, replied the Governor, that no goods shall be diſſembarked; you are welcome to land or ſend on ſhore as often as you pleaſe. But the cuſtom eſtabliſhed by the laws, being to ſend a ſoldier or guard wherever the boat puts into ſhore, I deſire you would not take it amiſs that I comply with it; it is for your quiet as well as mine; for I do not chuſe to lay myſelf open to any blame from my court. In every other reſpect, you may depend on my doing every thing in my power to oblige you; for I am prompted by my own inclination, as well as by the orders I have received, to treat the French with the ſame civility as the Spaniards. Matters being thus ſoftened on both ſides, the dragoons were ordered to the boat, and went accordingly.

The Governor afterwards deſired M. de Bougainville to permit him to take a copy of the orders he had received from the king of France for the command of the two frigates, becauſe he was obliged to ſend it to the court of Spain, together with a circumſtantial account of our anchorage. M. de Bougainville readily complied with his requeſt: the reſt of the converſation was carried on amicably, and we parted good friends.

The Governor had more reaſons than one for acting as he did: he told us ſome of them, ſo that it was not difficult to gueſs at the reſt. Don Joſeph Joachim de Viana (which was the Governor's name) being now, in 1763, about forty-eight years of age, knight of the order of Calatrava, brigadier of the troops of his Catholic Majeſty, was intruſted by the king of Spain with the command of the troops ſent into Paraguay againſt the Indians, who had revolted, as it is ſaid, at the inſtigation of the Jeſuits. The Jeſuits then held the ſway in that country, and had refuſed to ſubmit themſelves to the meaſures taken by the courts of Spain and Portugal, to fix the limits of their reſpective poſſeſſions. Don de Viana, conducted this buſineſs, and all his operations were crowned with ſucceſs, notwithſtanding the obſtacles of all kinds which the Jeſuits threw in his way. This certainly was not the method to

obtain

obtain their good will, and indeed he knew that they were not his friends.

At Montevideo they have a convent, in which there are but two priests, and one layman, who, as well as their emissaries, always keep their eyes open upon what passes, and are continual spies upon the conduct of the Governor of this city. The Governor of Buenos Ayres, whose power extends over the whole Paraguay, favours the Jesuits in every particular, and scruples not to be their slave, and the mean instrument of their revenge. The Jesuits knowing the misunderstanding there is between these two Governors, which perhaps they themselves have excited, would not fail, if Don de Viana was in any ways capable of conducting himself in a censurable manner, to take advantage of any little circumstance of that kind, and acquaint the Governor of Buenos Ayres with it: Don de Viana is thoroughly convinced of this. Being a man of great merit in every respect; a man of sense, abounding in military knowledge, and distinguished by probity; having none of that pride which the Spaniards are sometimes reproached with, he has acquired the esteem and respect of all who know him. All persons are unanimous in his praise, from which even the Jesuits themselves cannot dissent, at least publickly.

There are more than sixty Jesuits in the convent of Buenos Ayres, which is said to be very beautiful. The convent at Montevideo is but very small, without any remarkable appearance, distinguished from the houses of the rest of the inhabitants only by a bell, fixed under an arch, about three feet high, raised on one of the extremities of the top of the roof. I never saw the inside, though the Jesuits had sent me invitations two or three times to come and see them. The provincial, already spoken of, first made the proposal to me at the Governor's, and I came into it, promising to go the next day, or a few days after. A Spanish officer who was present told M. Bougainville of it, representing to him that it was not proper a Frenchman should pay a visit to the Jesuits, after what had lately happened at Buenos Ayres.

TO THE MALOUINE ISLANDS. 111

Ayres. He related the fact to Mr. de Bougainville, and taking me aside afterwards; you are a true Frenchman, said he, and you have just been promising to go and see the Jesuits. You must either break your word, or give up your pretensions to that title. About six weeks ago, one of them preaching at Buenos Ayres, when I was present, ran out in invectives against the Kings of France and Portugal, the Republic of Genoa, and against the other powers who have expelled the society: you cannot surely think of going to see them after this intelligence; besides, the visit would by no means be agreeable to the Governor. The last expression made me suspect that there was some partiality in this officer's discourse: so that I resolved to suspend my opinion. On coming away from the Governor's, M. de Bougainville repeated this caution to me as coming from the same officer; I promised not to go near the society, and kept my word. The officer told me in particular, the invectives the Jesuits had used against the King of France, which were so remarkably indecent, that I have thought it best to pass them over in silence.

Two days after I found an opportunity of coming at the truth. I inquired about it of two Spanish officers, who spoke the French language well, and who were going to embark on board the Saint Barbe Frigate, in order to return to Spain. One of them was a colonel, the other a captain. The captain's name was Simoneti. They each of them confirmed the fact, and added, that as the Governor of Buenos Ayres made it a point to protect the Jesuits, he took no notice of this rash and impudent discourse; but that some persons of quality and distinction, whose probity was well known, had ordered a particular account of it to be made out, and sent to the court of Spain; and that they were the officers commissioned to carry a copy of it to the said court *.

Two

---

\* These officers left Montevideo the same day that we did. The frigate upon which they embarked was commanded by Don Pedro de Flores, laden with 15 or 1,800,000 piasters, bulls hides, and other merchandize. She had set sail from Cadiz in 1755, bound to the coast of Guinea, fitted out on the English account, and
S                                                       destined

Two days after this conversation, I went to visit the chaplain of a Spanish frigate, which had been lying at anchor in the port of Buenos Ayres for five months; I knew he was much inclined to the Jesuits. It was even said pretty openly that he had been sent by them to Montevideo, in order to buy up any trifles he might find on board our frigate. He indeed bought up every thing we would sell him.

After the first compliments had passed between us, he asked me why I had not been to see the Jesuits, according to their invitation, and my promise. I told him it was true I had promised, but that I had been informed that one of those fathers, had lately spoken very ill of the king of France, my master, in a sermon preached at Buenos Ayres; and, if this was a fact, it was not proper that I, who was a true Frenchman, should pay a visit to the brethren of so rash a preacher. You certainly heard the sermon, said I.——I did; and it is certain that the Father did not express himself in the most cautious manner.—What said he then particularly of the King of France?——That he was a tyrant, a persecutor of the church, and many other things. But we should surely forgive them, for this is nothing more than the effect of their resentment having been expelled the kingdom of France.

We had scarce finished this conversation, when two of the three Jesuits of Montevideo came into the room where we were, the Abbé, M. Mauclair our surgeon, and myself. After having bowed to us, one of the Jesuits, addressing himself to me, said he was very glad to see me; and that in consequence of what he had heard from Joseph (this was the name of the provincial before mentioned) he and his brethren had expected me for two days. He afterwards asked me why I had not kept my word; I answered that

destined to carry over negroes to Buenos Ayres; but not meeting at Cape Verd with the English vessel from which she was to have received them, Don Pedro de Flores continued his course, and sailed into the Rio de la Plata. Here he had remained ever since that time, in order to avoid running the risk of being taken prisoner by the English during the last war, as he was laden for Spain. From the observations he had collected for making a chart of this river, joined to my own, the chart inserted in this work has been traced.

that I had just been giving my reason to the Abbé, who might explain it to him. I am not surprised, said he, I know the Benedictines do not think properly, and that they are not our friends. I told him he was mistaken, and that if they did not think properly, they would be his friends. As he did not like my answer, he made no reply; but took his leave of the company, and went away with his companion.

Between four and five in the evening, we spied a sail. We judged immediately by her course, that she was making for Buenos Ayres. But as we expected from day to day the arrival of the Sphinx sloop, which we had appointed to meet in the Rio de la Plata, many of us imagined this was she. As she advanced, and came more within our notice, we were so far confirmed in our opinion, as almost to persuade ourselves that we were assured of it.* Notwithstanding the uncertainty, M. de Bougainville dispatched the long boat with the lieutenants, Donat and Le Roi, to pilot her. The signals were agreed upon, powder and other necessary articles were given to put them in execution, and they set off about seven o'clock. The night grew very dark, the winds contrary, and the sea rather high, so that not having perceived their signals, we grew very anxious about them. The Sphinx had discovered us by the signals agreed upon, and in order not to lose sight of us, had done nothing but ply to windward, and make several tacks, which together with the darkness had prevented our long boat from boarding her: this she did however at midnight. The Sphinx then anchored, and setting sail the next morning, being the first of January, she came up, and cast her anchor near us about nine o'clock in the morning. The joy we had at seeing her, after a separation of more than two months, may readily be conceived. M. de la Gyraudais had been previously told of the defect in the maps, with respect to the bearing of the coast of Brazil; but though we had ourselves been upon our guard, we were very near running aground upon the bank which is not marked in the French charts. This bank lay in his course as it had done in ours;

nor are the Abrolhos made to extend so far upon the charts as they really do: all these circumstances contributed to make us uneasy, on account of her delay, especially after the stay we had made at the island of St. Catherine.

As soon as the Sphinx had cast her anchor, M. de la Gyraudais came to us in our long boat, and told us he had been obliged to put in at Togny on the coast of Brazil, because notwithstanding they had been apprised of the errors in the charts, yet they had fallen upon the Abrolhos at a time when they thought themselves at least thirty leagues distant from them. They found themselves stuck upon them in the middle of the night; it happened luckily that the weather was calm, and that the rock upon which they struck was of rotten stone.

The Sphinx being fast upon this rock, in order to avoid the dreadful consequences of a wreck, they quickly hoisted out the fishing boat they had, put the long boat and the yawl to sea; and having carefully examined the ship, they recovered a little from their apprehensions, when they found she had received no damage.

The next trouble they had was to disengage the Sphinx from the rock: as soon as it was day light, they found themselves surrounded with rocks of the same kind; and at the distance of half a quarter of a league, a vessel lying on her side, without masts. M. de la Gyraudais imagining they were then upon the Abrolhos, and that land could not be far off, sent the boat towards the shore for assistance. They met with several canoes of fishermen, negroes and Indians. They spoke to them in the Portuguese language, and six of them agreed to go on board the Sphinx, where they were well feasted. They promised to give them all the help in their power. Two of them were kept on board, and the other four dispatched in the boat, to bring up their comrades from the coast. They came back the next day attended by a great number of canoes. With their assistance, the Sphinx was at last disengaged from the rock, after having rested upon it for three days. M. de la Gyraudais came

off

off with the loss of the fishing boat only. The negroes piloted him as far as Togny, where the inhabitants treated him and his crew, for six days, with the greatest humanity, and as well as if they had themselves been of this country: although they are most of them negroes or Brazilians.

After this interview, we went to Montevideo to pay our compliments to the Governor upon the new year, not knowing that it was customary in this country to defer this ceremony to the sixth day of the month, the Epiphany. The Governor was holding a council for the nomination of officers of justice. Being informed that, after the finishing of this business, he was to go with all the retinue to the parish church, which they call the cathedral, we went to the spot, and waited for him upon our legs a whole hour, under the shade of a house, conversing with some officers of the garrison. At half an hour after twelve, he made his appearance in the midst of the new officers of justice, who had each of them large white wands in their hands, which they made use of, as walking sticks. He crossed the square, which is very large, in the middle of these officers, all ranged in one line, having their large black cloaks on, and their small sticks; as the Oviodore of the island of St. Catherine. We followed them into church. Mass was performed by the priest, whom they called le Signor Vicari; when this was over, we paid our compliments to the Governor, who invited us to dinner. As we were already engaged to dine with him the next day by appointment, M. de Bougainville thought proper to decline the acceptance of this kind invitation, and went on board with M. de Nerville.

I stayed behind in expectation of dining with the vicar; M. Duclos our captain having told me the evening before that I should do this gentleman a great pleasure, and that they had talked about it. After having saluted the governor, I went up to the vicar in the vestry, but did not speak a word to him about dinner. We came out of church with the two Spanish officers, who were to embark on board the St. Barbe; we went along with the vicar a little way without receiving any invitation to dinner;

dinner; and I took care not to invite myself. When we had left him, the captain asked me where I should dine. I answered that I did not know; that I had expected to dine with the vicar; but as he had not mentioned any thing about it, I intended to seek my fortune somewhere else. He immediately said, that I should go with the colonel to the Governor's. I started many objections to this, not thinking myself sufficiently known to go in this manner; the colonel insisted, and taking me by the hand, told me the Governor would be pleased with him for bringing me; and that he certainly would take it amiss if he should know that I had refused. I consented therefore, and was received by the Governor and his lady, with all possible marks of politeness and favour. He speaks French well enough to be understood; his lady understands it without being able, or rather without venturing to speak it. Her husband and the colonel were her interpreters. She was a native of Biscay, tall, well made, of a brown complexion, but her features were rather too masculine. She is a woman of great wit and vivacity, and about thirty-four or thirty-five years of age.

At eleven o'clock on Monday morning the second of January, M. de Bougainville, Messrs. de Nerville, de Belcourt, l' Huillier, the two Du Clos brothers, our first and second captain, Donat our first lieutenant, de St. Simon a Canadian, lieutenant of infantry, de la Gyraudais, captain of the Sphinx, and myself, all went to the Governor's, where we had as elegant a dinner as the country would afford; but the dishes were drest according to the custom of the place: that is to say, most of them with the fat of oxen clarified which they use instead of butter and oil; and seasoned with such a quantity of pimento and carthamum that the victuals were quite covered with them. Care had been taken however not to put these spices upon all the dishes, and many of us eat of none but these last. The only wines offered us were Spanish, and wines from the country of Chili; the plates and dishes were silver, and some of them china. The table was covered with a very short cloth, and the napkins were rather less

than

than handkerchiefs of a moderate fize, naturally fringed, or, to fpeak more properly, unravelled at both ends. The difhes were ferved up one after another. When drink was called for, it was neceffary to fay, whether one chofe wine or water, or a mixture of both; for the Spaniards generally drink nothing but water at their meals: at the end of which it is cuftomary to bring a large glafs of wine to every body in company, even without its being afked. When wine and water was called for, they were brought one after another, and we were obliged to drink them feparately. The wine of Chili is of the colour of phyfic, compounded of rhubarb and fenna, and very much of the fame tafte. It takes this tafte perhaps from the foil, perhaps from the goat fkins lined with pitch, in which it is conveyed. There is fcarce any other wine drunk in Paraguay. One foon accuftoms one's felf to this tafte; and after having drunk it for a few days, one finds it good. It is very warm upon the ftomach. But, whether from tafte or fancy, the Spaniards preferred the wine we had brought with us from France. The defert was entirely compofed of fweet-meats. The bread though made with excellent flour, was not good, becaufe it was not well leavened nor properly kneaded; neither do they know how to bake it.

In the evening M. de Belcourt, who had taken a lodging in the town, met with a ftranger in company, perhaps in difguife, who fpoke a gafcoun French. Prompted in all probability by the Jefuits, who had already taken care to acquaint themfelves by the people belonging to our frigates, of M. de Belcourt's military reputation; this man propofed to him to enter into the fervice at Paraguay, in order to form the troops. He made him promifes from the Jefuits, of the higheft emoluments to induce him to accept of the propofal. M. de Belcourt pretended to liften to him, but without entering into any engagements; and the very next day acquainted M. de Bougainville with this circumftance. This gentleman anfwered, that fome political advantage might poffibly be made of this, and that if he chofe to facrifice himfelf for the good of his country, it might then be proper to

give

give an ear to thefe propofals. M. de Belcourt anfwered, that in cafe he fhould think of engaging in this bufinefs, it would be neceffary that M. de Bougainville fhould give him a note, certifying that he went with his confent, and for the prefumptive good of the ftate.

The next day the ftranger renewed his folicitations to M. de Belcourt with greater earneftnefs, defiring him to take his refolution fpeedily; that he need not trouble himfelf about his cloaths or any thing elfe; that care fhould be taken to fupply him with every thing he might want; and that, in order to prevent the Spanifh government from knowing any thing of the matter, he fhould be conducted, by ways unknown to the Spaniards, to the place of his deftination. M. de Belcourt inquired which was the place, and what were the advantages propofed; but the ftranger not giving any fatisfactory anfwer, and having talked to him in a flighting manner of the Jefuits, on purpofe to conceal his defigns more effectually, M. de Belcourt declared at once, that he would not comply with his folicitations. But as he was under fome apprehenfions how he fhould get away he kept himfelf on his guard. About the dufk of the fame ev he found himfelf fo clofely preffed by three men, that he thought himfelf obliged to draw his fword, and carry it out of the fcabbard, to make his way, in cafe they fhould have furrounded him; which, however, they did not attempt. I had all thefe circumftances from his own mouth, and it is with his confent I make them public.

Towards eight o'clock in the evening, M. Mauclair, firft furgeon of our frigate, came and told me, that after having had a confultation with M. Paflé the fecond furgeon, and M. Frontgouffe furgeon of the Sphinx, upon the prefent ftate of the failor who had been wounded in turning the cap-ftern during the late ftorm, they had agreed that he was growing much worfe, and that he himfelf defired to be confeffed. I went down immediately, and finding him indeed very ill, received his confeffion.

He

He loft his fenfes an hour after; about ten o'clock I adminiftered the extreme unction, and at eleven he died.

On Tuefday morning the 3d inftant, having previoufly apprized the vicar, we fent away the corpfe in our yawl. It was depofited with the guard of the port, till the vicar fhould come to meet it. He came an hour afterwards, with his fexton. On his arrival, I made him a compliment in Latin, to which he gave no other anfwer, but a very low bow. He had a Roman furplice on, and a gown; his fexton, a lay-man, had a black petticoat on by way of caffock, and a very dirty furplice. Meff. Duclos, Guyot, his brother Alexander, his two fons, fix failors, and myfelf attended the proceffion. At each turning the vicar chanted a refponfe, and a prayer, and fang alfo the mafs for the dead. He did the failor all the honours he could have done to the captain himfelf, and had him buried in the church. The fervice being over, he invited us to dinner, and could not be prevailed upon to accept of any fee.

After dinner, I took a walk towards the extremity of the creek which forms the port, where our people were getting water. I went all over the coaft and the adjacent foil, in expectation of finding fome curious plants or fhells; but my fearch was fruitlefs. I met with one fingle plant only in a ftate of perfection; the ftem, which is eight or ten inches high, and the leaves were covered over with a fhort white down, fo clofe and fo thick, that it concealed the green part from the fight. I am unacquainted with the name and properties of this plant.

At the diftance of two fhots or thereabouts from the creek or bay, there are two fountains. The people of the country wafh their linen in that which is neareft the river. It is forbidden to wafh in the other; becaufe that is the one from whence they draw the water ufed for drink in the town, which is at the diftance of half a league from it. This fountain is bordered with a little wall of ftone, and is very badly kept up, though at the king's expence; fo lazy are the inhabitants, and fo carelefs even of what concerns them nearly.

As I was paffing by this fountain, I faw three or four Mulatoes, who had brought there fome ftones upon a cart, drawn by four large oxen; and three others, who were filling a cafk with water, in order to carry it into the town. An Indian or Mulatto woman, with a negro woman coming to the fame place to draw water alfo, one of the Mulatoes, who looked very much like an Indian born of Spanifh parents, took the negro woman by the hand, and they both of them danced together upwards of a quarter of an hour, the dance called Calenda. Travellers who fpeak much of this dance in their accounts, do not exaggerate, when they defcribe it as the moft lafcivious of all dances, at leaft judging of it by our manners.

It is thought, that this dance has been brought into America, by the negroes of the kingdom of Arda, upon the coaft of Guinea. The Spaniards dance it as well as the natives, throughout all their eftablifhments in America, without making the leaft fcruple about it; although the dance is fo very indecent as to aftonifh people who are not ufed to fee it. It is fo univerfally, and fo much liked, that even children, as foon as they are able to ftand, imitate in this particular perfons more advanced in life.

It is danced to inftrumental as well as vocal mufic, by two or by feveral perfons together. They are all difpofed in two rows, one before the other, the men oppofite to the women. Thofe who grow tired, as well as the fpectators, form a circle round the dancers, and the mufic. Some one of the dancers fings a fong, the chorus of which is repeated by the fpectators, with clapping of hands. All the dancers keep their arms half raifed up, jump, turn round, make contorfions with their backfides, advance within two feet or thereabouts of one another, then fall back in time, till the found of the mufic or tone of the voice brings them together again. Then they ftrike their bellies one againft another two or three times following, and retreat afterwards, whirling about, to begin the fame motion over again, with jefts, which are extremely lafcivious, indicated by the found

of

of the inftrument or voice. Sometimes they mix their arms, turning round two or three times, and continuing to ftrike themfelves upon the belly, and to kifs . other, without being in the leaft out of time.

One may readily judge, how furprifing fuch a dance muft appear to French manners, and how much our modefty muft be offended by it. Neverthelefs we are affured from the accounts of travellers, that it is fo very agreeable even to the Spaniards of America, and is become fo much an eftablifhed cuftom among them, that it is even introduced among their acts of devotion: that they dance it in church, and in their proceffions: that even the nuns themfelves, fcarce ever fail to dance it on Chriftmaseve, upon a ftage raifed up in their choir oppofite the grate, which is left open, that the people may partake of the fight; but they do not admit men to dance with them.

On Wednefday the fourth of January, while Meff. de Bougainville and de Nerville were gone to the Governor, to invite him to dine on board our frigate for the Sunday following, I went to fee an officer whofe name was Belia, who had been brought up in France, in our royal college of Pontlevoy near Blois. He had promifed me fome curious and medicinal plants of the country, and fome pieces of natural hiftory. With refpect to the laft article he had nothing worthy of attention; but he fhewed me the plants, which I fhall now defcribe: his brother-in-law and himfelf acquainted me with their names, properties, and ufes.

One called *Mèona*, is very much like the wild thyme, but the leaf is round, and the green not fo dark; the ftem red, creeping, taking root at each joint, affording a white milky juice, like the fpurge. The feed grows in a fpiral, briftly pod; this pod contains only a yellowifh feed in form almoft like a kidney. It throws off from its root feveral woody ftalks, which fpread themfelves circularly on the ground, as thofe of the biftort. This plant taken in infufion, like tea, is faid to cure a ftoppage of urine as by miracle.

*Ebreno*, or *Mio-mio*, is an almoſt repent plant, not riſing more than half a foot from the ground. The leaf is ſmaller than fennel, it has a very ſmall herbaceous flower, growing in cluſters, and pretty nearly umbellated: the root is reddiſh outwardly, and as well as the plant has the taſte of the parſnip. It is taken in infuſion againſt fluxions and colds. It ſeems to me to be a ſpecies of the *Meum*, or ſpignel.

The *Maté* has a round ſtrait branched ſtem, growing about a foot and a half high, and covered with a grey down a little inclining to red. The leaves are an inch and a quarter in length, only three or four lines in breadth, of a whitiſh green colour, and downy on the ſtem. The flowers ſhoot out one by one along the branches, and are compoſed of a ſingle yellow leaf, ſlit into four, and almoſt without ſmell. They are ſucceeded by a huſk or pod, of the thickneſs of a quill, an inch in length, which opens itſelf into four parts when dried, and lets fall ſome exceedingly ſmall ſeeds pointed at each end, of a grey brown colour. It is ſaid to be of admirable efficacy when applied to wounds, either recent or of long ſtanding. M. Simoneti told me, that, after having been ſix months under the care of the phyſicians and ſurgeons of the army, for a wound he had received in the ſide near the kidneys, and which had degenerated into an ulcer, he had cured himſelf in a ſhort time merely by the outward application of the leaves of this plant.

The *Cachen-laguen* or the *Cancbalagua*, which is alſo called at Chili, *Cachinlagua*, is in every reſpect like the leſſer Centaury of Europe. It is the Centaury of Chili, but does not grow quite ſo high as ours. A cold infuſion is made of it, by throwing ſix or ſeven of the plants whole and dry into a glaſs of water for the ſpace of the whole night, or from morning to evening. This infuſion is then uſed as a gargle, and afterwards ſwallowed, by which method a ſore throat is ſoon cured. Some freſh water is then poured upon the reſiduum, which is ſuffered to ſtand as long as the firſt; after which the gargling and deglutition is repeated. This is done alſo a third time. M. de Bougainville, and M. du

Clos

Clos our captain, had experienced the efficacy of it more than once. When the infusion is taken warm in the manner of tea, it heats very much but purifies the blood. This plant is very famous in Chili, from whence it is brought. I believe it to be a better febrifuge than the Centaury of Europe. Might not the latter be .ed with equal advantage in sore throats?

*Mechoacan*, is a name the Spaniards of Montevideo give to a plant bearing no resemblance to that which is sold in our shops under the same name. That of Montevideo, which is very common there, as well as in the neighbourhood of Buenos Ayres, is a small creeping plant, the root of which runs under ground like the liquorice. It is whitish, and slender as a writing pen; some short branches shoot out from this root, which creep upon the ground, are covered with a very few small leaves, and these only at the extremity, almost resembling those of the lesser Tithymalus, known in several provinces of France by the name of Réveil-matin. M. Belia told me, that the English who trade at the colony of St. Sacrament, always carry away several of these roots. It has a purgative quality like the Mechoacan of our shops. When it purges too violently, its effect is soon stopped, only by swallowing a large spoonful of brandy.

Another plant which they hold in great esteem is *he Guaycuru*; it bears a leaf of a beautiful green colour, rather thick, and shooting forth in great abundance from the root, which is of a red brown colour, externally shining, and reddish within, as the strawberry plant. From the middle of the root, the stem grows out to the height of half a foot, of the thickness of a common quill, solid, without leaves, of a greyish coloured green, spreading out at the upper part into a dozen small branches, bearing at their extremity very small herbaceous flowers, without smell, and forming altogether a kind of umbrella.

This plant, especially the root, is one of the most powerful astringents in botany; and experience has proved, that it never fails in drying up and curing ulcers speedily; and even, as the vicar told us, in curing the scrophula, and stopping a dysentery.

He made us a prefent of a dozen of the plants which he had fent for on purpofe, at the diftance of a few leagues, from a country place belonging to him.

The *Poyeo* is a plant, which throws out from its root feveral creeping branches: thefe are afterwards fubdivided into many others. The leaves are but three lines in length, and two in breadth, ferrated, thick, and fixed to the branches without any foot-ftalk. The flower is fo fmall that it is confounded with the feed, which fucceeds it, and with which the branches are almoft entirely covered. At firft fight, it might be taken for the *Rupture-wort*, or *Herniaria*, if the branches were fhorter. The whole plant is of a pale green colour, fometimes reddifh, as well as the ftem, when it approaches to maturity. It fmells like a lemon juft beginning to fpoil. It is an excellent remedy for diforders of the ftomach, and indigeftion. Its decoction is fudorific, and its virtues are much extolled in the pleurify. The method of taking it, is, by chewing one of the green ftems about the fize of one's little finger, and fwallowing afterwards the faliva together with the chewed plant. When taken in this manner it is a mild purgative. When there is none of the green plant to be had, it is taken in infufion like tea.

M. Delia fpoke highly of the anti-venereal virtues of the *Colaguala*, which fome call *Calaguela*. It grows in barren and fandy foils, to the height of feven or eight inches. Its .tem confifts of feveral fmall branches, which fhoot up through the fand or gravel. They are but two or three lines in thicknefs, full of joints placed at fmall diftances from each other, and covered with a pellicle which falls off of itfelf when it is dry. The leaves are very fmall, few in number, and arife immediately from the ftem.

The colaguala is looked upon as an admirable fpecific for diffipating impofthumations in a fhort time. Three or four dofes, that is to fay, three or four pieces of it in fimple decoction, or infufed in wine, and taken in the courfe of the day, are fufficient to effect this purpofe. Being a very hot plant, it would become
injurious

injurious if taken in too large a quantity. The root, which is the only part of the plant in use, is of a reddish brown colour outwardly, and resembles much the *Guaycuru* root. When cut horizontally, it has a brown spot in the center, and a whitish circle in the middle of its substance. A Franciscan named Father Rock, famous for his knowledge in physic, told me, that he prescribed the *Calaguala* in the epilepsy, as well as in the venereal disease; that when it did not succeed perfectly in the cure of the epilepsy, he had assisted it with the following prescription, which had never failed of success. He makes the patient drink, in the course of the day, a quart of water, in which a young virgin arrived at the age of puberty, or a sound healthy woman, has well washed the parts of generation on getting out of bed; with particular directions that two glasses of this water should be taken fasting, one half an hour after the other. This remedy is continued for eight or nine days consecutively, at the decline of the moon; and is repeated for several months, especially in the spring. The method of using the *Calaguala*, in venereal disorders, is by infusion in wine, or in boiling water.

The same Franciscan being with us at the Governor's country house, shewed me another plant which he called *Carqueja*, and which he told us was admirable, in infusion like tea, for dissolving coagulated blood in the body, for purifying it, and removing obstructions. But it must be used very sparingly, as it agitates the blood violently, especially the root of it.

The *Carqueja* grows like a small shrub, to the height of one foot, and its head is naturally rounded. It has no leaves distinct from the stem, which resembles much that of the Genista or broom, with which I fancy it may be classed. This stem divides itself into many branches to form the head. These branches are very flexible and thin.

The *Yguerilla*, the *Zarca*, and the *Charrua*, are plants greatly valued in this country; as well as the *Birabida*, or *Viravida*, which is reckoned refreshing and cooling in the highest degree. A French surgeon prescribed an infusion of the Birabida with good

success

succefs in a tertian. Frezier reckons it among the ever-greens. May it not probably be the fame as I mentioned before under the name of Doradilla?

But the plant they make the moſt uſe of is the *Séfran*. It is properly a kind of thiſtle, known under the name of Carthamum. The defcription of it is found in every botanical treatife. Its flower is called the baſtard faffron. It has the colour and form of the true faffron; but has not either its taſte or ſmell. At Montevideo and at Brazil they ſow the *Séfran* plentifully in their gardens; becauſe they uſe the flower of it to cover all their victuals, and even the ſoup. Parrots and Paroquetes are very fond of the feed, which is white, ſmooth, and made like that of the Corona Solis, or Sun-flower, but much ſhorter.

M. de Bougainville having told me, before he went to invite the Governor, that we ſhould ſet out early to go on board again, I went to the yawl at half an hour paſt four. There I found M. de la Gyraudais, and the ſurgeon of the Sphinx. After having converſed ſome time about the plants I had been collecting, finding that M. de Bougainville did not return, M. de la Gyraudais propoſed taking a walk about a mile off, behind the citadel, telling us, that the plant Maté had been ſhewn him; and that there was a great quantity of it near a fountain.

M. Frontgouffe, who had alſo heard of its properties, came with us in order to gather ſome. We collected likewiſe ſome of of the feed, which I gave, as I did all the feeds I collected in the courſe of my voyage, to M. de Juſſieu, to ſow them in the King's Garden at Paris. While we were ſupplying ourſelves with this plant, we heard a plaintive ſound iſſuing from between a large heap of ſtones and rocks, which cover and ſurround the fountain: we were not more than ſeven or eight toiſes diſtant from the found. We thought at firſt it proceeded from a cat confined among theſe ſtones, which might have eſcaped from a houſe about half a mile diſtant. As we came nearer the fountain, the cry ſeemed like that of a child. We were advancing

towards

towards it, when M. Frontgouffe defired us not to proceed, saying, it was not the cry of a child, but that of an alligator. He told us, he remembered to have heard them more than once in our iflands, and that had we proceeded it would have been to our coft. We found indeed that there were alligators in this country; M. de St. Simon having already told us, he had feen one of them on the bank of a fmall river, running behind the mountain, feparated from the town only by the bay in which the port is fituated. Not daring therefore to pufh our curiofity any farther, we contented ourfelves with gathering a few more plants, and went back towards the town, in order to go on board again. As we were walking along, we met with feveral Curlews, by thirty in a body. They came within piftol fhot of us, but we had only fticks in our hands.

About feven o'clock we reached the yawl, where we met with Meff. de Bougainville, de Nerville, de St. Simon, and Martin, Lieutenant of the Sphinx. It was very fine weather when we left the Port; and we had already made three parts of our way, when a South Eaft wind arofe fo brifkly as to oblige us to ply our oars, in order to get on board, before it fhould become more violent. It blew however harder and harder. Each cloud as it rofe on the horizon brought a frefh fquall, more violent than the preceding. The waters being confiderably fwelled by thefe repeated attacks, formed waves which grew bigger and bigger, and retarded our progrefs. Although the fea and the wind were againft us, we were now within gun fhot of the Sphinx, which was the neareft veffel, and on board of which we thought of fetting M. de la Gyraudais, with the other officers belonging to her. The fine clear fky had difappeared. The clouds made the night ftill more dark, fo that we could but juft difcern the figure of a boat, bearing towards us. We then imagined that M. Duclos, fufpecting our diftrefs, had fent out the longboat to our affiftance. We haied her, but received no anfwer. The fea however drove her towards us with fo much fwiftnefs, that we foon difcovered her to be our fmall boat, floating at the mercy of the waves, with no person in her. We shifted our course to try to save her; we came up with her, put two men into her with oars, and a grappling, and then endeavoured to get on our way. It might then be half an hour after eight. We strove in vain against the tide, the violence of the waves and the wind. While we were putting the men and the oars into the small boat, we had been driven to leeward more than three quarters of a league, on the side of the French island, situated near the coast, almost opposite the citadel. The darkness prevented us from seeing land, and indeed we could hardly discern the lights they had put out on board our two frigates.

Perceiving therefore, that we got farther and farther from the ships instead of coming nearer them, we determined to make for land, and steered to the point where we thought the city was, for its situation as pointed out to us only by two lights, at a great distance from each other. The waves which broke against our boat, had already thrown in a great deal of water, which we emptied with our hats; we were wet to the skin, and the boat-men were much fatigued. M. de la Gyraudais, after having rowed for an hour, had now taken the helm; we knew not where we were, and had no brandy to keep up our strength and spirits. In this distress we thought there was no better expedient for us, than to let fall our grappling, to give the men time to rest themselves. I then put on a great coat I found near me, and we distributed the quarter-cloths among the men, to cover themselves with; not indeed to keep them from the waves, for we could not be more wet than we were, but to shelter them from the wind, which made us so very cold, that we were ob-obliged to squeeze as close as possible to each other, in order to keep ourselves warm. We were almost resolved to remain in this condition all night, when M. de la Gyraudais thought he perceived, that we were dragging our grappling. He ordered the steersman to lay his hand on the hawser, that he might judge by the motion, whether our grappling was really aweigh or not. The steersman thought at first, that the motion he felt was

was caused by the shocks the boat received from the waves; but he soon found out his mistake, and gave us notice of it. He was ordered to sound with the boat-hook, which he did, and found only three feet water, with a bottom of rocks, which are on the borders of the whole coast, and advance pretty forward in the river. The oars were placed in the row-locks, the grappling was drawn up, and we rowed for a full quarter of an hour, sounding all the while, and finding the same bottom. At last we came to a muddy bottom, with seven or eight feet water. We were going to cast our grappling here, when the men foreseeing they should get no supper in this place, said, that as we were now in the way, we must continue, and go and lay on shore. We were extremely well satisfied with their resolution, and steered towards a light, which we imagined to be that of the guard placed at the only port where it is possible to land.

Soon after, as we were all looking about us, endeavouring to find our situation, we perceived a schooner, which we knew to be at anchor very near the port. The sight of this vessel revived our spirits, and we exerted ourselves so much, that in little more than half an hour we gained the port. The officer of the guard came out to reconnoitre us. Another officer was sent with the steersman to give the Governor notice of our being returned to the city, because we had not been able to reach our vessel. He sent us compliments of condolance, and at the same time invited us to supper, and desired us to take up our night's lodging at his house.

We were apprehensive of being troublesome to him, not only on account of the late hour, for it was midnight, but also because we were too numerous a company: besides, as we were very wet, and in a strange pickle, we thought it better to go in search of a Frenchman named Lacombe, of St. Flour in Auvergne, settled at Buenos Ayres, and having a house also at Montevideo: he was already known to many of our officers, from whom he had made several purchases. A soldier of the guard, who spoke French, offered to conduct us. Instead of leading us to the place where M. Lacombe lived, he brought us to the house of a friend of his, where the soldier had seen him several times. We knocked near a quarter of an hour before we could get any answer. At length they answered, the door was opened, and we found M. de Belcourt in bed in this house, as it was the place where he lodged. Thinking that we were playing him a trick, he did nothing but laugh at us. As we were not much in a humour for laughing, we enquired which was M. Lacombe's house, and were informed. We were making the best of our way to it when we met the Governor, who came on purpose to intreat us not to make use of any house but his. As we could not possibly refuse, after many civilities on both sides, we accompanied him.

When we came there we found every body up, and the cloth laid. Seeing we were all very wet, they offered us clean linen and cloaths. Those who had put on their great coats soonest, and were certainly not so wet as I was, refused even to change cloaths. The Governor's lady solicited me so often to put on at least a night gown, that I at last accepted of it. It was one of her gowns, which I had so much trouble to get on that the Governor gave me one of his own. We sat down to a light supper, provided hastily for us. Our adventure was the subject of much conversation; at last we drank a dish of chocolate, and, as it was now almost two o'clock, every body thought of retiring to bed.

Mess. de Bougainville and de Nerville were put into a small room of the court yard, in which there was no other furniture besides two chairs and two beds; one in a kind of alcove formed by a simple partition of wood, the other a camp-bed placed in the opposite angle. We had attended them to this apartment, and I took it for granted I was to pass the night in a place much of the same kind, when a negro woman pulling me by the sleeve beckoned me to follow her. She brought me back into the room where the company had been, where I found the Governor's lady and a negro woman employed in fastening
together

together some crimson damask stools, which before ornamented the bottom of the room. Not knowing why she was thus employed, I was talking in the mean time with the Governor. At length she interrupted me, saying, it is for you, Sir, I am preparing this bed; you will be near us, and will not fare worse than the rest. After having expressed my gratitude for her attention and politeness, I did all I could to prevent her from going on with this business, but all to no purpose; she still proceeded, telling me it was a great pleasure and satisfaction to her. When she had made me a very good bed, she retired with the Governor into the next room, where they slept.

A camp-bed was put up for M. de la Gyraudais, in the first room on coming in; and, as there were no more spare beds, a fire was made to dry our cloaths in the middle of the first hall, where M. de St. Simon and the rest slept upon the chairs.

About half an hour after four, one of these gentlemen came to wake me, telling me M. de Bougainville was up, and that we must go. I dressed myself quickly, and we were going without saying a word, when a servant from the Governor came in, and desired us to stay a little, that his master was getting up, and would pay his compliments to us. We told him to intreat the Governor from us not to rise, that he wanted rest, and that we were going away that instant, in order not to incommode him any longer. The wind and waves were considerably abated, and we got on board in a short time.

The squalls of wind and rain our vessels were exposed to since the preceding evening had been extremely violent. The storm having begun early in the spot where our frigates lay at anchor, because they were not under shelter of the town as we were; the crews had been in very little concern about us, being persuaded that we should not even have run the risk of coming from shore in such weather. At all events, however, they had taken the precaution to put out lights. The two men we had put into the boat to save it, had been luckily driven into a small sandy creek under shelter of the French island; and the long-

boat

boat of the Sphinx, which had been sent after her, had got to the bottom of the bay, in the place where we used to water. They were both returned when we came on board.

In the morning of the sixth of January we went back to the town, to return our thanks to the Governor, and to pay him the compliments of the new year. He detained us to dinner. The conversation turned much upon the curiosities of the country. This made the Governor recollect that he had a shell which he thought very scarce. He shewed it us: it was a papyraceous Nautilus, as large and beautiful as any I ever saw. He made a present of it to M. de Bougainville. It had been sent to him from Rio de Janeiro; and he told us, he had found a similar one on the coast of the island Maldonnado; but that it had been broken. The Governor's lady gave me a parcel of the Canchalagua, which was all she had left of it. A few days before she had made M. de Bougainville a present of a paroquete, which spoke very prettily, and had also given him a cup made of the Calabash of Peru, mounted in silver, with a *Bombilla*, or tube of the same metal, used to suck up the maté.

Many authors of voyages have mentioned the Paraguay plant, or Caflioberry bush, as one of the principal sources of the riches of the Spaniards, of the Indians, and especially of the Jesuits inhabiting this province. That my readers may be perfectly acquainted with this plant and its use, I shall insert the account given of it by M. Ulloa, which he had from the missionaries of the country; for as they suffer none but their own brethren to penetrate into the country, this account can only be had from them.

"It is affirmed, says M. Ulloa, that the sale of this plant was at first so considerable, and became so great a fund of riches, that luxury soon introduced itself among the conquerors of this country, who were at first reduced to the bare necessaries of life. As their taste for luxury was always increasing, in order to support their prodigious expences, they were obliged to have recourse to the Indians subdued by force of arms, or who had voluntarily

TO THE MALOUINE ISLANDS. 133

voluntarily furrendered themselves: of these they made their servants, and soon after their slaves. They worked them too hard, so that many of them fell under the weight of labour they were unused to; and more of them under the oppression of the cruel treatment they were exposed to, rather from the loss of their strength, than from their indolence. Others escaped by flight, and became most irreconcileable enemies to the Spaniards. The Spaniards fell into their former state of indigence; which however did not make them more industrious. Luxury had increased their wants so much, that the sale of the Paraguay plant alone was not sufficient to supply them: most of them indeed were now no longer able to buy it, for the great consumption of it had enhanced its price." Tom. I. page 13.

This plant, so famous in South America, is the leaf of a tree about the bigness of a middling sized apple-tree. Its taste is like that of the mallow, and in figure it nearly resembles the orange leaf. It also bears some resemblance to the leaf of the *Cocoa* of Peru, where a great deal of it is carried, especially among the mountains, and in all places where they work the mines. The Spaniards think it the more necessary, as the use of the wines of the country is hurtful there. It is brought dry, and almost reduced to powder. It is never suffered to remain long in infusion, because it would then turn the water as black as ink.

It is distinguished into two kinds, though they are both one and the same leaf. The first is called *Caa*, or *Caamini*; the other *Caacuys*, or *Yerva de Palos*; but Father *del Técho* asserts that the name of the genus is *Caa*; and distinguishes three species, under the names *Caacuis, Caamini,* and *Caaguazu*.

According to the same traveller, who passed great part of his life in the Paraguay, the Caacuys is the first bud, ju... ...ning to expand its leaves. The Caamini is the leaf in full ...th, from which the stalks are taken, before it is roasted: i... ...alks are left on, it is called Caaguazu or Palos. The leaves when roasted are preserved in pits digged in the earth, and covered
with

with a cow's skin. The Caacuys will not keep so long as the two other species, the leaves of which are exported to Tucuman, to Peru, and even into Spain. It is very liable to injury in the removal. It is asserted even, that this plant, taken on the spot, has a particular bitterness, which enhances its virtues as well as its price, and which it loses by transportation.

The manner of taking the Caacuys is by filling a vessel with boiling water, into which the leaf, powdered and reduced to a paste, is thrown. As it dissolves, any small portion of earth which may have remained sticking to it, floats at the top, so as easily to be skimmed off. The water is then strained through a rag, and being suffered to stand a little, is afterwards sucked up through a reed. Generally there is no sugar put to it; but a little lemon juice is mixed with it, or some kinds of wafers of an agreeable smell. When it is taken as a vomit, a little more water is thrown on it, and it is left till it is almost cold.

The most famous place for this plant is at *Villa*, or the new *Villarica*, which is near the mountains of Maracagu, situated to the East of Paraguay; about 25 degrees 25 minutes South latitude. This district is celebrated for the cultivation of this tree; it is not however upon the mountains that it grows, but in the marshy bottoms which divide them.

From this place are taken for the Peru only, one hundred thousand *Arrobes*, each of which weighs twenty-five pounds of sixteen ounces standard weight, and the price of the arrobe is seven crowns, or twenty-eight French livres, so that the whole profit of the hundred thousand Arrobes amounts to two million eight hundred thousand French livres. Yet the Caacuys bears no fixed price, and the Canmini sells for twice as much as the Caaguazu. The last of these, while we were at anchor at Montevideo sold for twenty-five livres, or five piasters per Arrobe. The Governor procured it us at this price.

The Indians settled in the provinces of Uraguay and Parana, under the government of the Jesuits, have sown some of the seeds of this tree, brought from Maracayu, which have hardly

degenerated

degenerated in the leaft. They refemble much the feed of the ivy. But thefe Indians do not prepare the plant in its firft ftate; they keep the Caamini for their own ufe, and fell the Caaguazu or palos to pay the tribute they owe to Spain.

The Spaniards imagine they find in this plant a remedy or prefervative againft all difenfes. Every body agrees that it has a laxative and diuretic quality, but I would not anfwer for all the properties the Jefuits attribute to it. I believe the moft inconteftible of thefe properties, which is however the one they are moft filent upon, is that of fupplying them with a prodigious fum of money every year.

It is reported, that fome perfons having at firft taken this plant too freely, it brought on a total deprivation of their fenfes, which they did not recover till a few days after. It appears indeed certain, that it often produces oppofite effects, fuch as to procure fleep to thofe who want it, and to rouze thofe who are lethargic; to be at once both nourifhing and purgative.

Cuftom renders the ufe of it neceffary; and it is often with difficulty that people abftain from an inmoderate ufe of it; for it is affirmed that an over-doze of it inebriates, and brings on moft of the inconveniencies which follow an excefs in drinking ftrong liquors.

According to Mr. Ulloa, the Paraguay plant, is called *Maté* at Peru. He fays, that in order to prepare it a certain quantiy is thrown into a calabafh, mounted in filver, which is alfo called *Maté*, or *Totumo*, or *Calabacito*.

Some fugar is thrown into this veffel, and cold water poured upon the whole, that the plant reduced to a pafte may be well moiftened: the veffel is afterwards filled with boiling water; and the plant being in very fmall pieces, the liquor is fucked up through a tube of a fufficient fize, but too fmall to admit the plant to pafs. The tube or reed made ufe of is called *Bombilla*. As the water diminifhes it is renewed, adding always fome fugar, till the plant floats no longer on the furface : at which time a fresh quantity of it is put in. It is often mixed with the juice of lemon, or Seville orange, and with sweet scented flowers. This liquor is commonly taken fasting: but many people drink it also after dinner. Perhaps the plant may be heathful; but the method of taking it is extremely difgusting. How numerous soever the company is, every person drinks by turns through the same tube or bombilla, handing the *maté* from one to the other. The Spaniards of Europe care very little for this drink, but the Creoles are passionately fond of it. They never travel without a supply of the Paraguay plant; and never omit taking it every day, preferring it to all other kind of food, and never eating any till after they have taken it.

Some, says Frézier, (Relat. du Voyage de la Mer de Sud, page 228) call the Paraguay plant, St. Bartholomew's plant; because they say this Apostle went into these provinces, where he changed the plant which was before poisonous, and made it salutary and wholesome. Instead of drinking the infused liquor separately as we do tea, they put the plant into a cup made of a calabash, mounted in silver, which they call *Maté*. They put sugar to it, and pour hot water over it; then drink it off immediately, without suffering it to stand in infusion, because it would grow as black as ink. In order to avoid taking up the plant, which floats on the surface, they make use of a silver tube, the end of which is formed into a round knob, perforated with several small holes: so that the liquor, which is sucked through the other end, comes up without the plant. The company drinks round through the same tube, pouring more hot water as the first is consumed. Instead of the reed or *bombilla*, some people remove the plant with a plate of silver, full of small holes. The aversion which the French have shewn to drink after all kinds of people, especially in a country where there are so many persons afflicted with the venereal disease, has introduced an invention of small glass tubes, which they now begin to use at Lima. In my opinion, the taste of this liquor is better than tea, it has an agreeable vegetable smell. The people of the country are so used to it, that even the poorest among them drink it at least once a day.

The trade of the Paraguay plant, adds the author, is carried on at *Santa Fé,* where it is brought by the river Plata, and by land carriage. There are two kinds of it: one of which is called *Yerva de Palos;* the other, which is a finer sort, and of a higher quality, is called *Hierba de Camini*. The last comes from the lands belonging to the Jesuits. The greatest consumption of it is made from *Paz* to *Cusco*, where it is twice the value of the other, which is sold from Potosi to Paz. Above 50,000 arrobes are brought every year from Paraguay to Peru; that is to say, 1,250,000 weight of one and the other species, the third part of which quantity at least is Camini; without reckoning about 25,000 Arrobes of the Palos, sent into Chili. Each packet, containing six or seven Arrobes, pays four reals duty, at Alcavala; and the expence of conveying it above six hundred leagues doubles the prime cost, which is about two piasters: so that at Potosi, it costs five piasters, or five and twenty livres of France, per Arrobe. It is generally conveyed in carts, which carry one hundred and fifty Arrobes from Santa Fé to *Jujui,* the last town of Tucuman; and from thence to Potosi, which is still an hundred leagues farther, it is carried upon mules. I have observed, that the use of this plant is necessary in places where they work the mines, and in the mountains of Peru, where the white people imagine wine to be pernicious: they rather chuse to drink nothing but brandy, leaving the wine to the Indians and Blacks, who are very well satisfied with it.

I was witness at Montevideo of the truth of the account given by these two authors. At whatever time of the day one goes into any house, one is sure to find somebody drinking *Maté,* which they never fail to offer to any one who comes in, even in the very hottest weather; being persuaded that this infusion is cooling, that it assists digestion, &c. The vessel out of which one drinks the *Maté* usually stands on a foot, fastened to a board. This was the general custom in almost every house; but some of the inhabitants held the veſſel alone, ornamented with ſilver, in their hands, without any board. There are alſo ſome *bombillas* or reeds, the end of which put into the liquor, is formed like an oyſter-ſhell, fixed to the tube by the top of its hinge.

While we were at the Governor's, two of our ſailors deſerted; ſome ſaid that one of them was a Malteſe, others that he came from Biſcay; they had given him the nick-name of Spaniard. The other came from lower Britanny. We ſearched for them in vain. We learnt afterwards that they had offered to enter on board the Spaniſh frigate, St. Barbe, but the owner aſſured me he had refuſed them. A few days after four ſailors deſerted from the Sphinx: one of them named Plaiſance, who had been formerly a dragoon, and had ſerved in Canada under M. de Bougainville. This man had been very preſſing to let him embark with us, when we left St. Malo. M. de Bougainville had always looked upon him as a very honeſt and brave man, very fit to become an inhabitant of a colony. He had given him two complete ſuits, and other cloaths. Two days before he had deſerted, he had been truſted with a fuſil, and a rich ſword to ſell. He gave out that they had been ſtolen from him. Whether this report was true, or whether he had really ſold them, it is certain that one of the inhabitants declared that Plaiſance had ſold the ſword to an officer's ſervant. Plaiſance finding himſelf ſuſpected, and not being able to clear himſelf properly of the accuſation, ran away, for fear of being puniſhed for his diſhoneſty. The Governor, at M. de Bougainville's ſolicitation, who had promiſed ten piaſters for every deſerter that ſhould be brought back to him, ſent ſome dragoons after them, but they came back without any tidings of them. I believe that if one had even promiſed a reward of one hundred piaſters, they would not have ſtopped any of them: for it is the intereſt of Spain to retain as many men as poſſible in the country for the ſake of population.

Monte-

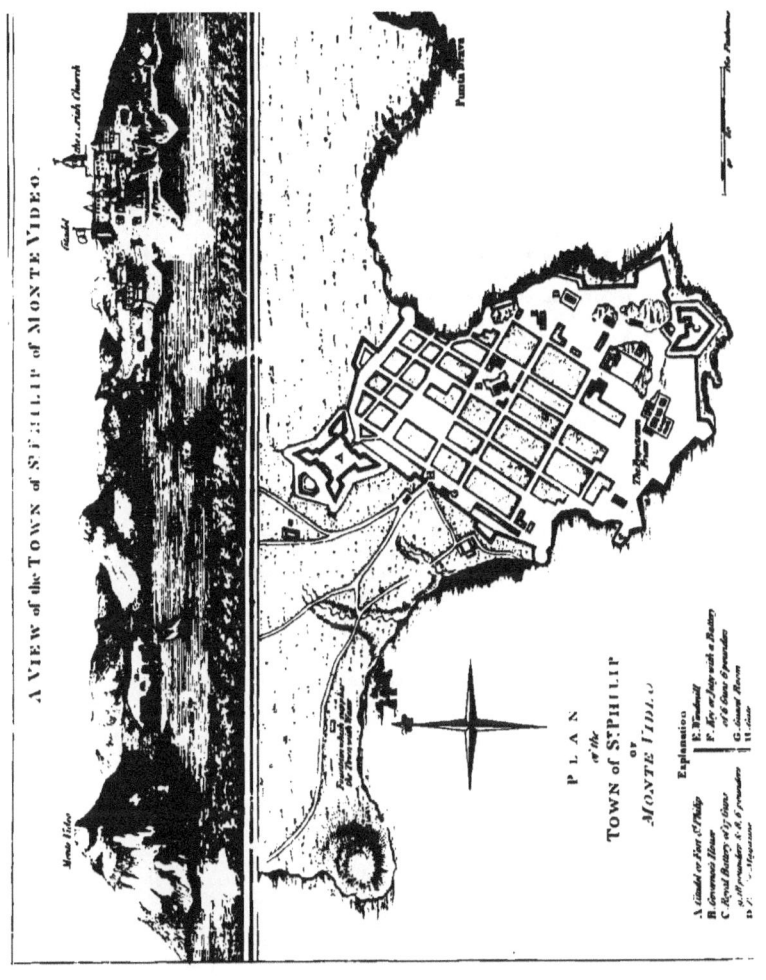

Montevideo is a new colony. Five and twenty years ago there were only a few huts in it. It is, however, the only tolerable place for the anchorage of ships that come up the Rio de la Plata. At present it is a small town which improves every day. The streets are made perfectly strait, and wide enough to admit three coaches abreast. I have given a view of it, taken as it appeared from on board the Eagle frigate, while we lay at anchor between the mountain and the town, according to the description I have given above.

The houses consist only of ground floors, under the roof; one of them only is to be excepted; this is situated in the great square, and belongs to the engineer, who built it and lives in it. It has one story, and a kind of a double roof with a pretty long projection, which supports a balcony in the middle of the front. I have given the plan of this town.

Each tradesman's house generally consists of a hall, which serves by way of entrance, a few bed-chambers, and a kitchen, the only place in which there is a chimney, and where they make any fire. These houses are therefore properly a ground floor, fourteen or fifteen feet high, including the roof. The entrance into the Governor's house is a long square hall, which receives light only from one small sash, half filled with paper and half with glass. The bottom of the sash is closed with planks of polished wood. This hall may, perhaps, be about fifteen feet wide, by eighteen feet long. From hence one goes into the room for receiving company, which is almost square, but rather longer than it is wide. At the bottom, opposite the only window in the room, made much in the same taste as that I have before described, there is a kind of alcove six feet wide, closed with bars of iron, and covered with tigers skins. In the middle of this is an arm chair for the Governor's Lady, and on each side six stools covered, as the arm chair is, with crimson velvet. All the ornament consists in three small bad pictures, and a few large plans, half-pencilled and half coloured, still worse in point of drawing than the pictures. The two other sides fides of the room are filled with feats for the men. Thefe are wooden chairs with very high backs, refembling thofe made in the time of Henry the fourth of France, having two turned pillars fupporting a frame which adorns the middle, covered with leather, curioufly ftamped and wrought, as well as the feat. The door which leads from this room into the next, where the Governor and his lady fleep, is only clofed by a kind of curtain made of tapeftry. The two angles of this room on each fide of the window are filled up, one with a wooden table, upon which the veffel for taking the *Maté* always ftands; the other with a kind of cupboard, having two or three fhelves, furnifhed with a few china difhes and cups.

The lady of the houfe is the only perfon who fits in the alcove when there are only men in company, except fhe fhould invite fome of them to fit on the ftools near her.

Thefe rooms have, generally fpeaking, neither flooring, nor pavement. From the infide of them one may fee the reeds which fupport the tiling of the roof.

The white people fpend their time in idle converfation, in taking the *Maté*, or in fmoaking a *Sigare* or *Cigare*, which is a kind of fmall cylinder, fix or feven inches long, and about half an inch in diameter, compofed of tobacco leaves rolled one over the other.

The merchants, and a very few artifts, are the only perfons who have any employment at Montevideo. There are no fhops, no figns, nor no outward fhow, by which they can be found. But one is fure of meeting with them, if one goes into any houfe fituated in an angle formed by the meeting of two ftreets. The fame merchant fells wine, brandy, woollen drapery, linen, toys, &c.

In the ftreets one meets with nothing but white or black people, or mulatoes on horfeback; and horfes ftanding at the doors of the houfes without being faftened. This country might well be called a hell for horfes. They often make them work three days following, without giving them either meat or drink;
fometimes

sometimes they are kept tied up for as long a time, with the same treatment, and doing nothing except running from the end of one street to another. At the end of three days, they are sent back again into the country to feed upon what grass they can find. The person who goes with them, takes off the saddle, and puts it upon another horse, whom he brings to the town to be treated in the same manner.

Notwithstanding this they are excellent cattle, having preserved the spirit of the Spanish horses, from which they are bred. They are extremely sure footed, and surprizingly swift. Their step is so sharp, and so long, that it is equal to the full trot, or small gallop of our horses. Some of them are so light that nothing can be compared to them. When they step they raise the fore foot and the hind foot at the same time; and instead of bringing the hind foot in the place where the fore foot was, they stretch it out much farther, bringing it opposite to and even beyond the fore foot of the other side; which makes their motion as quick again as that of other horses, and at the same time much easier for the rider. They are not remarkable for beauty; but deserve much encomium for their swiftness, mildness, courage, and abstemiousness. The inhabitants make no provision of hay or straw for these animals. Their only food all the year is in the fields. It is true, that in this country it is never cold enough to freeze either the rivers or the plants.

The environs of Montevideo are an extensive plain. The soil is a black thick earth, extremely fertile with very little manurement. This country only wants some persons to be employed in cultivating it to become one of the best in the world. The air of it is wholesome, the sky serene, and the heat not excessive. It is rather deficient in wood, which is found only a long side the rivers. Here tigers, leopards, and other wild beasts chiefly resort. The tigers especially are rather numerous, larger, and more fierce than those of Africa. The Governor had one of these tigers brought up from a whelp in his court yard. He was fastened near the entrance of the door, with a

single

single strap of leather, passed round his neck. The dragoons and servants used to play with him, and he never gave any signs of his natural ferocity. They used to turn him about, to pull him, to throw him over and over, as one would do a tame cat. The Governor seeing that M. de Bougainville took a fancy to him, had him carried on board, and made a present of him. A cage was made for him of thick planks, six inches in square, and he was kept eight days. At the end of this time, he began to roar now and then, especially in the night. It was then apprehended that he would grow furious, or that, even in play, he might swallow the arm of some of the ship boys, or children who went to see him, and who sometimes put their hands between the planks of his cage. Besides, it was necessary to supply him with fresh meat for his food, and we had none of that to spare. These considerations determined M. de Bougainville to have him strangled. He was then but four months old, and his height, when he stood upright, was two feet three inches. By this one may judge how high he would have grown.

The Spaniards of Montevideo live, as I have said before, in great indolence. They are clothed nearly as the Portuguese at the island of St. Catherine; but they very frequently wear white hats, the flaps of which hang loose over their shoulders, and cannot be made too large for them.

The women are pretty well shaped, but one cannot say with truth that they have a complexion of lilies and roses; on the contrary they are much tanned, have commonly but few teeth, and those not white.

Their dress consists outwardly of a plain white or coloured waistcoat, well fitted to the waist, the skirts of which fall four fingers in length upon the petticoat. This petticoat is made of stuff more or less rich, according to the circumstances or fancy of the person who wears it. It is edged with gold lace, or with a fringe of silver, gold, or silk; sometimes in double rows, but without flounces. They wear no caps of linen or lace. A simple ribbon passed round the head keeps the hair together at the top,

A Spaniard of Montevideo

*A Spanish Lady of Montevideo*

top, from whence paffing on the back part of the head, it falls in two or three treffes down the back; flowing fometimes as low as the bend of the knee. The longer they are the more beautiful they are reckoned.

When the women go out, and fometimes even in the houfe, they cover their heads with a piece of fine, white, woollen ftuff, trimmed with gold or filver lace, or filk. This piece of ftuff which they call *Iquella*, or mantle, covers alfo their fhoulders and arms, and falls down below the waift. They crofs the ends of it over the breaft, or under the arms, as our French ladies do their cloaks. When they wear this kind of mantle in the houfe, they feldom cover their head with it. The country women of Poitou wear fome nearly of the fame kind. But in the ftreets, and at church, the Spanifh women put this mantle fo clofe upon their heads, that one can hardly fee any of their face except an eye, and the nofe: in the houfe they often do not even cover their neck with it.

The women at home enjoy at leaft as much liberty as in France. They receive their company with much politenefs, and are eafily prevailed upon to fing, dance, play upon the harp, guitar, theorbo, or mandoline. In thefe things they are much more complaifant than our French ladies. When they are not engaged in dancing, they feat themfelves upon ftools raifed, as I faid before, under a kind of alcove, at the bottom of the room, where the company is. The men cannot fit near them, unlefs they are invited; and when this favour is beftowed upon them, it is looked upon as a mark of familiarity.

The manner of dancing among the ladies feems to partake of the indolence in which they pafs their lives, though they are naturally very lively. In moft of their dances their arms either hang loofely down by their fide, or are folded under their mantle, which they alfo call *Rebos*. In going through the *Sapateo*, one of the moft common of their dances, they keep their arms raifed up, and fnap their fingers in the air, as they fometimes do in France, when they dance the rigadoon. The Sapateo is performed

formed without moving much out of the fame place, and by ftriking the ground with the extremity of the foot and the heel alternately. The ladies hardly appear to move; they rather feem to flide along upon their feet, than to advance in cadence; this is owing to the lightnefs and celerity with which they move their feet.

The Governor and the military men are dreffed after the French fafhion, except that they always wear a hat upon their heads, and that they are never powdered or curled, any more than the women. They live alfo in a great ftate of indolence, as well as the other Spaniards; who are dreffed nearly in the fame manner as the Portuguefe of St. Catherine's ifland.

The common people, mulatoes, and negroes, inftead of a cloak, wear a piece of broad ftriped ftuff, of different colours, flit only in the middle, to let the head through. It falls down upon their arms, and covers them as low as the wrift. On the fore, and on the back part, it comes down below the calf of the leg, and is fringed all round. This garment is called *Poncho*, or *Chony*. Every body wears it on horfeback, finding it more convenient than the cloak or great coat. The Governor fhewed us one of them, wrought in gold and filver at Chili, from whence this garment has been brought. It had coft him more than three hundred piafters: fome of them are made at the fame place at the rate of two thoufand.

The Poncho keeps off the rain, and defends from the wind; it ferves for a bed covering at night, and for a carpet in the country. All thefe dreffes may be feen in the plates.

The Spaniards live in a very plain manner. The men, who are not bufied in trade, rife very late, as well as the women. The flaves, negro women, or mulatoes, prepare the *Maté*, while their mafters are dreffing, who put the reed into their mouths, almoft before they have put their feet into their flippers. The men afterwards fit ftill with their arms folded, till they take it in their heads to converfe, and fmoke a *cigale* with their neighbours. Four or five of them fometimes ftand together

*A Spanish Gentleman of Montevideo*

*A Spaniard of Montevideo.*

TO THE MALOUINE ISLANDS. 145

ther at the door of a houfe, talking and fmoking; Others mount their horfes, and go out, not to take a ride about the country, but through the ftreet. If they have a fancy for it, they get off their horfes, mix with any company they meet, goffip for two hours without faying any thing of confequence, fmoke, take fome *Maté*, then mount their horfes again; who has been all this while ftanding as ftock ftill as a wooden horfe, without being faftened, and as if he was liftning to the converfation. Sometimes there are as many horfes
 me⸺
 …g this interval, the women remain ….ed on a ftool at
 ‘tom of their apartment; having u. le. :.:ir feet next to
 a mat made of reeds, and over the …..t fome cloaks
 lavages, or fkins of tigers. There they play upon the
 o ., or upon any other inftrument, which they accompany with the voice; or they take the *Maté*, while the negro women are dreffing the dinner in the fame room.

About half an hour after twelve, or one o'clock, the dinner is ferved up; this confifts of beef dreffed in various ways, but always with a great quantity of pimento and fefran. Sometimes ragoos of mutton are brought up, which they call *Carnero*; and fometimes fifh, but very feldom any poultry, which is rather fcarce. There is great plenty of game, but the Spaniards do not go in queft of it, as that would be too fatiguing. The defert is compofed of fweetmeats.

Immediately after dinner, both mafters and flaves indulge in the *Siefta*, that is, they lie down; fometimes they undrefs themfelves and go to bed, where they fleep for two or three hours. Workmen, who live by the labour of their hands, do not deny themfelves thefe hours of indulgence. A great part of the day being thus loft, this is the reafon of their doing but little work, and makes all handicrafts exceffively dear. This circumftance may alfo proceed from the plenty of money there is here.

It is not furprizing they fhould be indolent and lazy. Their meat cofts them only the trouble of killing, fkinning, and cut-

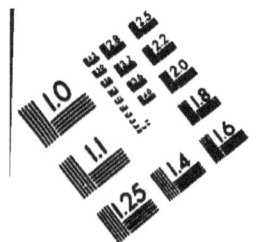
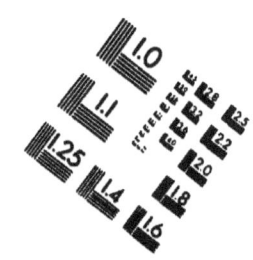

**IMAGE EVALUATION
TEST TARGET (MT-3)**

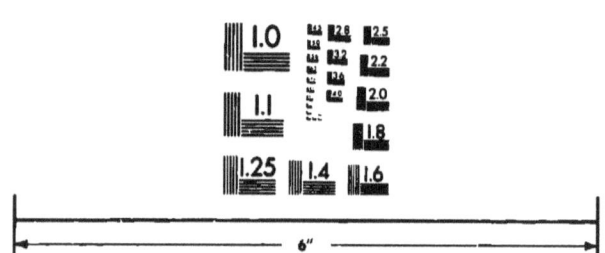

Photographic
Sciences
Corporation

23 WEST MAIN STREET
WEBSTER, N.Y. 14580
(716) 872-4503

ting up the ox to drefs it. Bread is very cheap. The fkins of
oxen and cows ferve to make them all kinds of facks, to cover
part of their houfes, and for a thoufand other purpofes, for which
different forts of materials are ufed in Europe. Thefe fkins are
fo common, that many flips of them are found fcattered here
and there along the ftreets the leaft frequented, in the fquares,
and upon the walls of the gardens.

Few of thefe gardens are cultivated, though there is one belonging to each houfe. The ground is left fallow. I faw but
one garden tolerably well kept, and this undoubtedly was becaufe
the gardener was an Englifhman. Vegetables therefore are
fcarce here. The plant they cultivate the moft is the fefran or
Carthamum, for their foup and fauces.

It is very common among them to keep a miftrefs. Thofe
who have children by them, give thefe children a kind of legi-
timacy, by acknowledging themfelves publickly to be their
fathers: after which, thefe children inherit nearly as the legitimates
do. There is no ignominy fixed upon illegitimate births; becaufe the laws authorife them fo far, as even to beftow the title
of gentlemen to baftards: in which thefe laws appear more
agreeable to humanity, not making the innocent fuffer for the
guilty.

I have obferved, while I was at mafs, that the Chaffuble was
compofed only of three flips of ftuff, fewed together lengthways,
without being in the form of a crofs. The middle flip only is
of a different colour from the other two. During the time of
mafs, one of the inhabitants plays upon the harp, in a gallery:
this harp certainly ferves inftead of an organ. I faw no particular demonftration of devotion, but that of ftriking their
breafts pretty hard five or fix different times, from the beginning
of the fervice till after the communion. The Rofary is much
in ufe here; and the Ave Maria is almoft the only prayer they
fay. Many of them wear the Rofary round their necks. The
Portuguefe of St. Catherine's ifland, white men, negroes, and
mulatoes, had likewife almoft all of them Rofaries; fome wore
them

them outwardly, especially the blacks; the others wore them under their cloaths. They are also very devoutly inclined to the scapulary of mount Carmel; which is worn by both men and women. They think the scapulary and the *Avillas* will preserve them from all dangers, and insure their eternal salvation. They are scrupulous only about the externals of devotion. These Avillas which one sees hanging at their necks are a kind of sea chesnut, resembling a flat round bean, of the size of a half-crown, and two lines and a half in thickness; the skin is granated, and very finely shagreened, of a pale chesnut colour; at its circumference there is a black band, which almost surrounds it. I picked up a great many of them on the sea coast, at the island of St. Catherine, without knowing what they were: and I have seen many of them mounted in silver, at a goldsmith's shop in Montevideo. He told me, that when it was worn round the neck it preserved from infectious air and witches.

At each altar there is a veil which reaches from top to bottom, always hanging before the principal image, in the same manner as that they place in France before the host, when taken out of the tabernacle, during the time of a sermon or a discourse. This veil always remains. At the beginning of mass, the string which fastens the veil is pulled up, and the veil raised like a curtain, so as to discover the image: when mass is over, the veil is let down again.

Two days after sailing from Cape Frehel, near St. Malo, we put into a small barrel of water a liquor which had been given us by M. Seguin, a chymist, who lives in the *rue des postes, près de l'Estrapade*, at Paris, as a preservative of sweet water from corruption, as well by sea as by land, and as having the property not only of preventing, but likewise of curing the sea scurvy. As we had hitherto kept the water we brought with us from St. Malo's, sweet; we now compared it with the other, and finding no difference, we determined not to open this cask again, in which we had put the liquor, till the fresh water should undergo some considerable change.

The very night in which the storm obliged us to lie at the Governor's, it produced more fatal consequences, at the distance of two cannon shot from our frigates. The thunder was very loud, and the lightning fell upon the Spanish vessel the St. Barbe, which had shifted her anchorage two days before, in order to be more at hand for sailing out of the river with the first favourable wind. Their change of position brought on this accident, by which they had one man killed, and fourteen wounded, five of whom were dangerously hurt; and their mizen mast was shattered.

The next day we carried to the Governor's house, the compass invented by captain Mandillo a Genoese, for finding out the longitude. We wanted to make some observations upon land, which we had not been able to do upon the vessel all the time of our voyage, even when it was calm; because the fault of this compass, is, that the least motion disturbs the steadiness of the needle. During a calm, even when it lies quite even, it is more or less agitated. Notwithstanding all possible care was taken to preserve this compass, yet the damp of the sea air, which penetrates every where, had affected the needles, so as to make them a little rusty at the center, and near the parts which keep them in equilibrio. They had therefore lost that property which is necessary, and their magnetic virtue was likewise somewhat impaired. We cleared them from the rust, and recovered their magnetic powers; but we remitted our observations till another day, because it was now lat     d we left the instrument with the Governor.

On this occasion we expressed our astonishment to the Governor, that the inhabitants of Montevideo should not think of procuring themselves shade in their gardens, and other extensive places, by planting of trees; and we mentioned our surprize also at observing, that the country seemed totally deprived of that benefit. He told us there were some trees along side the rivers, and that a country house which he had at the distance of about two leagues from the city was well furnished with them.

## TO THE MALOUINE ISLANDS. 149

them. He propofed a party to go there on horfeback the next day in the afternoon, after dining with him. We accepted of the ride with an intent not only of feeing the country, but at the fame time to convince ourfelves of the many wonderful and incredible things he and many others had told us of the horfes of Paraguay.

The party being concluded on, the Governor took upon himfelf to provide us with a fufficient number of horfes, which were to be ready about three or four o'clock.

The vicar had invited me to dine with him that day, in company with Meff. Duclos, the two brothers, firft and fecond captain, M. de Belcourt, the paymafter of the Spanifh troops, a Fleming who fpoke the French language well, and the two fons of M. Duclos the elder. We went there, and during the whole dinner time, a mulatto played upon the harp. About the middle of dinner, another man, whom they called a civilized Indian, joined the former and accompanied him with his guitar. Then the vicar, who was the only ecclefiaftic in town, called in four or five little blacks about eight or ten years old, and as many negro girls of the fame age. He made them dance to the found of his inftruments, and the caftanets they had in their hands. The children acquitted themfelves with furprifing agility and clevernefs. One circumftance a little tirefome in thefe Indian dances, is, that almoft all the fame motions are repeated in every dance. It muft alfo be allowed that there is no great variety in the tunes they fing or play. The mufick of fome of them, efpecially of the Sapateo is pricked down in Frezier's account of a voyage to the South Sea.

They knew in this country, not only what the King of Portugal had done againft the Jefuits in his dominions, but alfo what the parliaments of France, and the government, had enacted againft this fociety. The vicar defired me to give him in writing an account of what was reprefented in that famous picture found among the Jefuits at Billom, in Auvergne, at the time when an inventory was there taken of the furniture and

effects

effects of those fathers, after the condemnation and suppression of their institution in 1762, and 1763; and the secularization of its members. I satisfied his curiosity with regard to this authentic monument of Jesuitical folly. This vicar is a man of good sense, and generally beloved. He has thirty slaves, negroes and negro-women, great and small. It is his pleasure always to have somebody to dine with him. He gives his company a hearty welcome, and treats them well. He looks upon all his slaves as his children, and is beloved by them. He educates them well in order to give them afterwards their liberty, with forty or fifty cows or oxen, to put them in a way of keeping up their freedom. But he pays a particular regard, I may indeed say, he shews an uncommon degree of affection, for a little mulatto, almost white, who is the son of one of his mulatto slaves, as he was pleased to say by an Irish officer, but who bears in all the features of his face the strongest marks of being the vicar's own son. He told us he intended to send him into France to study, and to make a physician of him. The child is at present seven years old. When there is company, he makes him dine by himself, and when there is nobody, often with him. He has already settled five and twenty thousand piasters upon him. His living, and his own private income bring him in about four thousand, and he is now about sixty years old.

We were waited on at table by four negro women, by the mother of the little mulatto, who is also a mulatto, and by an Indian woman the wife of a Cacique, taken at the colony of St. Sacrament from the Portuguese, in the last siege the Spaniards laid to it. These women were all with child, though neither of them was married except the Indian, who knew not whether her husband was alive or dead. Neither men nor women in this country, are in the least scrupulous upon this article.

At the desert, Meff. de Bougainville, de Nerville, and l'Huillier de la Serre, came to meet us; and we all went together to the Governor's house, where we found horses ready for us. The

Governor's

Governor's lady, dreſſed like an Amazon, and having a gold laced hat on, cocked after the military faſhion, put herſelf at the head of our cavalcade, mounted upon a beautiful horſe, whoſe value anſwered to his appearance. M. de Bougainville's horſe was equally fine. With a kind of doubled pace, which reſembled ambling, they always left us behind. It was all we could do to keep with them, ſome of us trotting, others on a canter. We continued this pace till we reached the country houſe, which we did not do till more than a full hour after our firſt ſetting out, though they told us it was no more than one league diſtant from Montevideo.

Father Rock, a Franciſcan, was here waiting for us, with the Governor's ſon, a child of three years and a half, to whom this father was preceptor. We found a plentiful collation ready for us; and after drinking a glaſs, merely on account of the heat of the weather, we went to ſee the Governor's orchard, which he called a wood.

This country ſeat is nothing extraordinary with regard to the houſe; which conſiſts of one ſingle ground floor, as all the other houſes do; on account of the violent winds, very frequent in this country, which might blow them down if they were built higher. The only remarkable thing here is a tolerably pretty room, which however has no other ornament than ſome geographical maps, fixed on the bare wall, and ſome wooden chairs covered with leather, which is figured with flower work.

At the diſtance of two or three gun ſhots from the houſe, the orchard is planted: this conſiſts of apple, pear, peach, and fig trees, diſpoſed in alleys; which are not very regular, except the middle walk, which reaches from one end of the orchard to the other, and is about a mile and a half in length. A pretty conſiderable brook winds through the orchard; which has probably hindered the walks from being cut ſtrait. They are however extremely rural, on account of the number of tall, as well as low plants growing in them without cultivation. The balm eſpecially abounds there. I acquainted the Governor, M. Belia, and another officer, with its virtues. They were the more pleafed with my account, as the plant is extremely plentiful in this country, and they thought it might perhaps be ufed inftead of the *Maté*.

The trees were fo laden with fruit, that moft of the branches, unable to fupport the weight, were already broken. We advifed the Governor to have the others fupported with props, more efpecially as he told us, that all thefe fruits were of the beft and moft excellent kind. We could not judge of this ourfelves, as the time of their being ripe, was not till the end of February; at prefent however they had an exceeding fine appearance.

One might make a delightful walk of this orchard; but the Governor does not employ any body about it, becaufe it is his intention to return to Europe, where he propofes to fix entirely.

As we were coming back, I fpoke to father Roch, and held a converfation with him in Latin, upon feveral points of philofophy; which I foon found he had only ftudied in Ariftotle's fchool, both by the barbarous and obfolete terms he made ufe of, and by the fyftem he followed. He indeed confeffed himfelf to be much attached to it. He told me, he was *a Peripatetic and a Scotift, and would remain fo all his life*. He fpoke pretty good Latin, and with facility. The greateft difficulty to me was his pronunciation of u as ou, and his manner of pronouncing the g, which the Spaniards always lofe in their throats, pronouncing it nearly as an afpirate. Befides the attention this required of me in order to underftand him, I was alfo obliged to confider of what I had to fay, and at the fame time to endeavour to catch his pronunciation, without which, he might not perhaps have comprehended me. A few days before, for the firft time, I had been exactly in this fituation with him. Having heard that he was a man of learning, I had been to pay him a vifit at his convent. I inquired for him, in the Latin tongue, of one of his brethren who opened me the door. He made me a fign to walk in, without anfwering a fingle word. I went in, and

and meeting with three more brethren, I inquired for father Roch in the same language: and one of them answered me only, *Padre Fratre Roch? fuoras.* This was all I could get out of him. On this occasion as on many others I felt how disagreeable it was for a traveller to be unacquainted with the language of the country he is in. The want of comprehending exactly what others say; and the being obliged to be silent, when one has something of consequence to say, for fear of not being rightly understood, is a situation worse than that of a deaf man, who has at least the satisfaction of speaking, and making himself understood.

On returning a second time to the convent, I had the good fortune to meet with the superior, who answered me in good Latin, which he spoke, though with some little hesitation. He brought me into his cell, where we conversed together for a full half hour, after which father Roch came and joined us. In the course of this conversation, he informed me of some remedies, the success of which he had seen in repeated experiments. I give the receipts of some of them here, that any person who thinks proper may have an opportunity of trying them.

*Tooth-ach.*

Extract from the fuller's thistle, a worm which is always found in it when it is ripe. Rub this worm between the thumb and fore-finger, pressing it gently till it dies through weakness. One or other of these two fingers applied to the tooth will have, at least for a whole year after, the property of removing the pain.

*The Farcy in Horses.*

At the end of autumn collect the bearded protuberances, or kinds of chesnuts belonging to the eglantine: bruise the worm you will find in them, and make the horse swallow it in a glass of wine, or any other liquid; then cover him up warm.

*A foundered Horse.*
Let him take one or two spoonfulls of common salt, in half a pint of common water.

*Malignant Fevers.*
Under each sole of the patient's feet, apply a tench quite alive, without flitting them, or doing them any injury. Bind them on with linen rollers, take them off at the end of twelve hours, taking care if possible, not to infpire the fmell that comes from them, then bury them quickly, or throw them down the houfe of office; and the patient will foon recover.

*Quinfey.*
Take as many earth worms alive as will make up the fize of an egg; put them between two pieces of thin muflin, and apply them round the patient's bare throat. Renew the application every three hours for two days fucceffively.

*Bleeding of the nofe.*
Put into the patient's two noftrils, or behind both his ears, a fmall quantity of hair taken from the private parts of the fex different from the patient; and the blood will ftop almoft inftantaneoufly.

*An infallible plaifter for bringing out the fmall-pox when it has been driven in.*
Take fome rye meal; mix it up with fome rain water, fome verjuice, a new laid egg, and half an ounce of orpiment finely powdered. Beat the whole well together, and fpread it upon blotting paper. Sprinkle it with cloves in powder, and apply this poultice to the foles of the feet; it muft be left there for the fpace of four and twenty hours, then taken off, and thrown quickly into the fire.

*Flux*

### Fluor Albus.

Bruife the leaves of the plant called moufe-ear, and fqueeze out the juice to the quantity of two ounces, which the patient muft take fafting, in a cup of broth, or a glafs of white wine. The dofe muft be repeated for fome days fucceffively, after fome purging phyfic has been given to the patient, who will feed only upon meats of eafy digeftion, and will abftain from all kind of excefs. The father affured me that this medicine had cured women in five or fix days, who had been afflicted with this diforder for eight or ten years.

### Immoderate Menftrual Flux.

Torrefy, upon a new earthen plate, or upon the fire-fhovel well cleaned, as much hair, taken from the private parts of a healthy middle aged man, as one can hold between the finger and thumb. Reduce it to powder; and let the patient take it fafting in a glafs of good red wine. For a fuppreffion of the menfes it muft be taken in white wine. The remedy may be repeated a fecond time.

### Swelled Glands and other fcrophulous Tumors.

Apply one or two dead plantain leaves to them. Renew the application, with frefh plantain, twice a day. At the fame time, let the patient take, every morning fafting, a warm infufion of walnut-tree leaves, in the fame manner as tea.

### Colic, and Stitch in the Side.

Let the root of the fun-flower be applied under the armpit of the fame fide where the pain is. As foon as it is grown warm, there the colic goes off. This application was tried with fuccefs in an obftinate ftitch of the fide.

### Exoftofis.

Flatten a ball, which has killed an animal, and apply it immediately upon the part affected.

### Palfy.

*Palfy.*

Boil fome radifhes in water, with a fmall quantity of gin, and drink it for common drink. One may alfo put radifhes into the foup inftead of common foup herbs.

*Ulcers.*

Chew the dried treadles of fheep, and apply them by way of of poultice to the fore. Let the application be renewed morning and evening.

*Cancer and Ulcers.*

Put a large live toad into a new earthen pot, and over it put two ounces of rolls of fulphur in powder. Lute the pot well, and calcine the whole. Apply the afhes to the cancer.

*Corns and Warts.*

After having fcratched them and taken off the hard part, rub them well with the mufhrooms which grow naturally upon a dunghill.

*Pains after Child-birth.*

Boil two new laid eggs, and put into each of them a piece of fugar in powder, as big as a filbert; mix it well with the yolks, and let the lying-in woman take it, drinking over it a glafs of good wine dafhed with a little water.

*To promote the Difcharge of the Lochia.*

Put two drachms of flower of fulphur into two glaffes of boiling water, let this boil for a few minutes, then ftrain it through a linen rag, and let the liquor be taken.

*An Amulet againft the Falling Sicknefs.*

Put into a crucible, upon a flow fire, one ounce of Spanifh mercury, or mercury feparated from cinnaber. When the mercury acquires a little heat, and begins to fimmer, throw in one drachm of filver beaten very thin, and ftir the whole well with a rod of iron, a little heated. Afterwards remove the crucible quickly

quickly from the fire, and pour out the contents, leaving them to grow cold. Put this amalgama into a small leathern bag, closely sowed up. Fasten this bag round the neck with a string, so as it should fall upon the pit of the stomach, where it must be constantly worn. Before this amulet is applied, the patient must be blooded in the cephalic vein, at the new moon. The bleeding must be repeated, at the new moon, the two following months.

*Bronchocele.*

Apply some common salt, well dried and a little warm, to the tumor. When the salt grows damp, let it be taken off, well dried, and then applied again; this process is to be repeated till the disorder is cured.

*Specks on the Eyes.*

Take of dragon's blood, of succotrine aloes, and of myrrh, equal quantities, and let them all be very finely powdered. Mix a sufficient quantity of this powder with the yolk of a new laid egg, so as to form a plaister, which is to be applied to the temple on the same side as the eye affected. When the plaister falls off of itself, put another on, and continue in this manner till the cure is completed.

*Pain in the Teeth, and how to make them fall out without Pain.*

Put into the hollow of the tooth three drops of spirit of sal ammoniac, and a small bit of cotton over it.

*Corns in the feet.*

Take off the indurated part, without making them bleed, then apply several times, the red sediment found at the bottom of a chamber pot, when the urine has been left any time in it. Then cover them with a piece of thin leather, repeating this till the corns are removed.

*Fluxion*

### Fluxion in the Breast.

Set a pint of good cow's milk upon the fire; when it boils skim it two or three times, then throw in a large glass of good Spanish wine, and after it has boiled up twice, take it from the fire. When the milk is turned, strain off the whey through a linen rag, and let the patient drink a small glass full of it warm every quarter of an hour.

### To bring about the Delivery of a dead Child.

Take some of the seed of the greater burdock, reduce it to powder, and let the patient take one drachm of it in a glass of wine.

### Convulsions in Children caused by Teething.

Cut some of the root of wild valerian into small pieces. String them like the beads of a necklace, so as to make a necklace of them for the child; who is to wear it 'till the teeth have pierced the gum. The application may be renewed every fortnight.

### Dropsy.

Let the patient take, fasting, as much of the misletoe of eglantine in powder as will cover a farthing, after it is infused the whole night in a glass of white wine, which is also to be taken. Half of this dose only is given to women and children. This medicine was communicated to me by a Lieutenant of our frigate named Le Roy. He told me his father had tried it several times, and with success.

### Hysteric Vapours.

Rub the inside of a saucer with garlic laid on very thick. Then apply the side rubbed with garlic to the navel. Hold it on 'till it sticks, and let it not be removed till it falls off of itself.

*Fistula*

*Fistula of all Kinds.*

Take the leaves of St. John's wort, of the lesser wormwood, and of the round birthwort, of each one handful: succotrine aloes, and myrrh in powder, of each one ounce. Let the whole be infused in two quarts of good white-wine, in a pot well glazed, and strongly luted upon a gentle heat, for three quarters of an hour: let it afterwards boil for a quarter of an hour: strain off the liquor when cold, and add to it one pint of good spirit of wine. Keep the whole in a bottle well corked.

This liquor is to be injected into the fistula five or six times a day, applying a tent or compress dipped in the same to the wound. This remedy has been tried several times successfully, by M. Duvernay, a surgeon of Chambery.

*For Disorders of the Eyes, even the Gutta Serena, an Opthalmic wonderful in its Effects:*

Take thirty-one live cray-fish, caught precisely when the sun and moon are in Cancer, and not at any other time. Take also of the roots, stalks, leaves and flowers of the celandine, gathered before sun-rise, as much as will equal the weight of the crayfish. When all this has been well pounded together in a wooden or stone mortar, add of fennel-seed one ounce, of bean flower and camphor each half an ounce; cloves, hepatic aloes, prepared tutty, all in powder, of each two drachms. Mix the whole well in a mortar, and divide it afterwards into three parts. Put one of the parts into an alembic, and distil in B. M. till it is dry: take out the residuum, preserve it, and put a second part of the composition into the alembic, together with the water drawn off from the first distillation. Distil this again till it is dry. Take out the residuum a second time, keep it, and put in, in its stead, the third part of the composition, with all the water distilled. Let the distillation be repeated a third time. Afterwards calcine the three residuums in a close vessel, extract the salt by dissolution, filtration, and evaporation, *secundum artem*. Let the salt obtained be added to the distilled water, and

A a after

after the whole has digested on a flow fire, keep the liquor in a bottle well corked.

*Method of using the foregoing Application.*

Let the patient be purged at least twice with a mild cephalic medicine, leaving the interval of a day between the two doses; and if he is plethoric he must be blooded once at the decline of the moon. Two or three drops of this collyrium are afterwards to be introduced into the eye morning and evening, with the black feather of a fowl's wing, and let a flight compress dipped in the liquor be applied over the eye.

During the use of this remedy, which must be continued about forty days for a gutta serena, one must be careful to keep the body open. For this purpose, if it should be necessary, glysters may be used, composed of river water only warmed. All melancholy things, and employments of too serious a nature, are also to be avoided; and the patient must likewise abstain from spices, salt meats, sellery, strong liquors, and in general from all excesses in eating, drinking, sitting up, &c. For other disorders in the eyes, the collyrium is to be continued till the cure is completed.

*An excellent and almost universal Balsam.*

Put into a glazed earthen pan, which will bear the fire, and which holds about five or six quarts of water, three pints of fine olive oil, half a pound of fresh yellow wax, cut into small pieces, half a pint of rose water, three pints of good red wine, and two ounces of red saunders in powder. Let the whole boil together for half an hour, stirring the mixture all the while with a wooden spatula. When this is done, throw in a pound of fine Venice turpentine, not of the common sort, with four ounces of good honey, and two drachms of camphor in powder. The finer sort of Venice turpentine is not sharp to the tongue, and has no disagreeable smell; it is white and not yellow. Mix the whole together by stirring it well with the

spatula

TO THE MALOUINE ISLANDS.

spatula for one or two minutes: take the pan off the fire, strain the balsam through a linen rag, and let it be kept in earthen pots.

*Use of the foregoing Balsam.*

For wounds, ulcers, mortifications, contusions, burns, rheumatic and other pains, the part affected is first either washed or fomented with a little warm red wine; afterwards the part is very freely anointed with the Balsam, and a piece of blotting-paper, steeped in it is applied. This dressing is repeated morning and evening. If the wound penetrates any of the cavities of the body, the balsam is to be thrown up with a syringe, and the patient must take a drachm and a half, or two drachms of it, in each bason of broth, or in some decoction of vulnerary herbs. The same doze of this medicine may also be taken in the pleurisy, the cholic, and other internal pains, taking care at the same time to apply it warm externally, rubbing it in on the part where the pain is seated. I have tried this Balsam and always with success.

*For an inveterate Head-ach, caused by a Fluxion of Humours, and for an Hydrocephalus.*

Pound, in a wooden or stone mortar, ten or twelve tops of vervain, with some rye-meal, and five, or six, or more whites of eggs: the vervain may be omitted. Make a cataplasm of this, which must be applied to the nape of the neck, and over the shoulders, so as to cover almost the whole scapula. Let a fine napkin four times double be laid over it, and let it be left on for six or eight hours. If the patient is not then cured, a second poultice of the same kind is to be applied, which is to be left on as long as the other, or thereabouts. It very seldom happens that a third poultice is necessary. The patient must afterwards be purged. This poultice is equally beneficial in rheumatisms.

A a 2 *A weist*

*A swift Asthma, Colds, and Disorders of the Breast.*

In an earthen or very clean copper pan, let one pound of ripe juniper berries, well bruised, be boiled for half an hour, with a pound of fresh unsalted butter, which has not been washed. Then let the butter be strained off, with a very strong expression of the juniper berries. To the quantity strained off, add an equal weight of the best honey, and let it be put upon an exceeding slow fire 'till it has acquired the consistence of a syrup; which is to be preserved in earthen pots. The bigness of a small nut, or the value of a tea-spoonful, is to be taken in the morning fasting, suffering it to melt in the mouth like a lozenge. The same dose is to be repeated at night going to bed. When the disorder is dangerous, a third dose may be taken three or four hours after dinner.

In common disorders of the breast the juniper berries may be left out.

All these remedies have not been communicated to me by the Franciscan father whom I have before mentioned; but having seen the good effects of almost all those I have given before, I have been very glad of this opportunity of making them known for the good of the public.

The day after our party of pleasure into the country, which I have spoken of, four Indians or Natives of the country came to present themselves to the Governor, while we were with him examining Captain Mandillo's compass. As soon as the Governor saw them coming into his court-yard, he had all the doors of his rooms shut up. Upon our asking him the reason of this, he told us, that the room would be infected for eight days; if they were suffered to come into it; and that the smell which exhaled from them fixed itself even on the walls. This smell proceeds from their anointing their bodies with a certain kind of oil and grease to preserve themselves from insects.

These Indians finding the door shut, came up to the window where we were, and one of them pulled out of a bag made of a tiger's skin, a paper written and folded up, which he presented.

The

*An Indian of Montevideo.*

## TO THE MALOUINE ISLANDS. 163

The Governor received and read it, being written in the Spanish tongue. It was a certificate, in which several Spanish Governors declared successively, that the bearer of it was of the race of their Caciques or Princes, and that he himself was the chief of a village. The Governor returned the certificate, and the Indians asked him by signs for a sheet of paper instead of the one which before held the certificate, and which was now worn out in the the folds by much use: the paper was immediately given to him. It is most probable that these Indians were unacquainted with the Spanish language, as they did not attempt to speak a single word of it. A Spanish officer told us, that they had spoken the Paraguay language, mixed with that of the Indians, in the neighbouring parts. They had no other dress than a kind of cloke made of several deer skins with the hair on, sewed together, so as to form a long square pretty much like a napkin. It is fastened about the shoulders with two straps, and appears as in the plate. The side next the skin was white, and painted red and blue grey in squares, rhomboides, and triangles, the disposal of which forms various compartments, according to the fancy, I suppose, of the person who is to wear it, or of the painter. These Indians often come into the town in companies of five, six, eight or ten, bringing their wives along with them. Their dwelling-places are not more than six or seven leagues distant from Montevideo, where they come to drink wine or brandy. As they have no coin among them, they give their little sacks of tiger skins, their clokes, sometimes the skins of wild beasts they have killed, but more commonly those they have sewed together to cloath themselves with. They give them almost for nothing; for they exchange one of these kinds of clokes, composed of eight deer skins, for a real, which is about six-pence English. A sack of tiger's skin, fourteen or fifteen inches long and twelve inches wide, costs no more than half a real. When any body has a mind for the clokes of these Indians, it is sufficient to take hold of it with one hand, and to offer a real or half a real with the other. The Indian immediately unties the strap, takes the piece

of

of money, surrenders his cloke or little sack, which ever you want, and goes immediately quite naked to the first shop he can find to drink wine or brandy.

Their wives do the same. They have commonly no other clothing than the men, but now and then one sees some of them who have a piece of the same skin their dress is made of fastened round the waist with a strap.

It is prohibited to sell them such a quantity of wine or brandy as will make them drunk, for fear that drunkenness should lead them into some irregularities. M. de Bougainville being about to give a real to each of the four who came to the Governor's, the Governor desired him on this account to give them only half a one. Being one day at the vicar's, we were told that a company of eight or nine of them, men and women, were coming up to us. The clerk of our frigate immediately going to the door with a bit of bread he was eating, one of the Indians passing by took this bit of bread from him, stopped a moment, then eat it laughing, and afterwards went on to join the rest of his companions without saying a word. They were all of them bareheaded, their feet were naked, and they had no other clothing besides the cloke already spoken of. Some of them wore it upon their right shoulder, leaving the left arm and shoulder bare; others wore it on the opposite side. They wear the hair on the outside when it rains, and on the inside when it is fine weather.

Such of these Indians as I have seen, were perfectly strait and well-made, their arms and legs were well shaped, the chest well expanded, and all the muscles of their body strongly marked out. The women were much less than the men, who were all of a fine size. The women had, as well as the men, a lively look, a round but not a full face, pretty large eyes full of fire, a high forehead, a large mouth, and a wide nose, flattened a little at the tip; their lips are of a moderate size and their teeth white; their hair long, black, and harsh, falling carelesly about their necks, and sometimes even over their foreheads. As they greafe

their

their hair as well as their body with different ointments, it is gloffy; but always in diforder. Thefe ointments however have nothing in them more difagreeable or dirty than the pomatums of this country.

It is faid that when they are firft born they have not that red, copper, bronze colour, which is generally fpread all over their fkin. It is true indeed, that the climate, the action of the air to which their fkin, not covered with clothing, is continually expofed, the ointments and paint with which they fmear their whole body, may contribute, at leaft in a great meafure, to give them this colour. But when we confider that the Negroes themfelves alfo do not come into the world with their fkin black, which however is their proper colour, we may well imagine that the red copper colour of the Indians in South America is alfo natural to them.

The women are employed in the culture of manioc, and preparing it to make the caffavi, and their common drink; they are alfo employed in houfehold affairs, whch confift only in fowing together deer and other beafts fkins, which both men and women ufe for their clothing, and in preparing victuals for themfelves and the men, who fpend all their time in hunting, fifhing, and riding out on horfeback; and indeed they are moft excellent horfemen. The old men prefide in each hamlet of huts; and ftay at home with the young lads and girls, who have not yet acquired ftrength enough for any laborious work. Their form of government confifts entirely in refpecting their elders.

They are extremely dexterous at handling the fling, and at the management of the lance and the bow: they feldom mifs their aim with the fling even on horfeback and at full fpeed. A fierce bull, a tiger, or any other animal, or even a man himfelf, though ever fo watchful, can hardly efcape them. As it is neceffary that the halter, which is the name they give it, fhould confine the animal they have a mind to feize, they pufh their horfe at him ftrongly, fo as throw the halter in fuch a manner that the animal finds himfelf dragged away with fo much rapidity

that

that he has not time either to difentangle or defend himfelf. In their private quarrels with one another, they alfo ufe thefe flings, and a half lance. The only method of avoiding this fling, if in an open plain, is to lie down all along upon the ground, as foon as they take the inftrument in hand, and to keep clofe to the earth. Another method of avoiding it is, by fticking one's felf clofe to a tree, or to the wall.

Thefe halters or flings are cut out of bulls hides. They twift this ftrap, and make it flexible by greafing and ftretching it out, till it is reduced to half a finger's breadth. Neverthelefs it is fo ftrong that a bull cannot break it, and it refifts more than a hempen cord would do, which would alfo be lefs flexible, and therefore lefs fit for this purpofe.

One can hardly get the fkins of tigers and other wild beafts any otherwife than from the Indians. Neverthelefs they are not dear, though rather fcarce at Montevideo. One of the fineft of them may be bought for two or three piafters. I bought a very beautiful tiger's fkin of a middling fize, fowed up in form of a bag, for a piece of eight. The Indians kill but few tigers, though they eat them; becaufe they make ufe of thefe fkins only for the little bags I have mentioned. In thefe bags they carry the caffavi root, which ferves for their nourifhment, and the heads of their arrows, which they do not faften to the reeds, till they are going to make ufe of them. This head of the arrow has the figure and fize of a laurel-leaf, when much lengthened out at the two extremities. They fix it into the reed by either end indifferently, becaufe it is pointed and fharp at both extremities. Thefe arrows are the more fatal, as the head of them, not being firmly fixed, remains in the wound, upon attempting to draw out the reed.

When they want to catch an animal in the fling, they ride after him at full gallop, holding the horfes bridle in one hand, and in the other the fling, which they throw at the neck, legs, or horns of the animal. When it is a furious or wild beaft three or four of them together ride after him, each laying hold of a

limb

limb in the fling, then feparating, one to the right and another to the left, the fling is tightened by this means, and another of them comes up without danger, either to kill the animal with his half lance, or to tie him and bring him away.

The Indians have other methods of hunting, which are defcribed in the accounts of feveral authors, efpecially in M. Muratori's work on the Paraguay.

I fhall take this opportunity of acquainting the public, that M. Muratori's book is entirely written from the memoirs furnifhed him by the Jefuits or fome of their people, who were certainly fo much concerned as not to be willing to inform the public of all their tranfactions. Some Spanifh officers of credit, fent from the court of Madrid to Paraguay, in the time of the divifion of the refpective poffeffions of the courts of Spain and Portugal, have affured me, that all the pamphlets they had feen in that country relative to the conduct of the Jefuits, whether refpecting the Indians or the interefts of thefe two kingdoms, were always written with a great deal of caution in regard to the Jefuits. He alfo told me, that one of thefe fathers, among the chief in the country, had made the following anfwer in his prefence, to one of the Spanifh general officers, who was expreffing his aftonifhment at the obftacles which the Jefuits oppofed to the difpofitions concerted and fixed upon between the two courts. " I have much more reafon to be furprized, that thefe two kings fhould make difpofitions for dividing a country which does not belong to them. We Jefuits alone have conquered it; we alone have the right to difpofe of it, to keep and defend it, from all, and againft all." With fuch principles as thefe, one may eafily imagine what the conduct of the Jefuits would be. It is certain that the Indians of Paraguay are fubjects only to this fociety, either at home in their families, or when they go out in arms. When the Spaniards lately befieged and took from the Portuguefe the colony of St. Sacrament, which is about thirty leagues diftant from Montevideo, they were affifted by about a thoufand Indians, at whofe head was a Jefuit, who commanded them in

chief,

chief, and without whose order, these Indians would not have advanced one step, nor have fired a single musket. The Governor of Montevideo, who commanded the Spaniards, and several other officers present at this attack, told me, they were obliged to settle the plan of operations with the Jesuit, who afterwards gave out his orders in his own name to the Indians, who were encamped separately from the Spaniards.

Dragoons are almost the only troops of that country. Their horses are equipped in the same manner as at Paraguay. All the men wear the *Ponchos*, which they find more convenient than the cloke both for the horse and his rider.

The Ponchos, as I have said before, is a piece of stuff formed like the coverlet of a bed, two or three ells long, and two ells wide. One must pass one's head through a slit in the middle, to put it on. It hangs down on both sides, and behind as well as before. It is wore on horseback and on foot. The poor people and the negroes never take it off till they go to bed. It does not hinder them from working, because it may be thrown back at the sides over the shoulders; by which means the arms and the fore-part of the body are at liberty.

This kind of garment is fashionable on horseback, even for both sexes, and among persons of all ranks. It is easy, however, to distinguish ranks and sexes, notwithstanding the simplicity of the Ponchos. Riding on horseback is so common among the women, that they are as ready and alert at this exercise as the men. The differences by which the rank and sex may be distinguished with regard to the Ponchos, consist in the fineness, lightness and richness of the stuff.

The horses are not shod in this country. The saddle and furniture are also different from those used in Europe. They first put upon the horse's bare back a piece of coarse soft stuff, of a loose texture, which they call *Schuadéros*; over that a girth, then a piece of strong leather of the ha.. of the saddle, which hanging over the horse's crupper serves ... ..ig. This is called *Carseros*. Over this leather is placed the saddle, made like that we

5 use

use for pack-horses, and over the saddle they throw one or more sheep skins, sewed together. This they call the *Peilbon*. Above all this they put a second girth, or surcingle, to fasten the whole. The stirrups are small and narrow, for they only put the end of the shoe into them; and those who go bare-footed, rest only the point of the great toe. The bit of the bridle is iron, all of one piece, and without studs. The reins are composed of several small straps, interwoven with each other, as the strings of a bell or clock; and are at least six feet and a half, or seven feet in length, as they serve at the same time for a whip. A semicircular bar of iron, attached to the same piece which receives the horse's lower jaw, produces the same effect as the curb. That part of the Carrneros which projects beyond the saddle, and falls upon the crupper, is figured.

On the 9th instant, the Governor, the major of the troops, and their ladies, came on board the Eagle frigate about noon, where we gave them as good a dinner as we could. The air of the sea, or the motion of the ship, though scarce perceptible, were rather troublesome to the major's lady, and made her so sick, that she could neither eat nor drink any thing, except a couple of oranges, and was obliged to quit the cabbin where we were at dinner, to go and breathe the fresh air upon deck. This circumstance rather disturbed our entertainment, and obliged the company to return to the city very early.

As we were attending them to shore in our cutter, we perceived an exceeding fœtid smell, much resembling the putrid exhalation from the carcase of an animal that has been dead a great while. We thought at first that it had proceeded from the dead body of some bull, killed and left upon the shore till it was putrified, from whence the wind might bring it to us. The Governor undeceived us, assuring us, that it was the exhalation of the urine of an animal named *Zorillos*, who was either angry, or pursued by some other animal.

The Zorillos is of the size of a weasel, not quite so long, with reddish hair, lighter under the belly which is almost grey. Two

white

white lines extend the whole length of the back, forming, from the neck to the tail, almoſt an oval. The tail is very buſhy, and the animal always keeps it raiſed up as the ſquirrel does. When he finds himſelf purſued, or is provoked by any thing, he immediately expels his urine, which infects the air, to the extent of more than a mile and a half, with an almoſt inſupportable ſmell of carrion. We perceived this ſmell two or three times while we were on board our frigate, though we were more than four miles and a half diſtant from land: it is true indeed, that the wind blew from the land. M. Duclos, our captain, had already told us of this, but we had not taken his word for it. The fact was confirmed to us by the vicar of Montevideo, who made a preſent to M. Duclos of a fur lining made with the ſkins of this animal ſewed together. Theſe ſkins have no bad ſmell. The Zorillos is perhaps the ſame as the *Stinkbingſem*, or *enfant du diable* (devil's child) of Canada, the urine of which produces nearly the ſame effects. The *Chinche* of the ſouthern parts of America alſo reſembles much the Zorillos.

Another animal very common in theſe parts, and about Buenos Ayres, is the Tatu-apara, which we call *Tatou*, the Spaniards *Armadillo*, and the Portugueſe *Encubertado*. As this animal is very well known, I ſhall not give any deſcription of it. Ximenez ſays, that the ſcales of the Armadillo, reduced to powder and taken to the quantity of one drachm in a decoction of ſage, brings on a perſpiration ſo ſalutary, that it cures the venereal diſeaſe; and that it throws out ſplinters from all parts of the body: and according to Monades, liv. xv. pag. 552, the ſmall bones of this animal's tail cure a deafneſs.

Notwithſtanding the riſk there was in ſelling of any merchandize at Montevideo, and the difficulties our people met with in diſembarking them, to prevent their being ſeized; yet ſeveral of our officers and many of the crew, who had got together ſome few things, in hopes of ſelling them at the French iſland, and at the Eaſt Indies, where they thought they were going, got rid of them, and were ſelling them every day.

day. Our ship being the first vessel which had put in at this place since the peace, our things sold very well. The guards seized upon some packets brought on shore with too little caution. They even threw yesterday into prison two cockswains, on whom these packets were found. M. de Bougainville being informed of this, exclaimed and stormed very much against these cockswains, saying, they deserved to be treated as they were. He went to the officer, repeated the same thing to him, and desired only that his uniform, which the prisoners had on when they were taken up, might be delivered; that as for the men they might keep them, to intimidate the rest, and that he himself would put them in irons if they were released. By this behaviour, M. de Bougainville persuaded them that he did not countenance this practice. The parcels and the men were both given up, and it was even desired that the men might be excused. From this circumstance, it was easily found out that our people had not taken proper measures. A serjeant having complained on this occasion, that he had not received the value of one real, though he had assisted in bringing many parcels on shore, and that he had, as he said, wore out a pair of shoes in going about the town to shew such of our people as had any thing to sell, into the proper houses; this declaration made us understand that we should not meet with so many difficulties, if we did but distribute a few piasters among the officers and guards. We began therefore by giving away a few pieces of eight, a few shirts, &c. and every body was very ready to let us do as we pleased, even the officer himself placed there on purpose to prevent any kind of trade. As we were supposed not to have any Spanish coin, and that French coin was not current in that country, M. de Bougainville asked and obtained leave to sell some butts of wine, brandy, oil, and some other superfluous goods he had, in order to pay for the flour, and the fresh meat, the Governor had always taken care to provide for us every day at the port; as well as for the oxen, cows, horses and other animals, he wanted to buy. It was now time to think of quitting

ting Montevideo, in order to go to the place of our deſtination. We therefore provided ourſelves with every thing we thought neceſſary for this purpoſe; the quantity of water, flour, and animals M. de Bougainville aſked for, excited the curioſity of the Governor with regard to the deſign of our voyage. All the crew, even the officers themſelves, were perfectly ignorant as to this point, and thought, as I ſaid before, that we were going to the Eaſt Indies. This report had been propagated, and M. de Bougainville confirmed it, by telling the Governor we were going to the Indies, without ſpecifying to which of them.

The trouble neceſſarily attending theſe preparations prevented us from day to day from trying to make any accurate obſervations with the inſtrument or compaſs of captain Mandillo, ſo that we did not think of fetching it from the Governor's till we were juſt preparing to ſet ſail. As it is of the greateſt conſequence to take advantage of the firſt favourable wind, eſpecially in the harbour of Rio de la Plata, where the anchorage is ſo dangerous; and as we ſaw that this compaſs could not be of much uſe to us with regard to the longitude, M. de Bougainville reſolved to leave it with the Governor. He wrote to him by the captain of a ſchooner, to deſire that he would keep this inſtrument, and at his return into Spain * ſend it to him in France. All the reſt of the time we ſtaid in the harbour, was employed in preparations for our voyage. Our frigates were carefully inſpected, and every poſſible precaution taken. Having brought
on

---

* The Governor had told us, he expected to go back into Europe towards the end of the year; but we learned, on our arrival at Paris, that he would not quit his government ſo ſoon. M. de Grimaldi, the Spaniſh ambaſſador in France, aſked M. de Bougainville ſeveral queſtions, upon this Governor's behaviour to us. M. de Bougainville having given by his anſwers a proper teſtimony of the probity of Don Joſeph Joachim de Viana, and of his ſtrict obſervance of the duties of his ſtation; the ambaſſador confeſſed, that the Jeſuits and their friends had ſent over to Madrid memorials againſt him, to injure him in the King's opinion, that he might be recalled, and that they might have ſome Governor devoted to them in his ſtead. M. de Grimaldi juſtified Don de Viana to his court; which probably prevented the King from recalling him as ſoon as he wiſhed. The public news-papers have informed us of this gentleman's being continued in the ſame government.

on board twelve cows, or heifers, six mares, two colts, and two Hungarian horses, twelve goats or kids, eleven sows, and one boar, fourteen or fifteen sheep, two rams, and a great quantity of fowls and ducks, we set sail on Tuesday the 16th of January 1764.

At three in the morning, the wind, which for ten days past had been constantly South East, shifted to the North. The gale being moderate, we took this opportunity to unmoor. We heaved apeek to our best bower anchor, shipped the longboat and other boats, one of which had landed the Sieur *Sirandré* Lieutenant, with a letter of thanks to the Governor, from M. de Bougainville and the rest. At nine o'clock we set sail with the Sphinx and the Spanish frigate the St. Barbe, which we soon forereached, though she was at least two full leagues and a half ahead of us. We steered half a league S. E. $\frac{1}{4}$ S. about as far S. E. then directed our course S. E. $\frac{1}{4}$ E. in order to double a point, which consists of a chain of rocks on the South West of the fortress, extending near a league out in the river. When we set sail it blew a pretty fresh gale at North West. The wind abated gradually and a calm succeeded; insomuch that, at half an hour past three in the afternoon, the ship making no way, we anchored in six fathom and a half water, muddy bottom. The Sphinx, together with the St. Barbe, anchored at the distance of a long musket shot from our stern. During the calm we caught three very beautiful butterflies, particularly one delineated in the plate *.

Our anchorage in the road of Montevideo was not absolutely bad; but I am of opinion it would have been better higher up in the bay. During the whole time that we remained there, we were constantly on the alarm, as well on account of the *Pamperos*, which almost always rises on a sudden, as of the South East and South West winds, which blow full into the mouth of

---

* I gave it the name of the parrot, because the various colours of its wings exactly resemble those of the most beautiful parrot of Brazil. Its body is of the finest green, streaked with red.

the

the bay, and occafion fo high a fea as to make it impoffible to leave any of our boats along-fide the veffel. We were every night obliged to fhip them.

The little boat being only once forgot, it got loofe and had like to have been loft, as I have before related. When you are farther within the bay, you have nearly the fame depth of water, the fame bottom, and are fheltered by the mountain on one fide, and the town on the other.

We fet fail about eight in the evening, and continued our courfe the next day without any remarkable occurrence.

On the nineteenth, near two o'clock in the afternoon, an extraordinary kind of fifh paffed near the veffel. We had feen a great many before; but they being at too great a diftance from the fhip, we had not been able to catch any of them. Perceiving that they affembled to-day round the fide of the frigate, I got a failor to throw a bucket faftened to the end of a rope into the fea, and he had the good fortune to take one. Our mariners give them the name of *Galere*, or fea-nettle. It is a kind of bladder, which may be ranked under the fame genus with what the naturalifts call *Holoturia*, which, without any refemblance either of a plant or a fifh, are neverthelefs, really poffeffed of life, and tranfport themfelves like animals from place to place with a motion peculiar to themfelves, independently of the affiftance of wind and waves on which you fee thefe bladders carried like fmall veffels. Any one who did not obferve this appearance of a bladder with a nice and judicious eye, would take it for a bubble of air floating on the furface and driven by the waves and winds. But the failor who had caught it having brought it to me, I had fufficient time to examine it. I obferved in it a periftaltic motion, fuch as anatomifts afcribe to the inteftines and ftomach. I was juft on the point of taking it out of the bucket with my hand, when M. Duclos our captain caught hold of my arm, and bid me take care left I fhould foon have reafon to repent of fo doing, by the acute pains I fhould feel in every part of my hand, which fhould happen to

come

come in contact with the filaments, of a violet blue colour attached to this bladder. I therefore contented myself with viewing this sea-nettle and taking a sketch of it.

The captain's observation was verified the same day. A cabbin-boy having caught another of these fish, had the imprudence to take hold of it with his hand. The filaments, twisted themselves round it. The moment after, he began to cry out that he felt a smarting and very painful heat on all the back of the hand, and the wrist. He shook it immediately to get rid of the fish; but it was now too late. His cries hastened us to his assistance; he wept, and stamped, complaining that his hand seemed to be in a fire. It was bathed in oil; a compress dipt in the same liquid was applied to it, but the pain still continued more than two hours; when it went off gradually.

The sea-nettle is an oblong bladder, flattened underneath, rounded in its circumference, and blunted as it were at its extremities; from whence proceed those filaments, the touch of which occasions so much pain. One of these extremities is more rounded than the other; which is rather lengthened. The part which forms the base or resting point of this bladder is plaited about the edges. The whole is a membrane of a very delicate structure, transparent, and nearly of the same figure as those half globules, which rise on the surface of the water in summer showers, especially when they fall in large drops. It is always empty, but distended like a football. This membrane has fibres, some of which are circular, others longitudinal, by means of which the peristaltic motion is carried on.

At the longest of its extremities it contains a small quantity of the clearest water, which is prevented from communicating with the rest of the cavity by a membranous partition. The fibre which passes over the back, from the fore to the hind part, is raised, scolloped at the edges, plaited like a beautiful tuft, of a lively green, blue, and purple colour, extended in the form of a sail. It lowers, elevates or shifts, as it were to set itself for the wind. From the two extremities of the plait, proceed some filaments

filaments of different lengths, and of the same colour with this kind of sail: two of them are very short, and as thick as a large quill; these afterwards branch out into several others of lesser thickness, but much longer; and these again into others, still longer and smaller, to the number of eight in all. They are about a foot long; but not all of equal length. These strings, interwoven with each other, resemble a net whose mashes are of different sizes. They have a kind of articulation, formed by small circular rings, in which one may likewise observe a contractile motion. These filaments resemble loose tassels, composed of strings of a sky colour tinctured with purple, and of a greenish cast, nearly transparent, and of different lengths, the edges of which appear to be indented, and alternately intermixed with grey violet and flame colour.

The largest sea-nettles I have seen were about seven inches long at their under part, and five in height. It would be very difficult to determine precisely the colour of this extraordinary fish. The bladder is as clear and transparent as the finest chrystal; but its edges, back and legs may be said to contain the colours of the rainbow, or of the flame of sulphur. We saw a great number in our passage, particularly in the streight which forms the island of St. Catherine, at Brazil; and I believe they are common in these latitudes. If the bare touch of this animal causes so much pain, what can we think its effect must be in the bodies of fish or other animals who feed upon it? It has this surprizing quality, says Father Labat, that it taints and poisons the flesh of fishes without occasioning their death.—This is pretty nearly the effect of the fruit of the manchineel-tree.

On the 20th we perceived that the currents ran to the S.S.W. which confirms the observation in the account of Admiral Anson's voyage. The tides carried us 30 min. Southward; and there is reason to believe that their course is to the S.S.W. agreeable to the bearing of the coast.

On Sunday the 22d in the morning the wind, which the day before had blown very fresh till four in the afternoon, grew calm,

with

Cc 2　　　　　a very

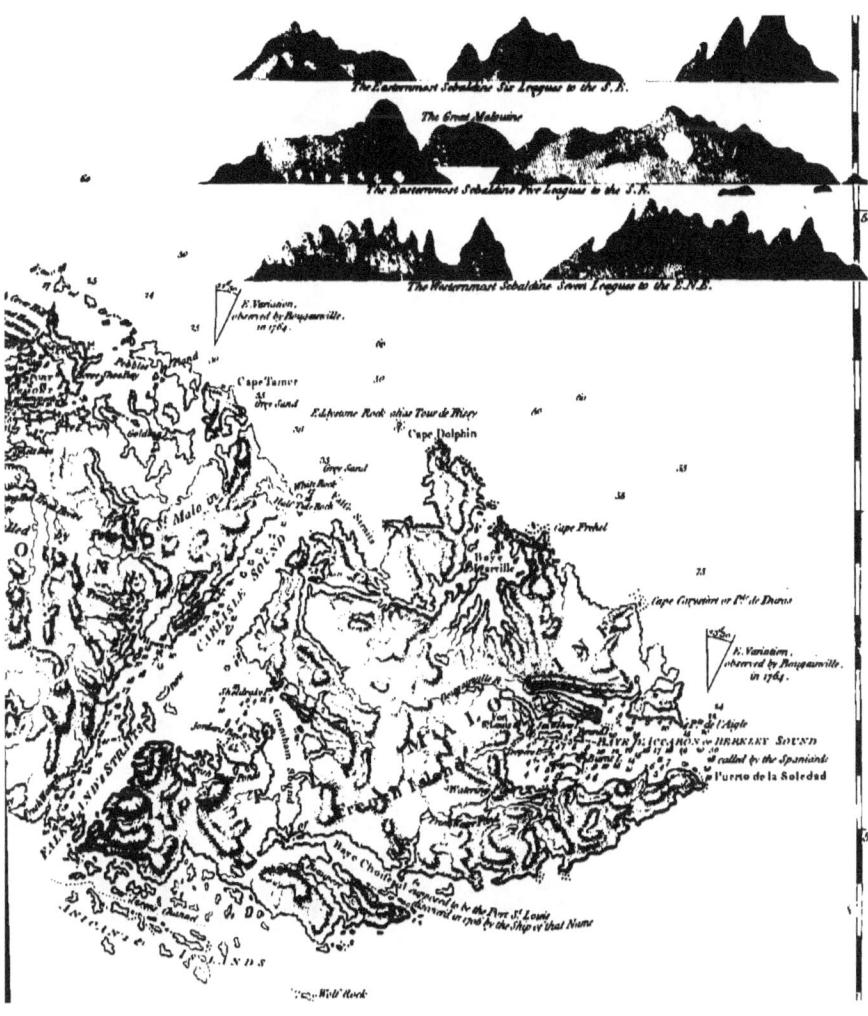

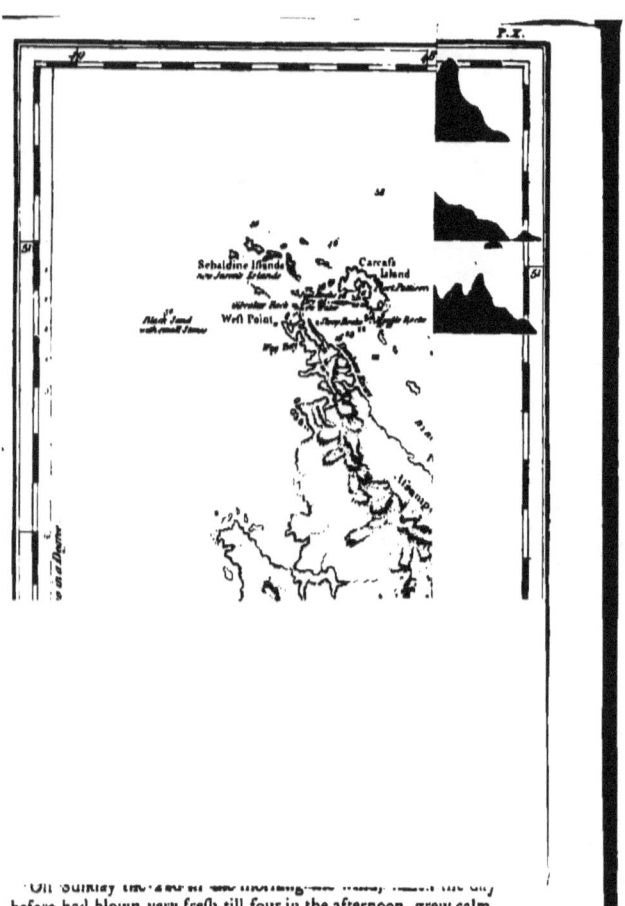

On Sunday the 24th in the morning, the wind, which the day before had blown very fresh till four in the afternoon, grew calm, with

## TO THE MALOUINE LANDS. 177

with fair weather and a fine sea. We saw some *Dadins*, sea-fowls which are found common in almost all latitudes, and some large birds called *Quebranta-buessos*, as well as some *King-fishers*, which our mariners call likewise *Puans*. 'Tis said that when these last appear, there seldom fails to be foul weather, and often storms, either on that or the next day.

In fact, the S. S. W. wind we had, soon after blew with violence: the sea ran high, the weather became foggy, and it rained a little at intervals.

In the evening of the 23d we saw several birds, and some very long and large and well formed beds of fishes fry, of a reddish cast. Most of them extended beyond our sight in length, and some were about a hundred feet in breadth.

On the 24th we saw eight or ten whales, a great number of birds, and a kind of sea-weed, which our mariners called *Baudreu*.

On the 25th the wind blew very fresh from the N. W. till five in the evening. The rolling of the ship was so constant and violent, that we lost a goat, two sheep, and three cows. Several others fell sick, as well as the horses we took on board at Montevideo.

The weather grew dark and rainy. At six o'clock the wind rather abated, and shifted to the West, then to the West South West, to the South, a gentle gale. The sea likewise gradually subsided.

On the 26th we observed that the tides turned towards the North. We again met with several birds, and some sea-grass. The sea still continued much agitated till seven in the evening. We were obliged to kill one cow and a goat, taken ill with the rolling of the ship. The sea soon after grew calm, and continued so almost the whole night. In the evening of the 27th we saw a quantity of birds, among which were several king-fishers. The wind blew with great violence, and the weather became dull and foggy. This lasted almost the whole night, and destroyed

C c 2        a very

a very fine ftallion, whom we were obliged to throw overboard, as well as a goat and a fheep.

On Saturday the 28th we faw a whale, two fea-wolves, and two penguins; in the afternoon there appeared great numbers of ofpreys, and fea-cobs, and we met with fome fea-grafs, with long leaves. On Sunday the 29th, about three in the afternoon, fome pretty large fifhes appeared near the furface of the water. Several of our mariners who have been ufed to fifh at Newfoundland, affured us, that they were ftock-fifh.

On the 31ft, at fix in the morning, we defcried land at the diftance of about fix leagues. We took this land for iflands. We had then a ftrong gale, which abating about eleven, we fteered E. S. E. till noon, when we made the fouthermoft point of land, bearing S. E. five degrees E. about a league diftant. The moft eaftern point bore E. ¼ S. E. diftance two leagues, and all thefe lands appeared to be iflands.

The figure of thefe iflands, which form a triangle, as the Sebald iflands are faid to do, and the idea we entertained of our being near thefe, induced us at firft to believe that thefe three iflands we faw were actually the Sebaldes.

On this account, according to our obfervations at noon, we found them placed in Belin's French chart thirty leagues too far to the weft; and we were the more deceived in our obfervation, on account of its agreeing with Father Feuillée's and with a manufcript chart which M. de Choifeul gave to M. de Bougainville, before we left Paris. See thefe iflands in the plate as they appeared to us at two leagues diftance, the Cape lying Eaft-South-Eaft.

This chart of M. de Bougainville's extends the eaftern verges of the Malouine iflands to 57 degrees 15 minutes longitude; and Father Feuillée places the fame extremity of thefe iflands in 57=45: the latitude agrees alfo pretty exactly. M. Belin fixes it at 62 degrees. We fhall be better able to determine which of the two is in the right when we land, as we intend to do.

In

In the afternoon we had a fresh gale at N. W. As we kept coasting along the shore we sounded at three o'clock, at 45 fathoms, a flinty bottom. At four we sounded at 40 fathoms, flinty bottom mixed with broken shells, we were then half a league distant from two flat islands, which at first view appeared to be covered with small copse, but these were only tall bulrushes with flat and large leaves called corn-flags, as we discovered afterwards on landing; the coast being quite full of these corn-flags, as it now appeared to us. Sounded again, and found a rocky bottom at twenty-four fathom.

In the afternoon of the 31st, we coasted along the shore, at the distance of about a league and sometimes only half a league, in order to observe it with greater advantage. We sounded from time to time at thirty-five fathom depth, grey sandy bottom.

The lands are of a moderate height from the sea, with eminences, some behind others; a proof that this is either the continent, or the largest of the islands. Almost all the shores were covered with bulrushes which looked like small trees. This appearance is occasioned by the corn-flags growing each of them about two feet and a half high, and afterwards shooting forth a tuft of green leaves nearly of the same height. This we had an opportunity of observing more particularly when we landed. We saw no wood, and at this distance the soil of the country appeared parched and dry; perhaps the heat of summer might have withered the grass.

At three o'clock we saw a small island two leagues wide of the coast. It nearly resembled in figure that on which the *Fort de la Conchée* near St. Malo is built. M. Bougainville gave it the name of the Tower of Bissy [*]. At five, we discovered a Cape, and a small island, resembling Cape Frehel, situated four leagues from St. Malo. This Cape seemed to terminate the land to the East.

On

---

[*] This is the entrance of the streight which divides the island into two parts, the eastern and the western. This streight runs from North to South.

On the firſt of February, we perceived another Cape and a ſmall iſland almoſt ſimilar to thoſe which reminded us of Cape Frehel; and after that, another ſmall one intirely covered with birds. At noon, the wind blowing ſtrong with ſqualls and rain, cauſed ſo violent a rolling of the ſhip, that our cattle ſuffered much from it. At laſt we determined to kill ſeveral ſick cows, fearing they ſhould die, and we ſhould be obliged to throw them over-board, as we had the fine bull we had brought with us from St. Catherine's iſland, as well as ſome goats and ſeveral ſheep.

At ſix in the evening the weather being then fine, with a gentle breeze, we determined to ſend out the fiſhing-boat which was manned for that purpoſe. Meſſrs. Donat and Le Roy the lieutenant, went on board with a ſufficient number of ſeamen, all well armed. They were ſent on ſhore to cut graſs for our cattle, who began to be in want of it. We were then about two leagues from the point which appeared woody. We were becalmed till about eight o'clock. The tide drove us towards the ſhore upon a ſhoal of rocks. In this embarraſſing ſituation, from which it was impoſſible to extricate ourſelves for want of wind, we founded with a view of caſting anchor, if the bottom ſhould be good. But the bottom proving rocky at between eighteen and twenty fathom, our perplexity increaſed, and with the more reaſon as the tide had already carried us towards the ſhoal, which lined a pretty large creek, and we were ſcarce half a quarter of a league from it. The Sphinx laboured under the ſame difficulty, and we were already contriving means to ſave our lives in caſe we ſhould be ſhipwrecked upon theſe rocks, which the mariners call *the Carpenters*; becauſe a ſhip which has the misfortune to run aground here, is ſoon daſhed to pieces. Fortunately, about eight o'clock, a very faint breeze blew from the ſhore; and our officers, equally attentive and able to avail themſelves of the ſmalleſt advantage, ordered the working of the ſhip ſo ſkilfully, that we got clear of the ſhore. The ſhip's crew were ſo fully ſenſible of the danger we were in, that in the moſt tempeſtuous weather, and even during the ſtorm we ſuffered near the Maldonnades, they never worked

the

the ship with so much alacrity and diligence. It was a fine sight to see every one at his post, holding in his hand the ropes he was to manage : all, in an attitude, in which was pictured anxiety and fear mixed with hope ; all, observing the most profound silence, their eyes fixed upon the captain, and their ears attentive to catch the first word of command : the two captains and the lieutenants, and all the ship's company, employed in looking, some on the side of the ship towards the sea, others towards the land, to observe if any one could perceive the smallest breeze rising, and ruffling the surface of the water which was almost as smooth as glass. One turned his cheek, another held his hand, and a third wetting his, extended it towards the quarter from which they imagined the wind began to blow in order to perceive the least motion. At length the long wished-for breeze arose, but blew very faintly ; fear gave place to joy and satisfaction, and to prevent our being again involved in the same difficulties, we steered away North East ¼ East, five degrees East.

About eleven our fishing-boat returned loaded with greens, and was taken on board. Messrs. Donat and Le Roy informed us, that they had seen at land, about the distance of a musket-shot from the place they were in, an animal of a terrible appearance and astonishing size lying upon the grass; his head and mane resembling a lion's, and his whole body covered with hair, of a dusky red as long as a goat's. This animal perceiving them, raised himself upon his fore-feet, eyed them a moment, and then lay down again; having afterwards fired at a bustard, which they killed, the enormous animal raised himself a second time, eyed them as before without changing his situation, and then lay down again. According to their account, this animal seemed to be as large as two oxen, and twelve or fourteen feet in length. They had a mind to fire at him, but they were terrified, and durst not fire for fear of wounding him slightly and hazarding their lives; or, according to their own account, they were unwilling to lose time, as it was late, and they were desirous of returning on board.

On the third about noon we difcovered an opening of a bay *, the entrance of which appeared fo fine, that we went into it full fail, as into a well-known and commodious harbour. We anchored about three leagues within the bay, which appeared to extend at leaft as many leagues beyond us. At the fartheft extremity we difcovered larger and fmaller iflands, where the fifhing boat founded at four, five, fix fathoms and more, in a muddy bottom. The Sieur Donat having been fent thither immediately after we came to anchor, informed us, on his return, at ten in the evening, that it was every where at leaft between eight and ten fathom, and between feven and eight to the Eaft of the ifland, with a bottom of muddy fand throughout, which fecured us a retreat in cafe of bad weather at fea.

This bay, the plan and figure of which is given in the plate, is capable of containing at leaft a thoufand veffels, and as many more to the weft of the large and fmall iflands, which are fheltered from all winds, and are, as our mariners fay, more fafe than in the harbour of Breft.

As foon as we had dined, we fent out the yawl and long-boat, and Meffrs. de Bougainville, Nerville, Belcourt, l' Huillier, Donat, Sirandré and myfelf, landed on the fouth fide of the bay. As we were going to fhore, a prodigious number of black and white birds, of the fame fpecies, croffed in large flocks, no more than five or fix feet above our heads. We killed fome of them. Thofe which fell into the fea wounded, only dived when we attempted to take them up. Before we landed, we fhot buftards, geefe and ducks, which did not fly away when we approached them; but walked near us, as if they had been tame.

While we were at a diftance from the land, its appearance deceived us. We expected to find the face of the country dry and parched, but on fetting foot upon it, we found it entirely covered with herbage, or a kind of hay, a foot, or a foot and half high,

* See the entrance of this bay in the plate. It is fituated on the eaftern fide of the Malouine iflands; and may be feen at the diftance of three leagues.

high, reaching even to the tops of the hills, which we had much ado to climb, on account of this hay obſtructing our paſſage.

We aſcended in companies, while ſome took ſeparate routs for ſhooting, both upon the hills, and along the coaſt. We were much fatigued in climbing theſe hills, there being no road or path through this herbage, which is probably coeval with the ſoil.

We walked up to the knees in this hay; and the ſoil, which appears to be a dark brown, is formed into a mould by the annual decay of the hay, and riſes with a ſpring under your feet, owing to the roots which are intangled with it. Hence it is evident, that one cannot walk for any time over ſuch a path without being fatigued. But we were luckily provided with ſome ſmall bottles of brandy, and ſome ſea-biſcuit, which were of great ſervice, as we ſhould otherwiſe have ſuffered from the intenſe heat.

Here we met with ſome green hillocks, raiſed ſometimes more than three feet from the ſurface. I examined one of theſe with attention, and found that a reſinous gum oozed from it, which is white at firſt while it is ſoft, and of an amber colour when it hardens. I gathered ſome pieces of it, which I perceived had at leaſt as ſtrong an aromatic ſmell as frankincenſe: but could not determine at that time the exact reſemblance this gum bears to other gums or reſins which have hitherto been diſcovered. I brought away near the weight of half a drachm in grains or drops, ſome of the ſize of a round pea, others of that of a kidney bean. When I returned on board, I ſhewed them to M. de Bougainville and our two ſurgeons. I held ſome of it on the point of a knife in the flame of a candle; it burnt like the fineſt reſin, emitting an agreeable ſmell, and leaving behind it a blackiſh oil, which did not burn, but grew hard and brittle when it was cold. I attempted to diſſolve this oil in common water, but without effect: from which I concluded, that it would be very proper to make an excellent varniſh. Having mentioned it the next day to M. Frontgouſſe, ſurgeon of the Sphinx, he went on ſhore, and having collected ſome of this gum, conjectured from its ſmell and taste that it was gum ammoniac. On comparing these, we found they agreed in taste and smell, and were reduced to the same substance after burning. The smell is retained so strongly on the fingers, that tho' I washed my hands more than once with sea-water, I could not get rid of it all that day and the next. This resinous gum only dissolves partly in spirit of wine, which it tinges with an amber colour. The residuum becomes spongy and burns as it did before it was dissolved: the third residuum does not dissolve in common water. Aqua-fortis has no effect upon it.

These hillocks are formed by a single plant, from which proceed small spongy stalks gradually dropping their leaves like the palm-tree. These leaves are tripartite, as may be seen in the plate, where the plant is represented in its natural size. They are of the thickness of those of purslain, but of a fine green, ranged very close to each other, disposed in a circle, and forming a cavity in the center which is scarce discernible. This is a kind of very flat funnel, the inside of which is lined with these leaves placed close one above another, imbricate like those of an artichoke. See the figure of it in the plate.

From the center and edges of these leaves, when they are bruised or only scratched, or when the resinous juice is too plentiful in them, this resinous gum, which congeals in the air, is produced. On cutting, scraping or even rubbing the surface, there issues a kind of cream which is white and viscous, and ropes between the fingers sticking fast to them like glue. I have given it the name of the *varnish plant*.

The inside of these hillocks is formed into a vault, supported by stalks and branches, whose leaves, having no air, are brown and withered. Other plants sometimes shoot forth on the inside of this vault, penetrate through the hillock, and rise above it. These hillocks, when they are not broken, are sufficiently firm, not only to support a person sitting upon them, but walking over them. The vault, however, is easily broken through, by stamping upon it with some force, and it is easy to tear off large pieces with one's hands. The root and the stalks when broken,

broken, yield the same white resin, which flows out like the white juice or milk of the plant called Tithymalus, which I shall speak of hereafter.

In the evening our sportsmen returned loaded with geese, bustards, ducks, teals, and a black and white bird already mentioned. I had separated from my companions, and wandered alone along the coast a league beyond the place where the boat had landed. I shot some ducks four or five feet from the shore. As I did not care to go into the water, I imprudently drew them to me with the end of my piece. The plenty of game engaged me to load again without recollecting that the barrel might have taken water. The powder was so wet that it would not take fire: and having no screw, I resolved to repair to the boat. I had scarce advanced twenty steps, before I perceived in the grass a path eight or nine inches broad, very much worn, which ran parallel to the shore at ten or twelve feet distance from the sea. I then imagined, that the island was inhabited, if not by men, at least by quadrupeds which frequented that spot. But as I did not know what these animals were, they might possibly be of the savage kind; and I was apprehensive lest I should meet with some of them in my way. Unattended as I was, without any other defence than a musket now become useless, I was rather anxious for my safety. I fixed my bayonet to the end of my piece, and pursued my journey in this tract, being desirous to know where it terminated. At the distance of about two hundred steps from the place where I entered it, it led into a thicket of those kinds of corn-flags I have already mentioned. Not daring to venture into it, I stopt a few minutes as I passed near it: I observed it attentively, and listened to hear whether any thing stirred. I could perceive neither motion nor noise. I continued my march, and re-entered the path on the other side, till I discovered the boat, in which, our seamen perceiving that night was approaching, and that the several parties who had gone on shore to reconnoitre and hunt were not returned, came to meet, and take us on board. It was almost full of game, and the night

obliged

obliged us to throw into the fea a great part of what we had procured in the day.

On Saturday the 4th at fix in the morning we got the yawl and fifhing-boat ready to make fome difcoveries relative to the depth of the bay, which appeared to us to be a large river when we faw it from the heights the evening before.

Meff. de Bougainville, de Belcourt, de St. Simon, l'Huillier, and Alexander Guyot, embarked in the yawl, well armed, and furnifhed with provifions for four or five days, and a tent to ufe on the fhore. The failors too were armed with mufkets, cutlaffes and bayonets. Their defign was to proceed to the northern part, and to find out whether it was covered with wood. Meff. Donat and Arcouet, in the fifhing-boat, were to make difcoveries on the fouthern part, an idea having been entertained that the bottom of the bay was divided into two branches which loft themfelves in the vallies.

Meff. Alexander Guyot and Arcouet returned on board the fame evening in the yawl, having left M. Donat with the fifhing-boat to join M. de Bougainville and his affociates. M. Guyot brought fome buftards, three young fea-wolves with hair of a brownifh grey, and five fea-lioneffes. They were about feven feet long, and three and a half in circumference, though their inteftines were drawn. Thefe gentlemen had landed on a fmall ifland, where they found a prodigious number of thefe animals, and killed eight or nine hundred of them with fticks. No other weapon is neceffary on thefe occafions. A fingle blow with a bludgeon, three feet or three feet and a half long, aimed full at the nofe of thefe animals, knocks them down, and kills them on the fpot.

This is not altogether the cafe with the fea-lions: their fize is prodigious. Our gentlemen encountered two of them for a long time, with the fame weapons, without being able to overcome them. They lodged three balls in the throat of one while he opened his mouth to defend himfelf, and three mufket fhot in his body. The blood gufhed from the wounds like wine from

from a tap. However he crawled into the water and disappeared. A failor attacked the other, and engaged him for a long time, striking him on the head with a bludgeon, without being able to knock him down: the failor fell down very near his antagonist, but had the dexterity to recover himself at the instant the lion was going to gorge him. Had he once seized him, the man would infallibly have been lost: the animal would have carried him into the water as they usually do their prey, and there feasted upon him. In his retreat to the sea this animal seized a penguin and devoured him instantaneously.

There are several kinds of sea wolves and lions; all which I have seen. The former, when at their full size, are from ten to twenty feet in length, and upwards; and from eight to fifteen in circumference. Their skin is covered with hair of a clear tan colour, or fallow like a hind's, and as short as that of a cow. The head is shaped like a mastiff's, supposing the lips of the upper jaw were divided under the nose like those of a lion of the forest, and were not pendulous; and that the ears were cropped close to the head. I shall describe them more fully afterwards.

The other species, which is not so large, has the same appearance; the snout is rather rounder and shorter. Instead of fore paws, it has two fins consisting of articulations, covered, as with a glove without fingers, with a very hard skin or membrane of a dark grey colour. These articulations are not distinguishable on the outside, and can only be discovered by dissecting the fin. The two hinder feet have visible articulations like the fingers of the hand, five in number, and of unequal length. These fingers from the first to the third articulation are joined by the membrane: which afterwards divides itself, and runs along the side of each finger, in the same manner as the membrane in the feet of a diver or water-fowl, and extends much beyond each finger. Its feet are situated almost at the extremity of the body; where they form a kind of split tail when they lie down or are not in motion. Each toe is armed with a claw

which

which is not sharp, but rather projecting, and of a black colour. See the figure in the plate.

Both kinds are bearded like tigers, and have thick strait hairs directly over their eyes by way of eyebrows. The female appeared to have a longer and more graceful neck than the male, and had dugs.

In these animals the fat, which is white and flabby, is so redundant, that it is several inches thick between the skin and the flesh. They are full of blood, which, when they are deeply wounded, gushes out with as much force as when you open a vein in a fat person.

The animal which Mess. Donat and le Roy saw when they went on shore for greens, was probably a sea-lion, of which I shall speak afterwards; though they described it with hanging ears, as long in proportion as those of a spaniel.

Such is the form and figure of the sea-wolves which we saw in some little islands in the bay where we anchored. Those whose description and shape admiral Anson has given are sea-wolves of the larger kind. He calls them sea-lions improperly for the reason hereafter assigned. See the plate.

These animals are all amphibious, and most commonly pass the night and part of the day on shore. When you pierce the thickets of corn-flags, in which they make their retreats and where they form a kind of apartment, you almost always find them lying asleep on the dry leaves of those plants. When they are in the water, they every now and then raise their head and part of their neck above the surface, and remain some time in this position, as if attentive to what is going forward. They make a noise much resembling the roaring of a lion: the young ones seem to utter a hollow sound, sometimes bleating like sheep, sometimes lowing like calves. The larger and the smaller kinds move heavily, and seem rather to drag themselves along than to walk, but with as much expedition as their bulk will allow. They live upon grass, fish, and other animals when they come in their way. On the little island where our gentlemen killed

so

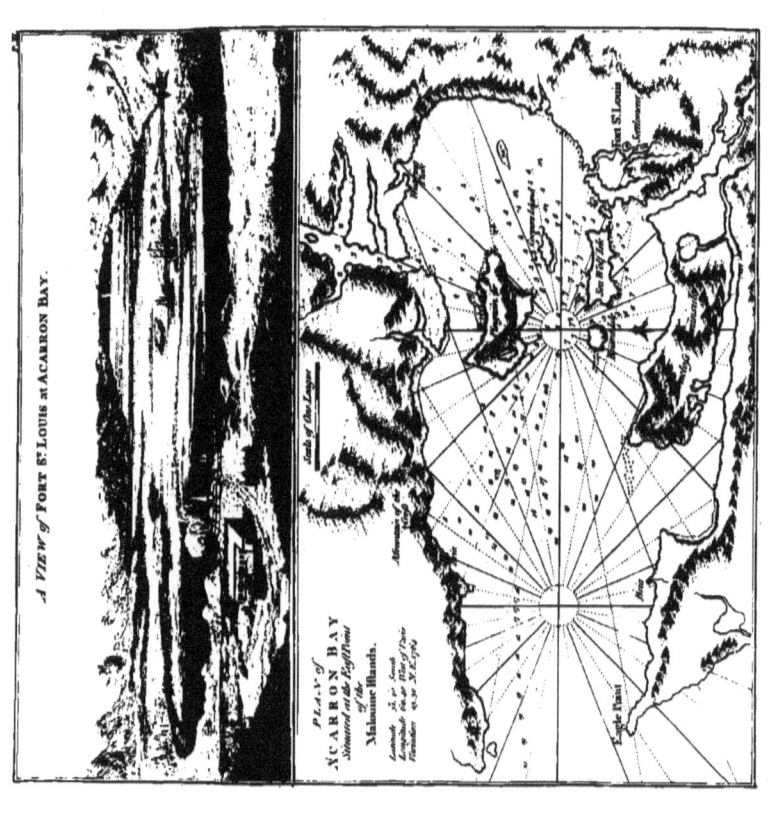

*A VIEW of* FORT ST. LOUIS at ACARRON BAY.

## TO THE MALOUINE ISLANDS.

so many of these animals; one of the females seized a penguin at the instant it fell by a musket-shot. The sea lion-wolf carried it into the water, and devoured it so entirely in a moment that nothing remained but a slip of skin floating on the surface. M. le Roy had, the day before, brought one of these penguins on board, which was at least two feet and a half high. We shall give the description and representation of this hereafter.

On the same day, while some of the company were employed in shooting, M. Duclos our captain and M. Chenard de la Gyraudais went to the top of a kind of hill toward the South, where they planted a cross of wood about three feet high on the summit between two rocks, and called this eminence the *mountain of the cross*.

On Sunday morning, the 5th instant, the weather being pretty fine, with a tolerable breeze, the longboat was sent on shore, to get hay and water, which we did conveniently on the southern coast, to the S. S. W. of the ship, where there seemed to be a kind of fountain. These people returned on board with our sportsmen, who brought a quantity of game of the same kinds as before mentioned.

About noon, M. de Bougainville and his associates returned from their excursion, much disappointed in their hopes of finding wood. They set fire to the herbage of an island, which they have since called the *Burnt Island*, and to a promontory of the continent. They brought with them ten young penguins.

A large piece of wood which M. Duclos found on the beech gave us fresh hopes of finding some on the island. Among several others, the journals of Wood Rogers describe the face of the country in the Malouine Islands, as consisting of mountains and hills covered with woods. As we had not hitherto discovered any in the places we had visited, we concluded that they had only viewed it at a distance, and had, like ourselves, been deceived by appearances. The difficulty however of accounting how this piece of wood should be found on the shore, unless it

was

was produced on some coasts of these islands, inclined us to suspend our opinions till we had made some farther discoveries.

The island which M. de Bougainville set on fire, was at first called Penguin island, because these birds were found there in such numbers, that upwards of two hundred perished in the flames. There remained however a prodigious quantity; and we found some of them at every step. The setting of this island on fire, which is near a full league in length, and half a league in breadth, may be said to be of no consequence, as the flames could not extend farther: but the same cannot be affirmed of the continent. M. de Bougainville imagined, that by destroying this useless herbage he was doing a piece of service, as it would save trouble whenever these lands were cleared. I represented to him, that as the whole country was covered with the same herbage, the flames might probably spread over the whole face of the continent, unless their progress was stopt by some rivers; besides, that they would destroy the game. He paid no regard to my remonstrances; and set fire that very evening to several parts of the continent.

On the 6th of February in the morning, M. de Bougainville, on the credit of the journal of a Malouine captain, asserting that he had seen wood in the eastern part of this island, determined to pursue his discoveries. As soon as we had put to sea with our cutter and longboat, the wind began to blow with some violence from the W. S. W. which determined us to postpone our expedition; especially as M. de la Gyraudais proposed to dispatch M. de St. Simon, with three or four other officers belonging to his vessel, to make discoveries by land; which was agreed to.

M. de St. Simon, a lieutenant of foot, who had lived many years with the savages of Canada, young, hardy and enterprizing, and in every respect qualified for an expedition of this nature, set out this very evening with Mess. Donat, officers of the Sphinx, and two seamen, to reconnoitre the N. N. W. part of this island.

The

The longboat of the Sphinx having likewise landed some of its crew, they found on the shore a bough of a dry tree fifteen or sixteen feet in length, which confirmed us in our expectation of finding wood upon the island.

On Tuesday morning the 7th instant, the weather becoming clear, we hoisted the anchor which had been cast the evening before on account of the hard wind which had then arisen. We sent to get in some ballast and some water, and our sportsmen came back about noon laden with game.

M. de la Gyraudais dined on board the Eagle, and a seaman brought a pretty large dry root which he found on the northern coast. It seemed to be a species of the cedar.

All these specimens of wood determined us to make an accurate search on the South West coast. With this view M. de Bougainville, M. de Belcourt, and the Sieur Donat la Garde, lieutenant of our ship, embarked in the boat. They took in provisions for three weeks, and being all well armed, directed their course to the South East.

On the 8th, the sons of M. Duclos Guyot our captain, happening to throw some hooks at the stern out of the windows of the cabbin, caught a large quantity of fish of a most delicate flavour, though not more than eight or nine inches long. Their eyes were red, their gills edged with gold, and their fins of the same colour; their skin smooth as that of a tench. I do not know their name.

On Thursday the 9th, at four in the morning, the wind being northerly, we got every thing in readiness to penetrate farther into the bay. When we were under sail the wind shifted to the North West, which obliged us to make several tacks, sounding all the while. We constantly found between twelve and fifteen fathom, the bottom of muddy sand: at eight, the wind veering to the West and blowing fresh, we anchored in a green, smooth, slimy bottom, at fifteen fathom.

On the 10th, the wind continued to blow fresh from N. to N. W. the weather was hazy, with showers of rain and hail.

We sent out our longboat however to the peninsula on the
N. W. of us, to see whether we could find pasture for our
cattle. Here we killed a great deal of game. I saw many sea-
wolves of the lesser kind, with a smooth skin of a dark brown.
They had five claws on their fore fins which served instead of
feet, but were not divided into distinct toes. On our return we
proposed to send our cattle on shore, not only for the sake of
recovering them from the very feeble state to which the tossing
of the vessel had reduced them, but to free ourselves from the
necessity of employing a boat and men every day to procure
fodder for them.

On the 11th, the wind blew too violently all the day W. S. W.
to permit us to execute our design. At six in the evening, the
yawl belonging to the Sphinx came on board, to inform us, that
their longboat had just then brought back to their vessel, M. de
St. Simon and the rest of his companions; who acquainted us
afterwards, that on their return they were three days on the
shore opposite to us; and had fired several times to give us
notice. We heard no firing, or at least none but what
thought proceeded from our shooting parties, which sometimes
returned very late; though always loaded with as many bustards,
teals, ducks, snipes, curlews, &c. as they could carry.

The gentlemen of the Sphinx farther added, that the supposed trees which we thought we discovered on a small island
when we passed near the verge of the current, were nothing more
than a plant of the bullrush kind, with flat leaves, known to
our seamen by the name of *glajeux*; that the hillocks formed
by their roots afforded a retreat for the sea-wolves, three of
which they killed as big and long as our boat, besides several
others. They likewise killed a kind of wild dog, much resembling a fox of the larger size: some of the company imagined it was a grey lynx. M. Martin, lieutenant of the Sphinx,
had killed two of them the same day.

These gentlemen met with no tree; but discovered a large and
fine bay some leagues distant from that in which we anchored.

On

On Sunday the 12th, I said mass at five in the morning, for the quicker dispatch of the longboat intended for forage. M. l'Huillier went in the yawl to draw a plan of the bay where we anchored, and several others set out with him on a shooting party.

The wind being W. S. W. and the weather fine, the Sphinx's longboat put to sea on Monday the 13th, with three men to make oil of the fat of the sea-wolves, which had been killed on a small island some days before. These animals may with equal propriety be called porpoises; since, besides their having fat or bacon several inches thick between their skin and their flesh, they often grunt like hogs, and wallow in the same manner in the dirt and mire, where I have seen twenty of them lying down, particularly of the species described by the author of admiral Anson's voyage, under the denomination of lions.

At the same time our small boat was dispatched to another neighbouring island in search of penguins, which are as numerous as the ants in an ant-hill. Some hours after, it returned loaded with a hundred and sixty of these birds without wings, some of which we salted. At seven in the morning we discovered our fishing-boat, at the southern point of the entrance into the bay. We immediately hoisted our colours, and the Sphinx followed our example.

At noon, the Sphinx's longboat brought on board our vessel the Sieur Donat la Garde, and M. de Bougainville's servant, who we thought were still in the fishing-boat in which they embarked. The Sieur Donat informed us, that M. de Bougainville and M. de Belcourt, had been ever since yesterday afternoon on the southern coast of the continent which encompasses the bay. We immediately sent out our longboat, in which M. de Nerville, M. l'Huillier, and myself embarked, in quest of them. We found them exceedingly harassed and fatigued, with the expedition they had just made on foot, through a country where there was no beaten track. We reconducted them on board, together with a seaman who had accompanied them. Being

pressed

preffed with hunger, they as it were devoured the dinner we prepared for them, which however did not prevent them from playing the ir part well at fupper, though it was ferved up foon after.

They informed us, that they had traverfed the fouth-eaft coaft, till they came to as fine a bay as that we now anchored in, about eight leagues diftant by fea, and about four by land. Here they quitted their boat, and went by land to the fouth-weft part of the ifland, and particularly obferved that the coaft ran W. N. W. which is not probable. For there is great reafon to believe that our veffel was then ftationed on the eaftern point of the ifland, the point taken notice of by failors in their journals; who, as well as others, were certainly deceived themfelves when they reported their having feen fome large fine trees growing upon very beautiful hills. M. de Bougainville told us, that in the bay where the boat was left, he found upon the fhore three trees which were very dry, and one of them almoft as large as a wine hogfhead. As they met with none in all the parts of the country they had traverfed, there is reafon to believe that thefe trees had been tranfported thither from the Terra del Fuego, or from the neighbourhood, by the waves and currents which run towards the Eaft, the wind too ufually blowing from the S. W. and W. M. de Belcourt, M. de Bougainville's fervant, and a feaman, were attacked, if it may be called fo, by a wild dog of the fpecies I have before mentioned. This is perhaps the only animal that is favage of the quadruped kind in the Malouine Iflands: it is probable too, that it may not have been fierce, and that it only approached them out of curiofity becaufe it had never feen any of the human fpecies. The birds did not avoid us, but flocked about us as if they were familiar and tame. We have not hitherto feen any kind of reptiles, nor any venomous animal.

The whole night of the fifteenth was rainy, and very tempeftuous. At half paft eleven, the thunder fell at two cables length from us, and knocked down Le Sieur Guyot our fecond captain, who commanded the quarter deck. He received no inconvenience from this accident, except being frightened.

Our

Our longboat, which had been sent out since the morning to carry provisions to those who were employed in washing the crews linen, could not return, on account of a contrary wind which arose, and blew with violence from the S. S. W.

On the 16th, about six in the morning, the wind fell, and the weather became hazy. Some squalls came on afterwards, accompanied with rain and hail. The fishing-boat was however sent out to get forage. Our longboat returned about nine o'clock, and the other at three in the afternoon.

On Friday the 17th, at five in the morning, the wind blowing fresh from the South South-East, Messrs. de Bougainville, de Nerville, de Belcourt, Donat, de la Garde and myself, embarked in the cutter, with a tent and bedding, to establish a settlement on the land, and to form a camp on a small eminence almost at the bottom of the bay.

As soon as we landed, we set about pitching our tent on a spot which we judged to be the most commodious, at the distance of a musket shot from the sea. The little hill ran from East to West. The place where we fixed our establishment is open to the North, which makes the South of the country with respect to the equator. Below us, at about a pistol shot from the tent, ran a rivulet of sweet water very palatable to drink. In the front of the tent was a small eminence like that on the declivity of which the tent was pitched. Some paces from thence we dug a hole in the ground for a kitchen; where, for want of other fuel, we made use of broom. We likewise tried the large green tufts of the resinous gum-shrub I have mentioned. They keep up and continue a fire extremely well; but when green are not proper for dressing victuals.

As I saw the inconvenience attending the want of wood in a country where we intended to establish a colony, I endeavoured to hit upon some expedient to obviate it, at least till the government could take measures for dispatching some pinks and schooners to be stationed in this country, and to make voyages to the Terra del Fuego, to bring wood for fuel as well as for building

ing and carpenter's work. I thought we might possibly find some coal, or at least turf. Accordingly I equipped myself with a mattock, and proceeded on my search. Having observed, that the banks of the rivulet were rather marshy, I conceived, that, as the country had never been cultivated, the grass which grew there, might in process of time have formed a mass of earth intermixed with roots and decayed leaves, which would exactly furnish us with the sort of turf I was in quest of. In fact, after a few strokes with the mattock, I discovered a turf of a reddish cast, which was owing to its not being arrived at the maturity requisite to give it perfection. When I had gone twenty paces up the rivulet, and had found, on digging, some turf with the properties I wanted, I carried two or three squares of it to M. de Bougainville, and acquainted him with the discovery. He was so anxious lest it should not prove the right kind of turf, that he declared it his opinion that it was not. It was shewn to every body who landed with us, and those who were acquainted with turf, were of my opinion. M. de Bougainville still in suspence, wishing that it might be the true sort, and yet fearing the contrary, resolved to make a trial of it. Some dozen of these squares were dug up and ranged round the fire. Our impatience prompted us to throw a few into the fire, when we had the satisfaction to find, that as soon as the moisture of the turf was exhaled, it burnt as well as the best turf produced in France and other countries. We then sent three or four seamen to cut a quantity, and to pile it in the usual manner to dry, and be ready for any use we might think proper to make of it.

When some piles of this turf were raised, the Sieur Donat recollected that he had seen in company with M. l'Huillier along the coast, a black fibrous earth which was tolerably dry, and might answer the same purpose. But having forgot the place, Messrs. de Bougainville, de Nerville, l'Huillier and myself, went in search of it that day, but without success.

While we were thus engaged in forming our settlement, measures were taken on board to penetrate farther into the bay, with
a view

a view both to be nearer us, and to provide for the security of our frigates.

Accordingly, as soon as we were gone, the two vessels set sail, and by proper manœuvres came at last to anchor immediately under Pengu..s island, or the Burnt island, and within the narrow channel or entrance which one must pass to get into the creek, on the borders of which we had fixed our establishment. Near the place of anchorage there is a small island, which has since been called Cooper's island; our people having resorted thither to repair the casks belonging to the ship.

On Saturday the 17th, in the morning, we put into the great boat the two Acadian families we had brought with us to make a settlement on this island, and to people it. At nine in the morning they landed with all their clothes, furniture and necessary utensils, provisions, and some tents to accommodate such of the crew as were to remain on shore to assist in establishing the settlement.

Marks of the new anchorage. The northern point of the burnt island, which concealed the mouth of the bay from our sight, bore East North East, three degrees North. The center of the round island North East, three degrees East. The ..tern point of the island abreast of us, N. N. E. five degrees East. The highest mountain at the bottom of the bay, South West, five degrees West. The Sphinx was anchored about a cable and a half length nearer the mouth of the bay, than our frigate.

Till this time eight of us, Messrs. de Bougainville, de Nerville, de Belcourt, l'Huillier, Donat, and myself, with two servants belonging to Messrs. de Bougainville and Nerville, had lain in one tent. We placed our matresses upon hay and broom, to secure ourselves from the damp. Though we were very much crouded, eleven of us lay there on the night from the 18th to the 19th, our company being enlarged by the arrival of M. de St. Simon, Lieutenant of foot, Mr. Balé, second Surgeon, and a Pilot, who were not provided with a tent to sleep in.

On

On Sunday the 19th we landed a great quantity of provisions and tents, and every one disposed of himself as well as he could. We had notwithstanding no fewer than twelve in our tent on Sunday night. Finding ourselves so much crouded we resolved the next day to pitch some additional tents, and to separate from each other. I was the only person that remained with Messrs. de Bougainville and Nerville.

While some were employed in fixing the tents, others went a shooting, and returned laden with game of the several sorts I have described. M. de Bougainville, having in pursuit of game wandered a little way from his companions, discovered another creek, formed by the same bay, near three quarters of a league from our encampment. All along the banks of it he found a lamellated earth of a brown colour almost approaching to black, which was undoubtedly the same which Messrs. l'Huillier and Donàt had seen some days before. M. de Bougainville having shewn me a piece he had brought from the place, I pronounced it excellent for the same purposes as turf. We made a trial of it, and it succeeded extremely well. Those who intended to stay on these islands, with a view of establishing a new colony, were transported with joy at the discovery, especially as this turf is at present dry and ready for burning, and as, according to M. de Bougainville's accouut, it is found in such abundance that the boats may be loaded with it every day and brought to the settlement.

Walking along the coast in the afternoon, I gathered several shells, Patellæ, Cochleæ, Magellanic muscles, &c. among the roots of that sea-grass, called by our seamen Baudreu, which had been lately thrown on shore from the bottom of the sea.

We this day landed the horses, calves, cows, sheep and hogs, which we had taken on board at Montevideo. They were all so harassed by fatigue and sickness that a mare and her foal died on the beach a few hours after they were set on shore.

On the 21st we were much afraid that we should not be able to save any of our horses, cows or sheep, considering their mi-

serable

ferable and weak ſtate when they were landed; as they all ſeemed to be either lame or languiſhing. We left them on ſhore to take their chance, and thoſe which could not ſtand upon their feet, we dragged upon the graſs, which was at a little diſtance. Having ſent ſome perſons this morning to ſee whether they were dead or alive, they were ſurpriſed to find neither horſes nor ſheep, and the cows and calves diſperſed about the country. They were unable to conceive, that, conſidering their ſickly ſtate the evening before, they could in one night have acquired ſufficient ſtrength to run about the fields: and it was apprehended that they might be devoured by the ſea-wolves, or ſome wild beaſts unknown to us; but the carcaſſes of the mare and foal which ſtill remained on the beach, removed this ſuſpicion.

Since Sunday afternoon we were employed in chuſing a proper place for building an apartment for the reception of the parties who were to remain on this iſland. The ſame eminence on which the tents were pitched was judged to be the moſt convenient. M. l'Huillier, Engineer and Geographer to the King, marked out the foundation, according to a plan he had communicated to Meſſ. de Bougainville and de Nerville. From the Monday morning every perſon on ſhore took the mattock or the ſpade to dig the foundation.

I had ſeen the firſt plan; ſeveral alterations in which having been made in conſequence of my remonſtrances, I thought myſelf equally at liberty to give my opinion on the choice of the ground. I obſerved that in heavy rains, or when the ſnow melted, the great quantity of water which would come down from the hill would overflow the building, and if it did not inſtantly demoliſh it, would at length effect its ruin by ſapping the foundation; the declivity being rather ſteep in this place. M. l'Huillier propoſed to obviate this inconvenience by cutting a trench above to receive and carry off the water; but this did not appear to me a ſufficient expedient, as the trench could not ſtop the impetuoſity of the torrent; beſides that the water which would be detained in it, by gradually oozing through the earth, would cause a dampness in the apartments very prejudicial to the health of the inhabitants, their provisions and furniture. My opinion seemed at first to be disregarded : M. l'Huillier defended his own, and had already caused some lands to be cleared on the spot to which he gave the preference. But on mature deliberation he fixed upon another situation on the same hill, at a musket-shot distance, where there was a very gentle declivity. The workmen were immediately set to dig the foundations. The sailors belonging to the two frigates were employed in this service; M. de Bougainville paying them for their day's work, exclusive of their seamen's wages.

On Wednesday the 22d there were only ten men left on board the Eagle; all the rest were employed in the building.

On the 23d some provisions and utensils were brought on shore from the vessel; and our sportsmen furnished an ample supply for the subsistence of both the ships companies.

M. de St. Simon, one of the keenest of our sportsmen, meeting with a sea-wolf larger than any we had yet seen, near the creek where we discovered the turf, killed it instantly by a lucky shot. On his return he related his adventure at supper, assuring us that this sea-wolf was so thick and long that our boat could not contain it. Every body thought the account exaggerated. But from the description he gave of its figure, I began to think that it might probably be of the species mentioned in Admiral Anson's voyage by the name of *sea-lions*.

Full of this idea, and being curious to know the truth of the matter, I determined to go to the place the next day, being the 24th, with M. de St. Simon and two others.

When we came within something more than a thousand yards distance of this animal, it appeared like a small hill, rising from the level of the ground where it lay. M. de St. Simon added to the deception of our sight, by pointing out this pretended hill, telling us that the animal lay dead near it; so that we did not observe the sea-wolf till we were near enough to see it distinctly. On measuring we found it nineteen feet and some inches long.

We could not at that time measure its bulk, being unable to raise or turn it in order to pass a cord round it.

After we had thoroughly examined it, M. de St. Simon led us to the borders of another creek, thirty paces from this spot, where there was a great quantity of cornflags. On coming to the place, he fired at a sea-wolf, no bigger than a very large calf, and killed it. We immediately heard on all sides, from among these cornflags, cries resembling the grunting of hogs, the bellowing of bulls, the roaring of lions, succeeded by a sound like the blowing of the largest pipes of an organ. We could not help being rather alarmed; but recollecting immediately that these different cries must proceed from these animals, and knowing that we might approach them without danger, taking care only to keep off about the distance of their length; we entered among these cornflags. M. de St. Simon fired at a sea-wolf which was nearest to him. The shot entered an inch above his eye, the animal fell under the stroke, and died almost instantly. A fountain of blood issued from the orifice, and spouted to the distance of at least half a foot. More than thirty pints ran out in less than half a quarter of an hour.

Thirty of these large sea-wolves were lying two and sometimes three in the same hole or pit, full of mud and dirt, where they wallowed like hogs. M. de St. Simon singled out such as lay on dry ground, as it was more easy to remove them when dead, and less troublesome to skin them, in order to get their grease or lard for making oil. He killed eleven of them successively. Two others, rather larger than the rest, being only wounded, though they had already lost twenty pints of blood, had strength enough left to get out of their holes, and escaped to sea, where we soon lost sight of them. The rest which were not wounded remained quietly in their retreats, without shewing any signs of fear or rage. Only one of those which were mortally wounded, in his last struggles seized some of the cornflags that surrounded him, tore them in pieces with his teeth, and

scattered

scattered them about; but without bellowing or making any noise.

An Acadian who accompanied us skinned a young sea-wolf, the first that was killed, as well as two other small ones which were killed after the largest. These are of the same species with that which we took for a hillock. They are exactly the same monstrous animals, as are described by the author of admiral Anson's voyage, under the article of the island of Juan Fernandes, situated at a small distance from the continent of Chili. The whole of his relation is pretty near the truth, except that in these sea-wolves, which he calls lions, the two feet are furnished with toes having distinct articulations, but connected by a membrane or black pellicle, and that these toes are armed with claws; a circumsta... wanting in the figure inserted in the 100th page of that admiral's voyage.

The least of these large sea-wolves which were killed by M. de St. Simon, was from fifteen to sixteen feet in length.

When they see any one approach them, they usually raise themselves upon their paws or fins as described in the plate. They open their mouth wide enough to admit easily a ball of a foot diameter; and keep it open in this manner, at the same time filling a kind of trunk they have upon their nostrils with wind. This trunk is formed by the skin of the nose itself; which subsides and remains empty when they cease to bellow, or do not fill it with their breath. Their head is shaped like that of a she-lion without ears.

Among the numbers that were killed, I observed several which had no trunk, the skin of their nose had no wrinkles, and their snout ended rather in a sharper point. Perhaps these were the females. All those we skinned were males: but six were left lying upon their bellies in the mire without being turned; and these were just the number we saw without trunks. If these were really the females, there should be much less difference in size between them and the males than is represented by the author

thor of the voyage juft now quoted; for the difference is not even apparent.

While thefe animals kept their mouths open, two young people diverted themfelves with throwing large ftones into them, which they fwallowed as we would a ftrawberry. They move their bodies with fome difficulty, but can turn their head and neck to the right or left with tolerable agility confidering their bulk. It would be dangerous to come within their reach; as they could bite a man in two with a fingle bite. They have the fineft eyes imaginable, and there is no fiercenefs in their countenance: I remarked that when they were expiring their eyes changed colour, and their cryftalline lens became of an admirable green. Some of thefe animals were white, others tawny; the major part of the colour of the beaver, and fome of a light fawn colour.

On Saturday the 25th, M. d. Bougainville propofed at breakfaft to both land and fea officers, to undertake the erecting of a fort upon the rifing ground forming the hill, on which the habitation or place of refidence was built for the colonifts, who were to remain on the ifland. We all unanimoufly agreed to erect it with our own hands, and to complete it without the affiftance of the reft of the fhip's company.

As foon as breakfaft was over, M. l'Huillier and M. de Bougainville went to choofe the ground, and M. l'Huillier affifted by two pilots marked it out upon the fpot.

In the mean time fome perfons were difpatched in fearch of tools for the execution of our defign; others went a fhooting to procure provifions for the company. We had hitherto killed more game than was fufficient for the fubfiftence of the crews belonging to the two frigates. We had more than once confidered it as a fingular circumftance that we fhould come with an intent to form a fettlement in a defert and unknown country, having no other provifion than bread, wine, and brandy; and yet free from any care for the next day, in full confidence that the game we met with would furnifh a fufficient fubfiftence for

above

above a hundred and twenty perfons, who had landed and were encamped under the tent. So far from experiencing any want hitherto, we had made fo plentiful a provifion, that there was no probability of our being reduced during the ftay we propofed to make. Neverthelefs each mefs, confifting of feven perfons, was allowed one buftard and a goofe, or one goofe and two ducks, or two geefe, or two buftards and fome diving waterfowl, which we call *Becfics*, or *Nigauts*, and which I fhall fpeak of in the fequel.

About three in the afternoon, we met at the place where the fort was marked out, which we agreed to call *Fort du Roy*, or Fort Royal. Every body fet to work with fo much cheerfulnefs, and fuch incredible ardor, that we had the very fame evening dug part of the ditch fix feet broad and one deep; M. de Bougainville's example animated us all.

On Sunday the 26th, both the fhips companies affembled at the habitation to hear mafs. There remained on board the Eagle only three men and two officers, one of whom had received a hurt in his leg. They all dined on fhore, and the boat did not return to the fhip till evening, when the wind which had all day blown with fome violence, was abated.

On Monday and Tuefday, the longboats took in ballaft for the Sphinx. Some poultry, beams, planks, &c. were carried on fhore. The works were continued at the building and the fort. In my walks, I now and then took notice of the foil of the adjacent country. I found a pretty large quantity of fpar and quartz; which is an indication of mines. I likewife met with fome earth of a reddifh caft, refembling oker, and fome ftones of a rufty colour and very ferrugineous, which I fhewed to M. de Bougainville.

I am perfuaded that there are mines of different ores in this ifland: I broke a piece of fpar mixed with quartz with an iron crow; and perceived in the crevices a greenifh fubftance which appeared to me like verdigreafe. On touching it with my tongue

the

the taſte and ſtyptic quality of this mineral was ſo ſtrong, that it made me ſpit for a full quarter of an hour.

On Thurſday the firſt of March the weather which was hazy, with ſqualls of wind and ſome rain, retarded our works; but we got ballaſt for the two frigates. M. de Bougainville came to a reſolution that the Sphinx on her return home ſhould touch at Guadeloupe, to diſpoſe of ſome of the merchandize we had on board; and that our frigate, after we had made ſome farther diſcoveries of the land, ſhould return to France, inſtead of going to the iſland Mauritius, which was intended if the Malouine Iſlands had not been fit for eſtabliſhing a commodious and advantageous ſettlement.

On the ſecond of March, at nine in the morning, we landed four pieces of cannon out of the ten which the Eagle was to furniſh for the defence of the fort we were erecting. Four more will be added from on board the Sphinx; two braſs field pieces, which were bought at St. Malo's two days before our departure, and ſix pedereroes.

As we had determined to raiſe a pyramid in form of an obeliſk in the center of the fort, I propoſed to place a buſt of Lewis the fifteenth upon the top, and undertook to execute it in terra cotta. I had ſeen ſome grey-coloured earth on the banks of a creek, which I thought very fit for this purpoſe. At ten o'clock I ſet out with our captain M. Duclos, to ſearch for it, and to obſerve what progreſs was made in extracting oil from the greaſe or lard of the large ſea-wolves, which we had killed ſeveral days ago, and left upon the ſpot. We went thither in the fiſhing-boat.

Though they had been killed ſo long and were expoſed to the heat of the ſun, which had melted a great part of the fat, the people employed in extracting this oil, aſſured us, that every ſea-wolf yielded at leaſt two hogſheads and a half, and would have afforded more than four, if the experiment had been made ſooner.

I wanted

I wanted to get the two largeſt teeth drawn from the jaw, but it was not practicable. In breaking the jaw-bone with a hatchet, the ſtroke unfortunately fell upon the teeth ſo as to ſplit them. They are ſolid and full only towards the point: the whole of what is inſerted into the jaw-bone being hollow. I at firſt intended to have diſſected the whole head, but the enormous ſize of it obliged me to relinquiſh my deſign, on account of the difficulty attending the carriage.

I employed the remainder of the time in ſeeking ſhells among the ſea-weeds, lately thrown on ſhore by the waves. There were ſcarce any other than ſome Neritæ, with ſtripes of different colours.

The bottom of the ſhell is compoſed of the fineſt mother of pearl. I likewiſe met with ſome cochleæ and Magellanic, as well as common muſcles. Some of the laſt were between five and ſix inches long and two broad, at their greateſt diameter. At ſix in the evening we loaded the fiſhing-boat with the potter's earth and turf. Finding that it was aground, owing to its being overloaded, we lightened it to ſet it afloat. We were deceived by the ebb; becauſe the ſea, which is not very regular in theſe bays, except at the time of the new or full moon, did not riſe ſo high as we expected. It was near an hour before the boat could be ſet afloat; and that it might not be overloaded, M. Duclos and myſelf determined to return by land, and to keep along the coaſt. We marched almoſt a league over flints, ſtones, and rocks, which line this coaſt. The boatmen had orders to come to take us in at the entrance of the bay, where we told them we ſhould wait for them. We reached the place with great difficulty, the weather being hazy and the wind very high. Having waited for them three quarters of an hour in vain, and while it was very dark, we concluded that the tide, which was running down, and the high wind, which was contrary, had induced the boatmen to bear away for the veſſels. We reſolved therefore to finiſh our expedition by land, by going round the bay, which is at leaſt three quarters of a league, when
we

we heard the boat coming towards us. We hailed her and she answered. After attempting in vain to put ashore at two or three places, they came near enough at last to give us a fair opportunity of jumping into the boat. We intended only to cross over to the other side of the mouth of the creek, and to perform the rest of our journey along the shore on foot. But the steersman assuring us that the sea still rose, and that the tide was in our favour; persuaded us that we should easily get the better of the contrary wind, and that they would engage to land us in a short time near our habitation. Our captain suffered himself to be prevailed upon, and we got into the mouth of the bay; but we had scarce rowed ten or twelve yards when the wind blew with excessive violence, the waves ran high, and the ebb of the sea joined to a contrary wind was so troublesome, that we could not get the better of it. Notwithstanding all our efforts we could scarce proceed twenty yards. The sea grew terrible; every wave broke with violence against the boat, and partly beat into it, so that we were already overflowed. Tired with struggling in vain against the waves, and finding ourselves in danger of running aground upon the stones which lay along the coast, to which the waves and the wind drove us in spite of all our efforts, M. Duclos said we must return to the mouth of the bay, and there run aground. In less than three minutes, in spite of the oars and rudder, we found ourselves driven towards the shore at the distance of about four fathoms from land. The sea which was then extremely furious, was near dashing the boat in pieces, and we ourselves were in danger. Our captain told us we must jump into the water, and set the example himself. I followed him at the instant that a large wave was just breaking against the boat, and overwhelmed it entirely: shock it gave made me fall into the water when I was coming to the ground. I recovered myself so soon, that I only got wet on my left side, and had my boots filled with water. It was scarce more than two feet deep. I immediately steered my course towards our habitation, and told M. Duclos our captain, that I was going to give tidings of him, while he was engaged in getting the boat afloat in order to fecure it. When I arrived at the habitation, I found feveral of our company, who were under apprehenfions on our account. Finding the weather fo bad, fome of them imagined that we had put ourfelves on board one of the frigates, to avoid the danger of ftruggling againft the wind and angry waves in a boat: others fancied that the darknefs had compelled us to land, and that we might have loft our way. It was near ten, and they ftill waited fupper for us. While I changed my clothes, the fupper was ferved up, and I played my part at it handfomely. M. Duclos arrived half an hour after me, and went to-bed without taking any other refrefhment than a glafs of wine.

We imagined till now, that the creeks and the bay which formed the port of our habitation, were not well ftocked with fifh: that the fea-wolves and the water-fowl, which were very numerous, deftroyed the fifh for food, and allowed it no time to grow large. M. de la Gyraudais yefterday convinced us of the contrary, by bringing us fome fifh which made part of our fupper. Being a fhooting at the extremity of a creek about a league from our encampment, he came to the mouth of a fmall river when the fea was at ebb; where, as he told us, he caught with his hands a dozen fifh, which were left aground upon the gravel, and were endeavouring to get back to fea. The fmalleft of them was about a foot long. They were fome of them dreft *au courbouillon*, others fried. Every body found them excellent.

On Friday morning Meff. Duclos, de la Gyraudais, Baflé, M. Duclos's youngeft fon, and myfelf, being defirous of making the moft of this difcovery, without communicating our defign to the reft, got ready a net of the fize of only three fathoms and a half, and repaired to the fifhing place. We placed two catch nets at the fame place, when the fea ebbed, and caught thirty fifh and upwards, the leaft of which weighed near a pound and a half a half. We afterwards caſt a third net at the mouth of a ſmall river two hundred paces from thence, and caught a dozen of the ſame ſort of fiſh.

Encouraged by this ſucceſs, on Saturday the third inſtant we returned to our fiſhing. But the ſea having ebbed, we did not catch a ſingle fiſh. We then concluded that this fiſh came into freſh water with the tide, and went back again with the ebb. Having obſerved that numbers eſcaped through the holes of our net which was a bad one, or jumped over it, we determined to go a fiſhing with the ſeamen the next day, when the high tide occaſioned by the new moon was expected. Accordingly M. Duclos went on board, and ordered the ſean to be got ready. M. le Roy carried it in the boat to the entrance of the creek in the morning, and came to acquaint us with it. A party of us, to the number of ſixteen, ſet out immediately after dinner, with Meſſrs. de Bougainville and de Nerville at our head. On caſting the ſean only once, we took more than five hundred large fiſhes, and thouſands of others half a foot long; three-fourths of which we threw into the ſea. We kept but one ſort of the ſmall ones called by the Spaniards *Pajes*, and by our mariners *Gras dos*. This fiſh is almoſt tranſparent and of a moſt exquiſite delicacy. It is excellent when fried, and not inferior to the eel pout.

The net was ſo full, that notwithſtanding the joint efforts of ſixteen perſons, it was with the utmoſt difficulty imaginable that we dragged it on ſhore. Several fiſh jumped over it, and a great number eſcaped both at the extremities, which could not be brought together, and through the holes that were in the net. However we loaded the boat, which could not reach our encampment till the next day. The fiſh were diſtributed in great plenty for two days, among the crews belonging to the two frigates: they were eaten with variety of dreſſing; and that the reſt might not be waſted, we ſalted a barrel full of them.

This fiſh reſembles in ſhape what is called *Meuille* in Saintonge. It weighs four pounds and an half upon an average.

The fame day, juft as fupper was over, M. Martin lieutenant of the Sphinx came loaded with game. While he was a fhooting, he went to difcover the fource of the river at the mouth of which we had caught fo much fifh. He informed us, that there was a vaft bay, three or four leagues north-weft of our encampment, of which he was not able to difcover either the entrance or the bottom from any of the heights; that this bay appeared to him to run at leaft eight or ten leagues within the land, and that at different diftances he faw rivers and iflands. We were charmed with this difcovery, and refolved to pay attention to it.

The great quantity of fifh we had caught induced us to make a fecond trial. On Monday the 5th, we returned to the place, but whether the fifh had taken the alarm, or the fea was not rifen to a proper height, we caught only fome fmall fifhes and a dozen large ones.

While we were engaged in fifhing, others went a fhooting, and took a furvey of the newly difcovered bay. As they were doubtlefs lefs fatigued than M. Martin, they found the journey not fo long, and declared it fhorter by two leagues. This determined M. de Bougainville and feveral others to go thither the Wednefday following, being Afh-Wednefday.

The whole company being returned about noon, and the fort, on which the officers alone had been employed, being finifhed, M. de Bougainville propofed to mount the cannon which were upon their fea-carriages at the bottom of the hill. We immediately fet about this bufinefs. Accordingly we laid planks upon the ground, to make what is called a bridge, to prevent the wheels of the carriages from finking into the earth. By the mere ftrength of our hands, without the affiftance of any inftruments or engines except crows, levers and ropes, we managed to mount one cannon, notwithftanding the height and fteep afcent of the hill. When we had planted it in its proper place, it being almoft time to conclude our day's work, we loaded and fired this cannon by way of fignal. We then cried feven times *Vive le Roi!*
which

which exclamation was repeated by the workmen employed in building the apartments.

Ever fince we fet about building our habitation, we fired a field-piece with a pound ball, and rang a bell at five every morning, and half paft feven every evening, to fummon the men to their work, and give them notice when to leave off. At eight we rang to breakfaft, and at one to dinner. Befides thefe meals M. de Bougainville now and then ordered them an allowance of brandy by way of gratuity. Thus the work was actually in, as great forwardnefs as if two hundred workmen had been employed.

While we were thus bufy on fhore, the few hands which were on board the frigates were by no means idle. They landed fomething every day for the' ufe of the encampment, as ordnance, balls, provifions, utenfils, &c.

On the 6th we began to ftow our ballaft of flints, and in the courfe of the afternoon mounted feven cannon in the fame manner as the firft. It muft be confeffed, that feamen may challenge all the world in point of dexterity in moving great weights.

When this operation was finifhed, I ordered fome bafkets to be filled with potter's clay mixed with argil for want of fand proper for the purpofe, and contrived fo as to go on board the next day, that I might work at the King's buft without interruption, which I found to be impracticable on fhore, where I fhould have been obliged to do it in our tent, into which fomebody was entering every quarter of an hour.

On Shrove Tuefday, at feven in the morning, I got into the boat in order to return on board the Eagle. I took up my quarters again in my cabbin; after dinner, I began to model the buft in M. de Bougainville's, and being unprovided with a piece of iron to fupport the earth upon the die, I fupplied its place with a cylinder of wood. The head was already roughly fketched the fame evening.

I. de-

I dedicated the 8th wholly to the finishing of the first sketch, which was already reduced to a form. Two or three officers who saw it in this state, encouraged me to finish the bust, and I was in hopes of succeeding in my attempt.

Animated with this expectation, I went to work at six in the morning on the 9th, and was not a little disconcerted to see crevices and cracks in the forehead and several other places, though the earth was very well mixed. M. Guyot and M. Baſlé coming a quarter of an hour after, were almost as much chagrined as myself, to find that the earth was not proper for the use I designed to make of it.

I asked M. Guyot, if he had not seen on the coast a fine sand, which when mixed with this earth might remedy its defects. They set out for the encampment an hour after, and gave M. de Bougainville an account of the difficulties I met with from the bad quality of this earth.

I thought I had nothing to do but to make another attempt with fresh earth mixed with sand, but M. de Bougainville, apprehensive that a new trial might prove abortive, determined to substitute a Flower de Luce in the room of this bust. M. Guyot returned on board to dinner, and communicated this resolution to me. I then desisted from my undertaking; and passed the evening upon the Burnt island in company with M. Mauclair, where we killed ten bustards: he had killed sixteen the day before. While we were in quest of game, two of our officers amused themselves with fishing with the hook from the cabbin windows, and caught fish enough to furnish a dish for three successive meals. The angle-rod would supply an equal quantity every day, if the line was but thrown one hour before the meal.

These fish are of three kinds. The first resembles a pike in shape, the flesh as it were transparent, with a stripe of blue, one line in width, which runs from the gills to the tail between two yellow stripes. The Spaniards of Chili call them *Rovalos*. The second species may be ranked in the class of the eel pouts, called by some *Loaches*. The head of that here mentioned is flat and much

larger

larger than the eel pouts in France. The third species is likewise exquisite, and has yellow stripes round the gills, as if orpiment or gum had been rubbed upon it with a pencil.

These three sorts of fish, which were the only ones we caught on board, are no more than between nine and ten inches long; they are usually from six to seven. But all of them are excellent, particularly that which has the head, and nearly the figure of a pike. They bite so freely, that they are caught as soon as you throw out your line. This fish was one resource, when the weather did not permit us to go a shooting.

On the 10th I returned to the Burnt island, in hopes of gathering some *Lépas* or Patellæ, but the sea was too high; M. Duclos's youngest son and myself, after killing four wild ducks and three *Becfics*, returned on board at five o'clock.

The wild gander is of a dazzling white; its bill is short and black like a bustard's, and its feet are yellow. The bill and feet of the female resemble those of the male, but the feathers upon its back are grey. The border of the white feathers which cover the neck and breast is black, and forms a spot which takes the round shape of the feather. The wings of both resemble those of the bustard; and have likewise a hard knob like a horn at the articulation of the pinion. After stripping the large feathers from the body of the female, there appeared a grey down extremely fine and very thick. The down of the male is at least as beautiful as that of a swan. They would both make beautiful muffs *.

The teal of this country are much superior in beauty to those of Europe. Their bills and feet are blue, their wings green and gold, and the rest of their bodies much more shining and beautiful than those of the Guinea hens. I skinned one of them, and having preserved the head and feet, and stuffed the coat with fine

---

* Their beauty induced several of our officers to order a great number of these geese and bustards to be skinned with a view of carrying them to France; but for want of proper care, they were most of them lost. Mine shared the same fate for want of room to stow them in my cabbin.

fine mofs, placed it in its natural attitude. I made a prefent of it to a virtuofo of St. Malo. I likewife brought to France and depofited in the cabinet of natural hiftory, in the Abbey of St. Germain des Prés at Paris, the head and feet of a large water-f... .... .... carnivorous kind, which I have mentioned under the ... ... Quebranta-hueffos. I have given its figure, on account of the lingularity of its bill.

It would have been a defirable circumftance to have poffeffed the art of preferving the eyes of thefe animals in their natural ftate. Diamonds and rubies can by no means equal the fire, the beauty and t... ... ... of the eyes of a certain fpecies of water-fowl or diver, which is frequently feen on the fea-fhore.

The pupil is furrounded with a circle of the fineft vermillion or carmine. The head is black, but the feathers from the eye to the back of the head are of a fhining white mixed with fome ftreaks of b ick.

In thefe iflands there are likewife prodigious numbers of fmall eagles or brown hawks, of the fize of the largeft of our cocks; but the wings of which when extended, were at leaft three feet acrofs. The large feathers of the wings are of a bright yellow, mixed with brown in tranfverfe ftripes. There is likewife a kind of eagle, of the fize and colour of a turkey hen, whii , red, or yellow. In this kind of eagle, at the bottom of the bill here is a fkin of a very fine red, ftrewed with pretty long black hairs. When this bird is dead, the red colour fades, and the fkin c'... ges to a very pale rofe colour. Its talons are fcaly and of a light grey, as well as thofe of fome of the fmaller kinds I have mentioned. The reft have yellow feet. The talons of this laft mentioned fpecies are as ftrong and large as thofe of the larger kind. Sparrow-hawks are likewife found here, with white breafts and necks; thofe of others are variegated with white, grey and red.

Mufcles are very commonly found along the coaft. We more than once attempted to eat fome of them; but found them fo full of pearls, that it was impoffible to chew them: as thefe pearls being very ' rd endangered the breaking of our teeth, and when they

they were broken in pieces, they left a kind of sand in the mouth which was very disagreeable. As I believed the production of these pearls to be owing to some disorder in this shell-fish, I imagined that this disorder might be owing to this animal's suffering from the want of water during the ebb of the sea. I therefore fancied, that if we took such as were constantly supplied with water, we should find them without pearls. The muscles I had found among the roots of the sea grass, confirmed me in this opinion. I opened some both of the common and Magellanic sorts; they were without pearls and excellent. I carried two or three dozen to the encampment; they were liked by all the lovers of this shell-fish, and we afterwards ate them frequently.

No remarkable occurrence happened from the 11th to Thursday the 22d of March. Provisions and other articles were landed for the use of the people who staid to establish this new colony. On the 21st, we laid the first stone of the pyramid.

There was one circumstance however that deserved notice, and occasioned various reflections among those who were witnesses of it. It was related to me on my return to the encampment.

On Thursday the 22d of March, I was desirous of knowing the truth of this circumstance, and have since been convinced of it more than once by ocular evidence. We carried over about a dozen hogs male and female. One of these was castrated. After they were all landed they went to seek their livelihood in the fields, and never failed to return every evening to pass the night together near the encampment. At first they had a kind of litter of hay made for them, which though in the open air they certainly enjoyed very much, as they repaired to it so punctually. Somebody observed that the castrated hog generally returned about half an hour sooner than the rest, took several turns round the litter and placed the hay in order; that he took and carried it in his teeth to their lodging, and filled every place where it was wanting. When the rest returned they lay down together, and he took his place last. If any one of them found his situation uneasy, uneafy, he got up, and falling upon me caftrated hog, bit him, and obliged him to fetch more hay to make up the litter. The females in particular were very nice in this article.

During our ftay one of them brought forth eleven pigs, and another twelve. Befides thefe young ones, we left there eight fows and one boar. It is eafy to judge how faft they will multiply.

I returned to the encampment with an intention of ftaying only three days, and fetting out on the 23d, to go by land to a bay fituated to the South Eaft of the ifland. M. de Bougainville having feen it in the tour he made fome days after our arrival, thought it delightful, and called it *Beau-port*, as it was well adapted for a commodious harbour. I was to accompany M. l'Huillier, and two or three others thither to take a draught of it. But as foon as M. de Bougainville and myfelf came to the encampment, M. l'Huillier urged the neceffity of poftponing the expedition to *Beau-port* to the Thurfday following, his prefence being abfolutely neceffary to carry on the building. M. de la Gyraudais was the only perfon who returned on board the Sphinx. M. de Bougainville lay in his cott; I fpread a mattrefs upon fome hay in the fame tent, and lay in this manner nine nights. I employed the day in vifiting the adjacent parts, in botanical refearches, and in other inquiries into natural hiftory.

On Saturday the 24th of March, it was propofed that we fhould go in fearch of the three ftray horfes, to fecure them with ropes, and bring them to the encampment. A party of thirty who fet out on this errand, found and furrounded them. They fuffered us to approach fo near, that M. de St. Simon feized one of them by the mane; but the mare which he held difengaged herfelf by a violent effort which threw him down, and leaped with the reft over the ropes we had put round them. They ran fo far, that it was thought proper to give over the purfuit.

We had better fuccefs with the cows and heifers. Thefe were in the fame manner fcattered and difperfed over the country; but a little calf that had been caught being brought near the encampment, and tied to a ftake, the dam hearing it low in the evening came to give it the teat, and the reft followed her. By returning in this manner two or three days fucceffively, thefe animals became accuftomed to it, and repaired punctually every evening to the ftable that was built for them.

On the 27th, M. de Bougainville and M. l'Huillier ordered their cotts to be carried to the chamber in the new building, which was intended for M. de Nerville. They propofed to me the removal of my bed, but I rather chofe to ftay in the tent, as the damp iffuing from the walls, which were rough-caft this very day, might prove prejudicial.

I was near having reafon to repent of my refolution that very night. At ten in the evening, the wind fprang up at South Weft, and continued fo violent all day with frequent fhowers of rain, that it feemed as if the tent would be carried away, or blown down upon me at every blaft. I lay there however the next night, but was obliged to change my quarters the day after, being the 29th.

The tents were ftruck to furnifh wood for the building, I furrendered mine, and removed to M. de Nerville's quarter.

Meff. de Bougainville and de Nerville had, on the 21ft, laid the firft ftone of the bafe of the pyramid, or kind of obelifk, intended to be erected in the center of the fort. A round filver plate, about two inches and a half in diameter, was depofited in the ftone-work of the foundation; on one fide of which was etched with aqua fortis, the draught of that part of the ifland where the fort and habitation were fituated; on the middle, the obelifk with thefe words for the exergue, *Tibi ferviat ultima Thule*. On the other fide was the following infcription:

Difcovery.
Settlement of the *Malouine Iflands*, fituated 51 d. 30 m. South latit. and 60 d. 50 m. Weft long. E. of the mer. of *Paris*, by the Eagle Frigate Captain *P. Duclos Guyot*, Captain of a fire-fhip, and the Sphinx Sloop Captain *F. Chênard*, *Gyraudais* Lieutenant of a Frigate, fitted out by *Lewis de Bougainville* Colonel of Foot, Captain of the veflel, Commander of the expedition, *G. de Bougainville de Nerville* Volunteer, and *P. Darboulin* Adminiftrator General of the Pofts in *France*. Conftruction of a Fort and Obelifk embellifhed with a medallion of his Majefty *Lewis* XV. agreeable to the plans of *A. l'Huillier de la Serre* Engineer Geographer of the Camps and Armies ferving on this Expedition under the Miniftry of *E. de Choifeul*, Duke of *Stainville*. In *February* 1764.
[With thefe words for the exergue, *Conamur tenues grandia*.]

This kind of medal is inclofed between two leaden plates, and the whole in a hollowed ftone. Near it is placed a double glafs bottle well ftopped with maftic to refift the wet, containing a roll of paper on which were infcribed the names, firnames, ranks, and countries of all the perfons who compofed both the fhip's companies employed on this expedition, and of the volunteers [*].

This fort was called *Fort de St. Louis*. It is fituated on a rifing ground, not overlooked by the neighbouring heights which

---

[*] This lift roll which is inferted in the original, is omitted by the Tranflator, as not being in:erefting to the Englifh reader. The number of perfons on board the two fhips, including officers, failors, paffengers, fervants, &c. amounted in all to 138, and 28 of thefe, including women and children, remained in the ifland for the eftablifhment of the colony.

are

are at the diſtance of at leaſt two full leagues. It commands all the adjacent country, and eſpecially the entrance of the creek, at the extremity of which the new habitation is built. This entrance is with good reaſon called the *Goulet*, or *Gullet*; becauſe when the ſea is high, the opening is no more than a full piſtol-ſhot in breadth.

M. Baſſé and myſelf went on the 28th to ſee the large bay, where I gathered a great quantity of the moſt beautiful *Limas*, or cochleæ, with mother of pearl, and faſciated, and ſome flat patellæ, which were extremely fine. On the 29th, it blew a ſtorm, and there fell a great deal of ſleet, attended with ſqualls of wind.

On the 30th the wind blew very cold, with hazy and dark weather, which continued all night, a circumſtance unuſual in this country, at leaſt ſince our arrival. Till this day, the 31ſt, the ſky had almoſt conſtantly been fine and ſerene. We had white froſts two or three times, and once only the ſtanding waters were ſkimmed over with ice; but for ſeveral days paſt there had been a coolneſs in the mornings and evenings, which in hot countries we ſhould call *cold*. However from ten in the morning to five in the afternoon, you feel the warmth of May in thoſe places which are ſheltered from the wind.

The weather was hazy all night, and Sunday morning the firſt of April. About ten the wind diſperſed the fog, and veered to the North North Weſt, where it blew with ſome violence, but ſubſided at four in the afternoon, when I returned on board with almoſt all the officers who were not to winter in the new colony. M. de Bougainville and M. l'Huillier, were the only perſons who ſtaid to ſuperintend the work on the roof of the building, which was almoſt finiſhed.

The ſame day Laurence Lucas, carpenter of the Sphinx, put the finiſhing hand to the carving of the double flower-de-luce in ſtone, which was to be placed on the top of the pyramid. The two medallions in wood, one repreſenting the buſt of Lewis XV. and the other the arms of France, which were to be fixed on

two

two oppofite fides of the pyramid were in great forwardnefs. All the provifions and other articles which were intended to be left upon the ifland were landed, and lodged in the Magazine.

On Monday morning the 2d, M. Duclos Guyot went in the yawl to found the bay, round the fmall ifland covered with cornflags, which was the neareft to the place where we were moored, and was called *Ile au Tonnelier*, or Cooper's ifland, becaufe our cooper was fettled there in order to carry on his bufinefs. M. Duclos every where found a good bottom, and concluded from the depth, that the true channel of the tide is on the fide of this ifland oppofite to that where we were moored. The afternoon was very windy.

On Tuefday the 3d, it was calm all day, and the weather fine. M. de Bougainville repaired to the habitation, to make every preparation for taking poffeffion of thefe iflands, having fixed the day for Thurfday next.

M. de Nerville and myfelf, paffed the whole afternoon upon the Burnt ifland, where we gathered a large falad of creffes and celery upon the banks of a pond at the caftern point. The latter of thefe plants is very common in all the parts of this ifland that we have vifited.

On the 4th, the wind which blew very frefh, varied from the South South Weft, to the Weft North Weft, the weather was fine, and the fea ran very high; which did not however prevent our fportfmen from going out to kill buftards. Four officers belonging to the Sphinx, had brought from thence a hundred and three fome days before. Our officers, encouraged by this fucce.., determined to go thither, and killed eighty-three. Two of them killed but 36 this day, with fourteen ducks and teals. They gave 18 buftards to the Sphinx, on account of the preparations that were making for their departure, which was fixed for the next day. The fort fired one and twenty cannon to announce the ceremony of taking poffeffion, which was to be performed the next day.

At

At four o'clock on Thursday morning the fifth of April, our longboat was sent with her hawser and anchor, on board the Sphinx; after which she weighed her two anchors, and got under sail at half an hour past seven, with a favourable wind and fine weather.

At day-break the fort made a discharge of one and twenty pieces of cannon.

The moment the Sphinx sailed, we all embarked in our yawls and one fishing-boat to go to the fort. As soon as we landed at the gullet, the fort saluted us with several guns. A party of the inhabitants, who had taken the resolution to remain in this new colony appeared in arms at the gullet. They conducted us to the fort, at the foot of which we found all the rest under arms. After the parade they accompanied us to the fort with drums beating.

All the company being assembled at the fort, the pyramid was opened; I then solemnly sang the *Te Deum*; after that the psalm *Exaudiat*, then thrice *Domine salvum fac regem*. After this I rehearsed the verse *Fiat manus tua, Domine, super virum dexteræ tuæ*; the response was, *& super filium hominis quem confirmasti tibi*, then the prayer *Quæsumus, omnipotens Deus, ut famulus tuus Ludovicus Rex noster, &c.* for the prosperity of his reign. We cried *Vive le Roy* seven times and fired twenty-one cannon. We cried again seven times *Vive le Roy*. M. de Bougainville then produced the king's commission, appointing a governor in the new colony, which was delivered to M. de Nerville, who was immediately received and acknowledged as such. M. de Bougainville, in the king's name, likewise proclaimed the other officers, who were in the same manner unanimously acknowledged.

An altar was likewise erected in the fort at the very base of the pyramid. I intended to have said mass there, to make the ceremony of taking possession more sacred and solemn. But the wind blew with such violence, that notwithstanding a tent was erected there, it was thought proper to content ourselves with the ceremony I have described. We afterwards repaired to the apartments

apartments in the habitation, where at eleven o'clock we had a plentiful breakfaſt, the allowance to all the ſhip's company being doubled on the occaſion.

As ſoon as breakfaſt was over, we went to viſit the ſeveral ſpots on which different ſorts of grain had been ſown eight or ten days before; and found them ſprung up, and in a very healthy and flouriſhing ſtate.

On our return, I ſtopped at a place where I had obſerved a pretty common plant, which makes an excellent infuſion: this I ſhall deſcribe hereafter. Having only time to gather a little of it, we took our leave, and returned on board.

On Friday the 6th, at ſix in the morning, M. de St. Simon and two others went on ſhore in the longboat to water, and killed ſeventy buſtards, twelve ducks, ſome teals, and ſeveral ſnipes. Theſe buſtards, together with a great number that were killed before, were put in barrels; ſo that we had two tierces and ſome barrels to ſupply us on our return to France.

The calm and the fine weather at ſun-riſe, favoured the execution of M. de Bougainville's deſign to ſurvey and take draughts of the great bay where we lay at anchor, of its creeks and the environs. With this view, Meſſ. l'Huillier, Duclos, his two ſons, Meſſ. de St. Simon, Donat, le Roy and myſelf, embarked in the longboat, and landed at the bottom of the bay in a creek, which runs up a great way within the land. You ſee it in the chart of the harbour. Meſſ. de St. Simon, Donat, and le Roy, went out a ſporting, while Meſſ. l'Huillier, Duclos, Seigneurie, ſome others and myſelf, made obſervations from the eminence or mountain E. When we had finiſhed our obſervations, and taken a draught of the bay with the graphometer, we amuſed ourſelves with obſerving a ruin, produced, as it ſhould ſeem, by ſome earthquake. It afforded a proſpect ſo dreadfully pleaſing that I was extremely mortified at my want of time, and the neceſſary inſtruments, to ſketch out a perfect repreſentation of it. A painter might here find materials to compoſe a picture of the

fineſt

fineſt ruins. A ſketch of it is given in the plate, as alſo of a kind of amphitheatre ſituated a hundred paces from it.

We were no leſs aſtoniſhed at the ſight of the infinite number of ſtones of all ſizes thrown one upon another, and yet ranged as if they had been piled negligently to fill up ſome hollows. We admired with inſatiable delight the prodigious works of nature. I attempted in vain to engrave a name upon one of theſe ſtones, which formed a table a foot and an half thick, ten feet long, and ſix broad; it was ſo hard that neither my knife nor a punch could make any impreſſion upon it. I tried ſeveral in the ſame manner which were equally hard. I broke off a piece by ſtriking a corner with another ſtone, and all the pieces that were broken off had the appearance of freeſtone porphyrized.

This freeſtone as it is found in its beds, which run in all directions, is every where cut into tables of a different ſize and thickneſs; but in ſuch a manner as if art had been uſed.

Theſe ruins repreſented in the plate, reſemble in ſeveral places the gates of a city, whoſe arches are demoliſhed; and of which there remain only ſome walls to the right and left, ſtill raiſed twenty or five and twenty feet, in the parallel angles forming the entrance. They are like the walls of a town, the ſtones of which have been ranged according to the level and the perpendicular, as they are in our walls compoſed of freeſtone. Some angles are likewiſe to be ſeen here, both ſaliant and reentrant, ſome out-works more than fifteen feet high, and ſome rectilineal projections li. e corniſhes, advancing at leaſt half a foot, and which run at the ſame height all along the poſterior or internal, as well as the anterior or external parts of the ruins. The only things wanting are the mouldings.

To the left of the track leading from the ſpot where we landed, we met with the eminence on which the ſtones are ranged like the arches of an amphitheatre: the figure of which I have given. Beyond theſe ruins lies a valley more than two hundred feet deep, and about half a quarter of a league broad,

broad, the bottom of which is covered with stones thrown together promiscuously, and seems to have served as a bed to a river or some large torrent, which running through the hollows made by these eminences, probably discharged itself into the great western bay I have mentioned. The eminence which is beyond the valley appears to be covered with ruins, similar to those upon the eminence on this side. Before you come to these you meet with an esplanade, or platform of earth, about twenty or twenty-four yards broad, which runs from the base of the amphitheatre, beyond the first opening of these ruins, which I said resembled the entrance or gate of a city. The rubbish of these seeming walls obstructs the continuation of this esplanade where you see two pieces of water, or reservoirs, one nearly round, the other oval, at a small distance from each other; the first about twenty-five feet in diameter, the other thirty. A gentle declivity fifty feet broad leads from the esplanade to the ruins.

From the bottom of the hill you see kinds of hollows intirely filled with these promiscuous heaps of stones.

Between these hollows are irregular spots of ground, twelve, fifteen, twenty, and twenty-five feet in breadth, and twenty, thirty, and at least fifty in length, covered with herbage and heath, as if they had escaped the shock. Between these promiscuous heaps of stones, are every where left void spaces or interstices, whose depth cannot be estimated. The smallest of these stones, none of which are angular, the corners being rounded, are two feet in length, and one in breadth or thereabouts; their figure however is not regular. They are likewise composed of a species of freestone which is of a very hard quality. It is an hour's walk from the place of our landing to the rubbish, and the road is level all the way as far as the foot of the eminence on which the ruins are seen.

As we returned, I gathered a little bag full of a plant which I shall describe in the sequel under the name of *Lucé musqué*, or *Thé des Isles Malouines*: I ate twenty of the fruits of a small herb which

which our mariners call *Plat de bierre :* and we returned on board loaded with game.

After the ceremony of taking poffeffion, M. de Nerville invited us to a dinner he intended to give the Sunday following, by way of taking leave, and wifhing us a fpeedy return to France. We agreed to wait upon him. But our captain M. Duclos Guyot, having reprefented to M. de Bougainville, that the longer we deferred our departure, the greater would be our danger of meeting with bad weather and a tempeftuous fea, on account of the approach of winter in this country; that, two days fooner or later were of confequence, efpecially as M. de Bougainville wifhed to give the court as early an account of his expedition as poffible; and that, it was therefore neceffary to feize the firft opportunity of getting under fail: the refolution was accordingly taken on Saturday evening, to fail the next morning if the weather proved favourable.

On Sunday the 8th of April, we failed at half paft four in the afternoon, the fort faluting us with twenty difcharges of cannon. M. l'Huillier and fome others were difpatched early in the morning to the habitation, to make our compliments of departure, and to bring two hogs and two dozen of fowls to make broth for thofe who might have the misfortune to be ill.

When we arrived in the great bay, that is, when we had got beyond the iflands fituated in it, we lay by to wait for our longboat, which arrived at fix with our great anchor. When we had taken them and our yawl on board, we got under way at half paft feven. At half paft nine we were North and South of the ifland at the entrance of the bay. From this time to midnight, we directed our courfe to the Eaft, at the rate of three leagues and two thirds an hour.

I could not have conceived, that at fifty-one degrees and an half latitude, and fixty longitude from the meridian of Paris, a climate could have been found fo temperate as that of the Malouine Iflands. We landed at the eaftern point, a part of the ifland expofed perhaps more than any other to cold, white frosts, and other inconveniences incident to a situation almost intirely encompassed with the sea, or with bays, forming a peninsula swept by the South West and West winds, which are the most frequent in those parts. We had reason to draw this conclusion during more than two months stay in the country even in the time of autumn, when the cold might be expected to be felt early in that latitude; and from the herbage in all the parts we visited, inclining to the North East and East. Notwithstanding this, except the grass which was withered by the heats of summer, as is usual in all other countries, the other plants, and even the grass of the second growth, were still very green at the time of our departure.

In the quarter of the island which we saw, the land every where presents a very agreeable aspect. Mountains, or rather eminences which we called mountains, encompass plains farther than the eye can see, divided by little rising grounds and hills which communicate by gentle declivities. At the foot of each a rivulet, more or less considerable runs in winding mazes, and discharges itself into the sea through the numerous creeks of the bays. That in which we anchored (which might be called *Baye de St. Louis* on account of the fort of this name which is erected on the land which terminates it, or rather *Baye Royale*, on account of the pyramid dedicated to Louis XV. our well-beloved monarch) runs up more than six leagues within land, and naturally forms a good harbour in which more than two thousand ships may ride at anchor. There is every where a good bottom, islands of different sizes, peninsulas to the number of about twelve, which afford such shelter from the most violent winds, that perhaps there is never any swell in those parts.

The entrance of this bay is at least two leagues over, and is contracted by a pretty large island at some distance from the South East point, as may be seen in the chart.

This great bay which was discovered fifteen days before we left the island, has been examined and traced in part by M. de Belcourt and M. Martin, who made an excursion thither of two

or

or three days and nights. As we were defirous of obtaining a more perfect knowledge of its extent, Meff. de St. Simon and Donat fet out fome days after the return of the two gentlemen I have juft now mentioned. They went at firft to the place where it approaches nearest to the habitation, which is at the diftance of two little leagues, and then kept along the fhore till they came to the bottom of it. They paffed here to the oppofite fhore, and followed it ten leagues. The brooks and a confiderable river which it was difficult to crofs, obftructing their farther progrefs, they determined to climb the higheft mountain they could find; from whence they thought they fhould be able to difcover the entrance of this bay and the reft of its courfe. They judged at that time that it ran at leaft fifteen leagues within the land, and formed into a peninfula that part of the country where we had eftablifhed our fettlement.

According to their account, the coaft of this bay prefents to the view an excellent foil, and an agreeable profpect. At every quarter of a league it is watered by brooks and fmall rivers, one of which, that runs from the Weft, appeared to them to be fixty feet broad. They found a prodigious number of buftards in flocks of twenty or forty, and a great many other birds. Upon the whole, they counted twenty-fix pretty large iflands in that part of the bay which they furveyed.

It may be doubted, whether there is not actually a ftreight which divides thefe iflands, and communicates from North to South, as fome navigators have imagined, and whether the appearance of this bay might not have led them to form fuch a conjecture. Perhaps they faw only its entrance, or not venturing on account of its running fo deep within the land and its great breadth, to proceed farther into it, concluded that it formed a ftreight *.

After an attentive examination of the foil at the habitation, and that of its environs, I think I may venture to pronounce it

of

---

* It was found on a fecond voyage, that fuch a ftreight actually exifts; and that its entrance on the northern fide, is at the place called by us *la Comble*.

of a mineral nature. The ochreous earths, both red and yellow, the spars, the quartz, which are every where to be found, are evident proofs of it. The rocks which are commonly covered with grey and reddish flats, sufficiently indicate a great quantity of sulphur. On breaking the tops of the rocks of quartz which appear on the surface, with crows and mattocks, I found in the crevices, marks of a vitriolick and coppery matrix. I likewise discovered a substance of a greenish cast, which had the astringency and acidity of verdegrease: I applied a little of it to the tip of my tongue, and was forced to spit very much for a full quarter of an hour. Here you frequently meet with pyrites which are round, and sulphureous; and with others of irregular figures, which one would conclude belonged to an iron-mine, both on account of their weight and their brown colour, mixed with an ochreous earth of a reddish yellow, or of the colour of rust. In digging to lay the foundations of the houses, M. de Bougainville observed in the earth that was thrown up, several pieces of broken quartz, which exhibited to the eye spangles that glittered like gold. He picked up some which he brought to me, and I imagined at first sight that it might be *mica*, or the yellow talc. However as the talc is not usually found in the quartz, I thought it might be that species of sulphur which glitters in the pyrites. We were unfortunately unprovided with the necessary materials for making experiments; we had no coals, or wood, no furnace, or even aqua regia, nor could any be made with so small a quantity of aqua fortis. The crucibles I brought were useless to me. There was besides, too small a quantity of these little glittering particles, and we had too many other objects to engage our attention, to be at leisure to ransack the earth for such a collection of them, as would be sufficient to make an experiment. I therefore contented myself with visiting the place where the ground had been dug, and examining the earths that were thrown up. In a hollow at the depth of about six feet, I perceived a bed of earth lying obliquely, six inches broad in some places, the rest of an unequal breadth,

breadth, which entered the ground in the same direction. This bed was composed of quartz covered with a rusty earth, yellow and red ochre, and a sort of hollow flints, several of which were filled with a species of fine bole, of a flesh or rose colour in some, and of the colour of fine laccn in others; several, with a very fine earth of a brownish red colour. The cover, or stony crust which surrounds these fine earths, is commonly of the same colour with the inclosed substance. I have met with some of them grey, very much resembling silver ore. Their colour ... deeper when exposed to the fire, which gave me ... include that they are of an ochre ... ity, and ... chiefly of iron. On my return ... France, I ... these pieces of quartz to persons versed in expe-
rime... ossils, who likewise judged them to be iron ore.

Having therefore no hopes of making discoveries of this kind, I turned my attention on the plants of the country. I met with only four or five of those kinds which grow in France. Here is plenty of red and white celery, which has a sweet and pleasant taste, though produced without culture. We ate it in sallads and soups every day. Some of our mariners called it *Macedonian Parsley*, and were afraid of it at first, but ate it afterwards without scruple, especially as the country afforded no other greens.

M. Duclos, captain of the Eagle, found some hartshorn, or rocket which he called *Cressonette*, and brought it to the encampment. On tasting it, we found it rather too poignant. As M. de Nerville and myself were walking along the side of a pond, we met with some very good cresses, and frequently ate them mixed with celery. Along the banks of a little rivulet, I have seen the *Grenouillette* or crowfoot, as well as the ranunculus, which is cultivated in gardens for the beauty of its flowers.

Our pilots observing that we were fond of a plant which had rather a singular appearance, were induced to taste it. It has a milder and more agreeable acidity than even the round leaved sorrel. They found it so palatable that they put it into their

soup

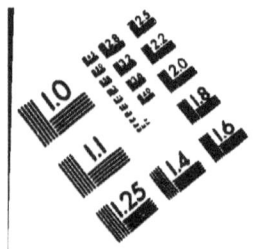
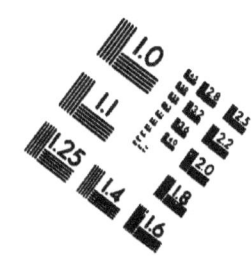

IMAGE EVALUATION
TEST TARGET (MT-3)

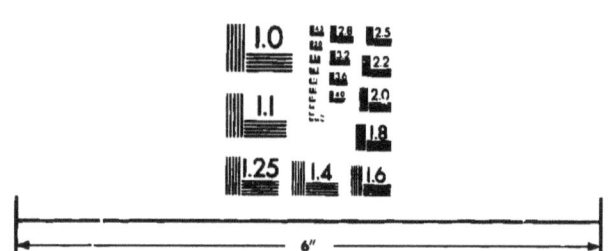

Photographic
Sciences
Corporation

23 WEST MAIN STREET
WEBSTER, N.Y. 14580
(716) 872-4503

foup the fame day, and as we did not perceive that they fuffered any inconvenience from it, we ordered fome of it in our own.

This plant produces leaves ranged in a circular form, fometimes eighteen or twenty in number, at the extremity of a cherry-coloured petiole as thick as a crow quill, round and generally from feven to eight inches high, always rifing above the plants which furround it. The leaf is of a light green.

It has only one ftem nearly fimilar to the footftalk of the leaves, which fupports a fingle white flower confifting of a pentaphyllus calix, and having the figure of a very fmall tulip; it expands in the fame manner, and emits a very fweet fmell like the almond. The leaf of the plant is fhaped like a heart, the extremity of which is very much lengthened: each leaf is faftened to the petiole or footftalk by this extremity, and forms a kind of hoop. See the figure in the plate. I have never feen any of thefe leaves quite expanded; they are almoft always funk into a channel. Ten, twelve, and often more of thefe leaves or leafy ftems proceed from the point of a long twifted root, covered with fmall pointed fcales of a red colour inclining to vermillion, lying horizontally two or three fingers deep. This plant is very common. We called it *Vinaigrette* from its tafte. Perhaps it belongs to the clafs of wild forrel.

The plant reprefented in the figure next to that of the *Vinaigrette*, may be ranked among the *Satyrions*: its leaf feems at firft fight to fuggeft this conjecture: however as the orchifes have ufually no more than two tubercles at their root, and this plant has twelve roots or more, fhaped like thofe of the goat's beard and very long, I think it ought not to be placed in the clafs of the orchifes. I take it to be the Epipactis, mentioned by Father Feuillée, page 729. pl. 29. under the denomination of *Epipactis amplo flore luteo* vulgo *gravilla:* the root of the Epipactis of the Malouine Iflands, bears however a greater refemblance to that of the *Epipactis floribus uno verfu difpofitis* vulgo *Nuil,* which he mentions p. 726. and is reprefented in pl. 17. It grows in the dry and barren parts of Chili, and the Epipactis

*flore*

*flore luteo* in the moist parts of the same country: that of the Malouine Islands likewise grows in low and moist places. The root of this consists of several knobs, which are formed into a bunch. I have seen from ten to twelve of them, and sometimes more. Their length on an average is three inches, and some of them are more than half an inch in thickness. They are covered with a small thin skin, inclosing a friable, soft, watery substance, which at first has a sweetish taste, but when it is chewed leaves so strong a flavour or relish of ambergrease in the mouth, that it a little resembles cat's urine.

I have not been able to discover the flowers of this plant, though I have seen several of every size. The highest of them have capsules filled with seed, and a kind of tuft at the extremity resembling a cluster of dried petals of a reddish cast, without any determinate smell.

The seed is a very fine red dust, that fills the hollow part of the capsule, which is divided into four or five compartments. After the most careful examination, I have not been able to discover any other kind of seed.

The stem of the plant never rises higher than seven or eight inches, and is covered with pretty long leaves, which frequently form a shallow channel; some are perfectly flat: they are all smooth, and of a green colour, resembling that of the leaf of the orchis.

In all places washed by the water there is found a species of spleen-wort, which grows like a fungus, and supports a stem with hollow leaves, in which the seed is contained : a circumstance not common in any species of the maidenhair, in which the seed is a dust adhering to the verge of the prone disk of the leaf. In this plant we are describing, the stem that supports the seed rises singly on the right side of the root, the leaves being at the same time circularly disposed, or vertical. The stem itself, or if you will, the only leaf in the whole plant, which supports the seed, is in proportion near an inch longer than the longest of thofe leaves which grow out of the fame root. This feed however, like that of the maidenhair, is a thick red duft.

In the fields, amongft the herbage which covers almoft the whole furface of the foil of the ifland, there is a pretty common plant with a white flower, radiated like that of the dandelion, but the petals are fharp pointed. The leaves the largeft of which are three inches long, and the ftem, which is about a foot high, are of a green colour and rather foft like cotton. Upon each ftem is a fingle flower, which fmells exactly like Benzoin.

There is another plant, whofe ftem and leaves refemble thofe of the preceding, which bears a bunch of yellow flowers, twelve or fifteen in number, equally radiated, and very pleafing both to the fight and fmell. This flower is fupported by a fquamous calyx. The root is a mafs of fmall fibres, all terminating at the bottom of the plant.

Here are alfo two plants to be met with, which both produce a red fruit: the fruit of one of them fo much refembles a rafberry, that it is eafy to miftake it when feparated from the plant: its tafte is fomething like that of the mulberry, but much more agreeable. It is a creeping plant, ftrikes root at each joint, and has a fmall leaf like that of the yoke-elm.

The leaf of the other plant is rather hairy, fomething like that of the mallow. The ftem which fupports the fruit is fo little elevated, that a part of it is frequently under-ground. It is fhaped like :lberry, but of a lively vermillion: the feed is dry and almo. .telefs.

Amongft the herbage and heath, there grows another plant full as remarkable as thofe I have mentioned. Its fruit is pleafing to the eye, and agreeable to the tafte. It makes an excellent liquor infufed only in brandy and fugar, as it has a very grateful odour of amber and mufk, which would not difguft any one who has even an averfion to thofe two perfumes, and would be infinitely pleafing to thofe who are fond of them. The Indians who inhabit the fouthern parts of Canada, prefer the

infufion

infusion of this plant to the best tea. They drink it both for pleasure and health; they say that it cheers the heart, restores and fortifies the stomach, cleanses the brain, and communicates a balsamic virtue to the blood. M. Duclos our captain, a Canadian, and some officers belonging to our frigate, who made a considerable stay in that country during the last war, assured me of this, and took great pains to provide a plentiful stock of it. They call this plant *Lucet musqué*. It has the delicate and sweet scent of myrtle. Its ligneous branches lie close to the ground, creeping like those of the wild thyme, which this plant resembles in its stems and leaves, with this difference only, that they are not quite so acute. I never saw it in flower; nor do any of our officers remember to have seen it; but whatever its flower may be, it is succeeded by a fruit resembling that of the myrtle, only larger when it comes to maturity. At first it appears red, and most commonly grows white as it ripens. It then becomes oval, and is crowned with four green points which expand themselves like those of the pomegranate. It contains a small quantity of seeds, like the *Vitis Idæa*; its juice is sweet. Most of these fruits are as large as that of the hawthorn, but I have seen some of the size of a sloe. See the plates.

Another plant whose name and properties I am unacquainted with, grows in sandy places upon the sea-coast: but it is uncommon. Suspecting that it might have some virtues, which, if discovered, might prove of advantage to mankind, I gathered the seed. The leaves of it, which resemble the head of a blunted spear, and are nearly oval, are produced on a long stalk which rises from the root itself. They are more woolly than those of the *Verbascum*, called *High-taper*, or *Mullein*. Its flowers are yellow, radiated, disposed in bunches, and supported by a calyx, which becomes round like that of an artichoke, and when the flower is fallen, contains a long angular seed much like that of endive.

We met with but one kind of shrub in that part of the country which we visited. It is found in moist lands, on the little hills through which the waters pass in their descent from the heights. This shrub grows to the size of rosemary, which it perfectly resembles in its leaves, except that they are shorter and rather smaller. The flowers are white, much like those of the Easter daisy, or the daisy of the fields. They are not ranged in the form of ears like those of rosemary, but each flower is placed at the extremity of each small branch, in such a manner that the shrub appears intirely covered with them.

The flowers and leaves have scarce any smell; and the little they have does not resemble that of rosemary. It is certainly not the plant which Frezier mentions in his account of the South Sea by the name of the P..... an Indian name, and which the author of admiral Anson's voyage affirms to be very common at Port St. Julian, on the coast of the Patagonians, situated in almost the same degree of latitude with the Malouine Islands, where the shrub I speak of is also very common: but he says, that it resembles rosemary and has the same smell. The bark of this on the Malouine Islands is greyish, tolerably smooth, and the wood is yellow.

Among the shrubs may be ranked a ligneous plant, which commonly grows in such parts of these islands as are supplied with fresh running water. At the distance of some paces it might be taken for a small rose-tree; but upon a nearer examination, the leaves, which come out in pairs, rather resemble that of pimpernel. It is indeed rather longer, and its taste as well as the top which elevates the seed, bear some affinity to it : this top is oval, not unlike the outward coat of the chesnut, or one of those red berries which the sweet briar or wild rose exhibits in autumn. This shrub has a creeping stem, sometimes an inch in thickness, and four or five feet in length. From this stem are produced branches eight or ten inches high, which are terminated by the flower and the seed. I did not see any of these in flower, it being too late in the season.

The drier soils produce two or three sorts of broom with a red fruit, which differ much from the European kind. They have

have all a refinous fmell. There is another pretty large plant which taftes exactly like the young fhoots of the pine-tree, called in Canada the *Sapinette*, of which is made a fermented liquor of the fame name, which is very wholefome. We tried to make the fame kind of liquor with this plant: thofe who had been in Canada affirmed that it had the fame tafte. We drank of it feveral times, and found it exceedingly good. It will be of great fervice to thofe who may hereafter fettle in thefe iflands; as this plant is to be found there in great plenty, and the liquor that is made from it may be ufed inftead of beer. The ftem and leaves are of a pale green inclining to yellow, and may be claffed with thofe creeping plants which have a round ftem very pliant, and fometimes as thick as the barrel of an eagle's quill, though oftner that of a goofe-quill. The leaves come out in pairs on the fides of the branches, being faftened to a very fhort footftalk, and are fhaped pretty much like thofe of the gum-tree, which I have fpoken of before. This plant flourifhes as well in low, as in high and dry grounds. The flower, which is herbaceous, leaves behind it a white tuft fhaped like a loofe brufh, and bears no fruit.

The leaves of the largeft of the two kinds of broom which produce it, are round, and of a whitifh green; they are crowded in fuch numbers round the branches that they quite conceal them. The fruit is of the fize of a pea, of a red colour, and is tolerably well tafted.

The leaves of the other are placed in the fame manner round the branches, but are fmaller, terminating in a point, and are of a very fine green. The fruit has a kind of berry like that of the hawthorn; but its colour is a fine carmine: and it is fmaller than that of the laft mentioned broom. The plant is likewife not fo large: it is pretty commonly found among the gum-trees, between which its branches infinuate themfelves in fuch a manner that you would take it for a branch of the fame plant, though with different leaves fupporting the fruit.

This

This gum-tree forms but one green head, as its leaves do not exceed each other in length more than the fourth part of a line. It requires a very close inspection to distinguish them. They are as it were glued one above another in the form of a rose. The flower so nearly resembles the capsule which contains the seed, that it may easily be mistaken for it. This capsule greatly resembles that of the aniseed, but it is of a grey earth colour. I have seen several of these gum-trees more than ten feet at their greatest diameter, and from four to four and an half in height. They are in general nearly circular, but the largest are shaped like a potatoe cut in two.

I have met with few remarkable sea plants except that which our mariners called *Baudreux*. Its stems rise to the surface of the water, upon which they extend a great way, and are supported by means of a kind of bubble filled with air, from which the stalk of the leaf is generated.

These baudreux are found in great quantities along the coast, and even a full league from land, in places from fifteen to eighteen fathoms deep: so that the stem, in order to reach the surface and extend itself so far upon it, must be twenty fathoms in length. I once amused myself with taking measure of one which the waves had by chance broken off, and thrown upon the surface; I thought I should never have seen the end of it.

The roots of these baudreux, as well as the stem of the plant, are yellow, interwoven with each other so as to form a large bunch, which affords a shelter to the finest muscles, both of the Magellanic as well as the smooth and common kinds. Here are likewise found purpura, cochleæ, and several other shells. The mother of pearl and fasciated limas live amongst the stems and leaves.

These leaves are two feet and an half in length, and their greatest breadth is four inches. They are of a yellow red, resembling in colour the leaf of a dead tree which begins to rot. Their superficies is uneven, as if the leaf was figured. See the plates.

This

This plant produces thirty stems from a single root, which is fastened to the bottom of the sea by one extremity, shaped like the broad end of a trumpet, or wide funnel. From this proceeds a bundle of roots or intertwisted stems, among which stones and shells of the kind I have mentioned are frequently found. The leaves grow upon the stem at intervals. A mucilaginous and frothy fluid oozes from the stems, and affords nourishment to the shell-fish that adhere to them. When the waves have dislodged these bundles from the bottom, and thrown them upon the shore, and when the leaves becoming withered by the action of the air, and the rays of the sun, are separated from them, our mariners call them *Goemon* or Sea-grass. If one is not careful to take out the shell-fish as soon as the sea which has thrown them on shore has ebbed, the shells are not worth preserving: the sun calcines them, destroys their finest colours, and reduces them to lime, so that they become friable between the fingers. In order therefore to collect such of them as deserve a place in the cabinets of the curious, these weeds must be pulled up from the bottom of the sea with the drag, or the shell-fish picked out from the weeds as soon as the sea has thrown them on shore.

The lepas, or patellæ, of the Malouine Islands are superior in beauty to any in France. They are for the most part oval. The inner surface exhibits the finest mother of pearl; the bottom of the concavity is often lined with the red brown tortoise-shell, which appears to be gilt. The outward surface is striated and channeled, the projecting parts are of a brown tortoise-shell colour, and the bottom is variegated with mother of pearl and gilt tortoise-shell.

I have seen some that were three inches and upwards at their greatest diameter. There are five or six sorts of them which are more or less oval; in some the cavity is of a considerable depth, in others, though of the same diameter, it is less deep by three-fourths. I have some in my possession an inch and an half broad at their small diameter, which are not three lines in depth;

depth; and others an inch broad whose cavity is an inch deep. The inner surface of these is most commonly of the colour of fine white porcelain, and the bottom of the cavity of gilt tortoise-shell.

There are some of this kind very large and beautiful, having an oval aperture in the center of the top, white within, and stained with stripes of purple and violet, which widen as they extend from the center to the circumference.

The fourth sort is by some called Dragoon's cap; the largest aperture I have had an opportunity of observing does not exceed from nine to ten lines in diameter, and six or seven in depth; the outward superficies is grey, almost smooth, and has sometimes stripes inclining to brown; the inside is usually of the colour of the lees of red wine with a little tincture of brown.

In many of these patellæ the perforation in their convex part is not placed directly in the middle, but rather towards one of the edges of the greatest diameter. In one of them it is situated as near as possible to one of the extremities. This patella is very flat; its shell is so thin, that it requires great nicety and care not to break it. The two surfaces are smooth, and silvered over when the external one is stripped of its outward covering, which is of a filemot colour. Here is likewise found a concamerated patella which is small and white, both within and without; I never saw any of this sort but upon the shore, and they were always without the fish. To these may be added that sort which our seamen call *Gondolas* or *Boats*; because it resembles them in figure when the bottom is turned uppermost: but their upper surface is like the coat of the millepedes. It is composed of eight pieces, inserted into each other in such a manner, that the fish can roll itself up, form itself into a round ball, and inclose itself in its shell. A fleshy substance runs quite round with rough hairs three or four lines in length. The shell is variegated with stripes or streaks of a fine bluish green, a milky-coloured white, and a darkish brown.

The Malouine iflands abound with four kinds of mufcles; the common, the Magellanic, and two other forts which differ in fhape both from the common and Magellanic. I have feen fome of thefe laft forts, the fhell of which was from five to fix inches long, and three inches broad. Thofe which are gathered from the rocks left dry when the fea retires, are commonly full of pearls, fome of which are pretty enough. Thofe which adhere to the fhell, or are difperfed over the body of the mufcle, are of a violet blue inclining to black; they are often uneven, and bear a great refemblance to turnip-feed. The pearls of the large Magellanic kinds are white, but feldom of a good fize, and clear colour. They are likewife very apt to break in attempting to feparate them from the fhell. Thofe which are found on the body of the mufcle, are properly nothing more than feeds. It is highly probable that thefe pearls proceed from fome diforder in the fifh, as they are feldom found in mufcles which are conftantly wafhed by the fea-water. The want of water, at a time when the fun darts his rays fiercely, undoubtedly occafions an extreme thirft, and a languor that impairs them, and creates an obftruction; from which thefe pearls are generated.

The fhell of one of the other two kinds of mufcles is white, tranfparent, and fo light that the leaft breath of air blows it off the hand. The other, though larger, is of a very fhining red brown gold colour, particularly when under water, and the fun fhines upon it. When empty, it is fcarce heavier than the preceding one, for the wind alone throws it upon the fhore. See the plate, &c.

The large and fmall Magellanic mufcles are of the whitenefs of mother of pearl, divided by purple ftripes, adapted to the circular figure of the fhell. The coat which covers the external furface is of a muddy brown; but when this is taken off, it difplays a fine fky-blue veined with purple ftripes. The channels diminifh infenfibly as they approach the fharp end, which is fine

L l                                  mother

mother of pearl, and from which they proceed as from their center. See the figure of thefe mufcles in the plate.

A great number of other different fhells engage the attention of the curious upon the coaft of thefe iflands: foliated buccina, fpinofe buccina, fcrew fhells, of different kinds, Purpura, fafciated Cochleæ, concamerated Cochleæ, Neritæ, fmooth Chamæ, ftriated Chamæ, Scollop fhells, Pectines, Echini, Sea-Afteriæ, and a fpecies of Concha, which our feamen call *Gueulle de Rayes*. This laft fhell has not till lately been known except among the foffil fhells, and it has been doubted whether it exifted in nature. In the fubfequent voyages made to the fame iflands, fo great a quantity of them has been collected, that they have been diftributed among the cabinets in Paris: fo that the only fhell of the kind which I depofited, on my return, in the cabinet of the Abbey of St. Germain des Prés, is no longer a rarity.

There are probably feveral other fhells along the coaft of the main fea, which I have not had an opportunity of feeing, becaufe the place where we anchored was about fix leagues in the bottom of the bay; and the fpot on which we pitched our tents, and fixed our habitation was near two leagues farther. Throughout this whole bay, I have feen no other kinds of fhells than thofe I have defcribed: nor did we meet with any fifh befides thofe I have mentioned, except fome white porpoifes, and feveral whales.

There are three kinds of amphibious animals very commonly found on thefe iflands; fea-wolves, fea-lions, and penguins. I have faid fomething of each of thefe; but fhould add, with regard to the fecond, that the name of *fea-lion* does not fo properly belong to thofe I have defcribed, (and of which the author of Admiral Anfon's Voyage treats pretty largely) as to another fpecies, in which the hair that covers the back part of the head, neck and fhoulders, is at leaft as long as the hair of a goat. It gives this amphibious animal an air of refemblance to the common lion of the foreft, excepting the difference of fize. The fea-lions of the kind I fpeak of, are twenty-five feet in length, and from nineteen to twenty in their greateft circumference. See the plate. In other

other respects they resemble the sea-lions, of which I have given the figure. Those of the small kind have a head resembling a mastiff's with close cropt ears.

The teeth of the sea-lions which have manes, are much larger and more solid than those of the rest. In these all the teeth which are inserted into the jaw-bone are hollow. They have only four large ones, two in the lower and two in the upper jaw. The rest are not even so large as those of a horse. I brought home one belonging to the true sea-lion, which is at least three inches in diameter, and seven in length, though not one of the largest. We counted twenty-two of the same sort in the jaw-bone of one of these lions where five or six were wanting. They were intirely solid, and projected scarce more than an inch, or an inch and an half beyond their sockets. They are nearly equal in solidity to flint, and are of a dazzling white. Several of our seamen took them for white flints when they found them upon the shore. I could not even persuade them that they were not real flints, except by rubbing them against each other, or breaking some pieces off, to make them sensible that they exhaled the same smell as bones and ivory do when they are rubbed or scraped.

These sea-lions that have manes, are not more mischievous or formidable than the others. They are equally unwieldy and heavy in their motions; and are rather disposed to avoid than to fall upon those who attack them. Both kinds live upon fish, and water-fowl, which they catch by surprize, and upon grass. They bring forth and suckle their young ones among the corn-flags, where they retire at night, and continue to give them suck till they are large enough to go to sea. In the evening you see them assembling in herds upon the shore, and calling their dams in cries so much like lambs, calves and goats, that, unless apprised of it, you would easily be deceived. The tongue of these animals is very good eating: we preferred it to that of an ox or calf. For a trial we cut off the tip of the tongue hanging out of the mouth of one of these lions which was just killed. About sixteen or eighteen of us eat each a pretty large piece, and we all thought

thought it so good, that we regretted we could not cut more of it.

'Tis said that their flesh is not absolutely disagreeable. I have not tasted it : but the oil which is extracted from their grease is of great use. This oil is extracted two ways; either by cutting the fat in pieces and melting it in large cauldrons upon the fire; or by cutting it in the same manner upon hurdles, or pieces of board, and exposing them to the sun, or only to the air: this grease dissolves of itself, and runs into vessels placed underneath to receive it. Some of our seamen pretended that this last sort of oil, when it is fresh, is very good for kitchen uses: this, as well as the other, is commonly used for dressing leather, for vessels, and for lamps. It is preferred to that of the whale : it is always clear, and leaves no sediment.

The skins of the sea-lions are used chiefly in making portmanteaus, and in covering trunks. When they are tanned, they have a grain almost like Morocco. They are not so fine, but are less liable to tear, and keep fresh a longer time. They make good shoes and boots, which, when well seasoned, are waterproof.

The Penguin is so singular an animal, that it is not easy to say to what genus or species it belongs. It has a bill like a bird, and feathers; but they are so fine and so unlike common feathers, that they have properly the appearance of hair as fine as silk; even when you are near enough to examine and touch them. You can only be convinced of the contrary by plucking one of them, upon which you discover the barrel and feathers of a quill. Instead of wings it has two fins, which are articulated in the same manner as the wings of birds, and are covered with very small feathers which might be taken for scales. At first sight it appears to have no thighs, and its feet, which are rough like those of geese, seem to come out directly from the body on each side of the tail, which is nothing more than a continuation of the feathers, nearly in the same manner as in ducks, but much shorter. The neck, the back, and the fins are of a bluish grey, blended

through-

## TO THE MALOUINE ISLANDS. 243

throughout with a pearl-coloured grey. The belly down from the neck is white. The old ones have a white stripe round their eyes mixed with yellow, which is not unlike spectacles. From thence this stripe extends on both sides along the neck, where it is sometimes double, and passing close to the fins, terminates at the feet which are of a darkish grey, and have very thick toes. Its noise is like the braying of an ass. Its aspect and its motion are different from that of birds. It walks upright, with its head and body erect, like a man. At the distance of an hundred paces, you would take it for one of the children of the choir in his habit. The largest of those we have taken may be about two feet ten inches high.

They live among the corn-flags like the sea-wolves, and earth themselves in holes like foxes. They suffer one to come so near them without stirring, that one may kill them with a stick. As you approach them, they look at you, turning their head to the right and then to the left, as if they made a jest of you, and muttered ironically *What a fine fellow have we got here!* They sometimes retreat when you are five or six feet from them, and run pretty much like a goose. If they are surprised and attacked, they run in upon you, and endeavour to defend themselves by striking at your legs with their bills; they have recourse to stratagem to gain their point, and pretending to retreat sideways, turn back in an instant, and bite so hard that they take the piece out, if you have nothing to secure your legs. They are usually seen in flocks, sometimes to the number of forty, ranged in order of battle, and eye you as you pass at the distance of twenty paces. Their flesh is black, and has rather a perfumed taste. We ate of them several times in ragouts, which we found to be as good as those made of a hare. We took off the skins from several, with a view of preserving them, but they were so oily that we threw them into the sea: it was likewise their moulting-season. I wrapped the skin of a young one in straw, which is in very good preservation: I have deposited it in the cabinet of natural

ral curiosities belonging to the Abbey of St. Germain des Prés. See the Plate.

When they take to the water, and find it deep enough to cover their neck and shoulders, they plunge into it, and swim as quick as any fish. If they meet with any obstacle, they spring four or five feet out of the water, and then plunge again, in order to pursue their course. Their dung exhibits only an exceeding fine earth, of a yellowish red, interspersed with small shining points like mica; it might be taken for the *Lapis fortuitus*.

As for the birds in these islands, there are but few found upon land. There is a flock of birds upon the shore like small thrushes, of a brown grey, so tame that they come flying almost upon your finger. I killed ten with a small switch in less than half an hour, without changing my place. They scratch among the sea-grass which is thrown on shore, and eat the worms and small shrimps, which we call *Puces de mer*, because they are skipping incessantly like fleas.

Blackbirds are likewise found here, and a kind of thrush with a yellowish belly. They feed in the same manner as the bird I have just now described. We killed a kind of starling in the fields, the upper part of whose neck, back, and wings, is marked and speckled almost like those in France; the bill is likewise shaped in the same manner: but the lower part of the neck and belly are of a very fine red, somewhat inclining to a flame colour; this red is besprinkled with some black spots. I could not give a true resemblance of it without making use of the minium or red lead. See the Plates.

Here are great numbers of wrens like those in France, snipes, curlieus and sea-larks: likewise a small bird, not often seen, like those that hover about flocks of sheep; these birds have all an excellent flavour.

Upon the sea-coast is almost always seen a kind of duck, which flies in pairs and sometimes in flocks: the feathers of its wings are very short, and only serve to support it in running upon the water, for it never flies. Its plumage is grey, its bill and feet yellow,

yellow. When it is not shot dead, it continues its flight upon the surface as long as the least breath of life remains. Its flesh is oily, and has a fenny taste: it was eaten however by our ships companies when no bustards were given them. These ducks usually weigh at least between nineteen and twenty pounds each. We called them grey geese, to distinguish them from the kind which affords that fine down of which muffs are made. They are not better eating than the ducks; their flesh has even a disagreeable smell, which their oily skin retains a considerable time, though exposed to the air. This disgusting circumstance prevented our making a collection of them. They may probably be of the kind called *Cabuitabu du Para*.

The large feathers in their wings are of an iron grey; the small ones a mixture of green and gold, and vary their colour like those of a wild duck; the rest of their body is white. The articulation of the wing is armed with a spur as hard as horn, not very sharp, but rounded like a cone, and about half an inch long. Their bill and feet are black. The strokes they give with their wings in defending themselves, are accompanied with such force that they bruise the flesh where the blow lights. The bustards are likewise armed with a spur of the same kind. I received a blow upon my hand from one that was even mortally wounded with shot. I felt a very acute pain for a full quarter of an hour, and the mark of the bruise remained more than two days.

The wild Ducks, which are here very common, are like those of France, but not near so good; having, in general, the taste of muscles: but the Teal and the Divers, which are no less numerous, are excellent.

There are likewise found prodigious numbers of another species of Divers which are tolerably good, though they have rather an oily taste. Our seamen called them at first *Becfics*, and afterwards *Coyons* and *Nigauts*, because they suffered themselves to be killed with stones, not attempting to fly away unless they were hit. They assemble in flocks upon the rocks near the sea-coast; sometimes to the number of an hundred and upwards. When

we

we went on fhore in the floop, feveral companies of them, confifting of two or three hundred, paffed only eight or ten feet above our heads. There are three kinds of them; all nearly of the fame fize. Some are quite black; in others the fore-part of the neck and all the belly is white: in the third kind, the belly and breaft is white, and the reft black. Their bill, which is of the fame length as their head, is black and fharp, like that of birds which are not aquatic. Their feet are of a dark grey and webbed; but inftead of four toes, they are only furnifhed with three, which differ in fhape from thofe of other water-fowl. See the Plate. Our feamen preferred them to wild ducks; and indeed they had not near fo difagreeable a tafte.

Red-fhanks and fea-pies are very good here; but the buftards in particular are exquifite, either boiled, roafted, or fricaffeed. It appeared from the account we kept that we ate fifteen hundred. It is indeed hardly to be conceived, that the fhip's company of our two frigates, confifting of an hundred and fifty men, all in perfect health, and with good ftomachs, fhould have found a quantity of thefe birds fufficient for their fubfiftence during a ftay of more than two months, within a tract of country not exceeding three leagues.

Thefe are almoft all the kinds of animals we faw in that part of the ifland where we fixed our encampment, except two or three kinds of fmall birds, fome of which refemble the Sifkin, others the linnet; and a kind of wagtail that has not fo long a tail nor fuch darkifh ftripes as thofe of France. There is likewife found a kind of white gull, and a carnivorous bird of the fize of a common hen, with reddifh grey plumage. The people on board called them grey gulls. They came very near us, and, when we were in purfuit of game, flew fo clofe to our heads that more than once they fwept off the caps and hats of our people. They make a noife much like a duck; and though they are water-fowl their feet are not webbed; but they feize their prey voracioufly, by means of the very fharp talons with which their toes are armed; and when their prey is either not large

enough

enough to support upon the surface, or too heavy for them to carry off, they tear it in pieces with their beak and talons, flapping their wings all the time. They settle however upon the water, and remain upon it like ducks, but I never saw any of them dive. Nobody thought it worth while to shoot them, concluding they would be very bad eating.

A small heron with a crown is likewise found here, whose feathers are of an ash-coloured bluish grey: the crown is composed of three white feathers three inches long, resembling in shape the crown of the peacock. Upon the breast, round the neck, under the wings, on the lower part of the back, and under the thighs, there is a down, part white and part of a citron coloured yellow, at least an inch long, exactly resembling a piece of the finest raw silk.

In the second voyage we saw some paroquetes, and a kind of swan with a red bill, the whole neck being of a most beautiful black, and the rest of the plumage white.

The climate and the air appear to be so wholesome, that all the persons we left behind remained on the island of their own accord, and live under the same roof, in the apartments provided for them in the building erected near Fort St. Louis; where they will subsist as well by shooting, as on the provisions with which their magazine is plentifully stored for two years. One of the two Acadian families which we carried over consists of the husband, his wife, two children, one a boy three years and an half old, the other a girl about a year old, and of two young women, sisters of the mother, the eldest nineteen, and the youngest eighteen. The other family consists of the husband, his wife, who is pregnant and ready to lie in, a son four years old, and the mother's sister, a girl of sixteen.

There remain here all kinds of artificers, as smiths, ironmongers, carpenters, joiners, masons, bricklayers, shoemakers, bakers, a captain of a ship, sailors, &c. The soil is very promising, and it is very probable that these artificers will make good use of the tools and seeds of all kinds that were left them, and that this colony will flourish, if the miniftry make a point of improving it. Befides provifions, we left feven heifers and two young bulls, eight hogs and two boars, a few fheep, a goat, two horfes and a mare, which range about the country.

We faw no kinds of reptiles or noxious infects here, only fome fmall common flies, fome fmall field fpiders called *Spinners*. There is no kind of quadruped except the fmall wolf or fox I have mentioned. This will not be furprifing if we recollect that travellers affure us, that no reptiles or infects are found in the fouthern part of Chili, which is pretty nearly in the fame latitude with, and almoft oppofite to the Malouine Iflands. See the chart of the coaft which we made a furvey of from our place of landing on the three iflands, which we took at firft to be the Sebalds, to the port or eaftern bay where we anchored.

In the fecond and third voyages the fhips, in returning from the ftreights of Magellan, failed along the fouthern coaft of thefe iflands, as it will be defcribed in the extract of the journals of M. Alexander Guyot, and M. de Bougainville; and they have made a chart of it, which is given in the plates.

On Tuefday the 10th of April, we perceived feveral whales and a great number of birds, among which were fome Petterils, called *Damiers*, or chefs-boards, on account of their plumage being chequered with black and white. The head and part of the neck, likewife the tip and middle of the wings, are black; the reft of the body is not white, though it appears to be fo at the diftance of piftol-fhot. On a nearer view you find that the extremity of the wings is black; they have the appearance of round fcales edged with black. It is of the fize of a large pigeon. As we had now very frefh gales, the rolling was fo conftant and violent, that it was impoffible to keep the difhes upon the table without holding them, and every perfon was obliged to have his plate in one hand and his fork in the other.

Notwith-

Notwithstanding every possible precaution, a soup-dish, some plates and drinking-glasses were broken at dinner. These rollings were so violent in the night-time, that those who did not lie in cots or hammocks, could not rest in their beds.

On the 11th, the same weather continued all the morning. In the afternoon we saw several birds and whales. We were still so excessively rocked with the rollings, that it was almost impossible to keep the deck. We saw a quantity of birds, and a very large whale, which accompanied the ship for a considerable time, at the distance of a musket-shot.

On the 14th, we saw a number of grey sea-mews, and some Quebrante-Uessos.

From the 14th to the 24th, nothing remarkable happened: but on this day, soon after seven in the morning, we saw a flying fish by some called *Adonis*, but for what reason I cannot say. There are several kinds of them. Some are distinguished by the colour, others by the length of their fins which serve them as wings. There is a third kind with four wings instead of two, which is the usual number. None of those we caught between the tropics had more than two wings, some of a larger, others of a smaller size. They were all of a fine deep blue, silvered over on the back to half the breadth of their body, and the whole belly was of a very bright blue, silvered over in the same manner. The largest of them which fell into our frigate was eight inches in length, including the head and tail. In some the wings were only two inches long, in others they extended as far as the tail.

Few animals have so many enemies as the flying fish. They spring out of the sea to escape being devoured by thunnies, bonitos, sharks, &c. and in the air meet with birds that are always upon the watch for them. They rise so high above the water that they strike against the sails and shrouds of ships into which they fall: and this is the only way of catching them. Their flesh is good and delicate. You see them spring out of the water by hundreds like flocks of larks, at which time their wings make them appear white.

On the 25th in the morning, we passed the Tropic of Capricorn, and entered a calm and warm climate. Accordingly last Sunday, which was Easter-day, we all put on our lighter clothing.

On the 27th, we spied land before us, and steered N. E. ¼ N. then directed our course so as to pass within half a league of it. At half an hour past six we found by observation that this land was the island of Ascension, which appeared to us as described in the plate. We computed its distance at about six leagues. As we approached this island, it appeared to me to be composed of several rocks joined together, or of a single rock having different summits, between which there was a little earth or sand, covered here and there with some herbage, which gives a little verdure to the sloping declivity which runs down to the sea on the side towards the N. E. and E. N. E. At half an hour past nine, several of our people fancied they saw trees, but on taking an accurate view of the whole with perspective glasses, we concluded that what had the appearance of trees was nothing more than broom or shrubs. At the bottom of the declivity just now mentioned, you see a kind of sandy flat, slightly covered with verdure, upon the coast and to the N. N. E. of the island. At half an hour past eight, we were at two leagues distance or thereabouts.

At eight o'clock, we discovered another island to the E. ¼ N. E. about six leagues from the island of Ascension; three small islands soon after appeared close to the last discovered one.

This island, with the islets about it, might probably be the same that some seamen passing too far eastward, and not seeing the island of Ascension, have called Trinity island; since many navigators pretend that the island of Ascension, and Trinity island are one and the same; at least an island, and three rocks or islets, are found E. ¼ N. E. of that of Ascension, as they are laid down in the charts. This island of the Trinity

Trinity will then be the largest, or rather the largest of the four islets I have been describing. Indeed the latitude in which Trinity island is placed, and the latitude of Ascension, would not be found to coincide: but the charts, which are so faulty in placing other islands, may possibly be mistaken in the position of these. The largest of the islets, which I took for Trinity island, was seen by us at the distance of five leagues or thereabouts, but appeared less extensive than the island of Ascension, when observed at the same distance. The two islets, or rocks, at first view had greatly the appearance of ships under sail.

We passed between these two islands without altering our course; and saw nothing but steep rocks, several of which appeared almost perpendicular. We saw no inhabitants but sea-fowl. As we coasted so near the land, we should have seen some tortoises if there had been any in these islands. One of these animals, a foot or rather less at its longest diameter, passed alongside our frigate four days before: but we were then at too great a distance from these islands to think it probable that it came from thence.

On Sunday the 29th, in the morning, we saw some flying-fish; some birds called *Taylor Birds*, others called *Frigates*, and some Tropic birds, called *Paille-en-Cul*, or otherwise *Flèche-en-Cul* and *Fétu-en-Cul*. The sailors, who name things according to their ideas, give the bird this name on account of the two feathers of its tail which are very long. Some of this kind, which hovered over our ship for a considerable time, appeared to be of the size of a pretty large red partridge. The Tropic bird has a small well-shaped head; its bill is about three inches long, pretty thick and strong, rather crooked, but pointed and red like its feet, which are webbed. The wings are very large in proportion to the body; and indeed this bird flies very well and to a great height. It makes excursions three or four hundred leagues from land, rests upon the water, and lives upon fish.

Its

Its plumage appears to be intirely white. Our seamen who have had a near view of it affure me, that it is variegated with white and blue. The tail confifts of twelve or fifteen feathers from five to fix inches long. The two middle ones, which are from fifteen to eighteen, are joined in such a manner that they appear to be one.

Some of our officers who had been at the ifland of Mauritius, or the ifle of France, communicated to me a fingular obfervation they made there, that the Tropic birds never appeared in the port of that ifland, except on the very day, or about twelve hours before the arrival of fome French veffel. Accordingly, when one of thefe birds is feen, the inhabitants are in a manner certain that a fhip will come into port foon after.

On the 4th, 5th, and 6th, we faw many flying fifh; and on the 8th, a great number of porpoifes paffed very near our veffel; we endeavoured to harpoon them, but without fuccefs.

On Thurfday the 10th, in the evening, we caught a fhark, faw a quantity of porpoifes, fome thunnies, and feveral bonitos.

On Friday the 11th, at fix in the morning, we caught a fhark. We attempted to catch fome thunnies with the lofs of two hooks, which were thicker than the barrel of a goofe-quill. One of thefe thunnies broke two of them which were faftened to the fame line. The bonitos would not bite.

On the 12th, we caught one porpoife among a prodigious number, and a fhark; at three o'clock we caught a bonito, in the belly of which was found a fifh called *Cornet*, which it had probably juft then fwallowed, as it was ftill intire, and preferved its natural colours. I immediately made a drawing of it, reprefented in the plate.

The reader muft not form his idea of the fize of this fifh from the figure I have given of it. In the opinion of the feamen who frequent the South Sea, the *Cornet* is the largeft of all fea-fifh. It feizes its prey by the affiftance of the moveable claws at the end of its fnout. Thefe feamen likewife tell us, that faftening upon, and catching hold of fhips with thefe claws,

claws, it climbs along the tackling: that if it does this in the night-time unperceived, its enormous weight throws the ship so much upon her side that she is in danger of being overset. They accordingly take great care to keep a good look-out, with hatchets, and other sharp instruments to cut the claws of this fish, as soon as they see them fastened upon the ship. Our captain, and his brother Alexander Guyot, who have made several voyages in the South Sea, confirm this account; but add,. that they never saw any of such an immoderate size, that they have tasted some that weighed an hundred and fifty pounds, and had an excellent flavour. If one may judge of them by the small one described in the plate, they must be very delicate. The scales of this fish, which are a kind of sheath to it, as well as the fish itself, were almost transparent.

On Sunday the 13th, we continued to see a great number of porpoises all the morning, and a large shark which would not take the bait.

On the morning of the 14th, we saw several bonitos, thunnies, and a great number of flying fish, several of which falling into the ship made an excellent dish for dinner.

On the 15th, about four o'clock, we caught two thunnies, and two bonitos with the harpoon.

The thunny is a fish well known in the Mediterranean. But whether the description which M. Valmont de Bomare gives of it, in his dictionary of natural history written on the plan of Lemery's, is not exact, or whether the fish whose figure I give in the plate is not the thunny, or whether the thunny caught between the tropics differs from that of the Mediterranean, it does not agree with M. Valmont's description. In those we caught; the scales are neither large nor broad, nor the back of a blackish cast, but of a fine deep blue, which brightens insensibly towards the fins, which are shaped like scythes, and placed near the gills. These two fins, as well as the two smaller at the bottom of the belly, are of a very deep grey, or bluish black, inclining to grey. That on the back, and the two on the belly,

situated

situated at about two-thirds of the length of the body, are of a gold colour, as well as some parts resembling the teeth of a saw and extending from the fins to the tail, which is arched. On the outside, their gills do not appear to be double. Their snout, which is not thick, is pointed, and has small teeth that are very sharp. M. Valmont says, that this fish dies soon after it is out of the water. That which I delineated, lived near half an hour hung up by the tail near the main-mast. It would probably have lived much longer, if, by struggling to disengage itself, it had not disgorged its heart, which fell upon deck in my presence, and on taking it into my hand continued its palpitation near a quarter of an hour. In voiding it, it discharged a great quantity of blood through its gullet, some drops of which I have represented upon the surface of the lower jaw. Its flesh is something like veal; but drier and more firm.

The bonito is a large fish; its figure from the head to three-fourths of its length is round; from thence it begins to grow flatter, and terminates in a pretty thick tail, which is forked, and like that of other fishes. As it has little or no neck, it has two fins which are pretty long, but not broad in proportion to the bulk of the bonito. On the back is a fin, which, as it approaches towards the tail, seems to form there, as well as on the opposite part under the belly, triangular projections of a gold colour. On each side are placed two other fins of a blue colour, terminating in a point at the tail. Two small fins appear under the belly. The back is of a very deep blue, which grows brighter towards the middle of the body. The belly is white with a cast of greenish yellow, and is variegated with several stripes of a greyish colour, which seem to be blended together promiscuously. The eye is large, and has a circle of gold round the pupil. Its head is not so long as that of the thunny. It is necessary to lard it well, as its flesh is very dry. See the plate.

These fish always appear in shoals; the sea sometimes seems to be intirely covered with them. They are caught with the spear, or a hook baited with an artificial flying-fish. The flesh

of

of the bonito, which is taken on the coasts of the kingdom of Angola, is said to be hurtful. In the middle of the flesh of some we found some live worms. They were white, of the thickness of the barrel of the feathers in a hen's wing, and about four lines in length.

On the evening of the 25th, we again met with some sea-grass, which the seamen call *Goemon à grappes de raisin*. I have already observed, that the seeds with which it abounds are small bladders, of the size of the largest swan-shot. They are not collected into separate clusters, but dispersed over the stems and branches. When the seeds grow dry, they dwindle to the size of a middling pin's head. The leaves which are very small, almost like those of parsley piert, become brittle. Some of the stems, and a great number of the seeds, are incrusted with a very small kind of shell, or spawn of fish, which is white and hard, and when rubbed against wood, acts as a file, or the herb called shave-grass.

On the 26th, in the morning we saw such a prodigious quantity of the sea-grass I have been speaking of, that the sea was almost covered with it. Among some large bundles of it, we found crabs of different sizes, of a light red, marked with brown spots. They have eight feet, and two claws. The body, or cuirass, is almost square on the side of the head. The eyes project from the extremity of the two angles that form this square. See the plate.

Several beds of this sea-grass, some of which were almost as broad as our vessel, and longer, passed close to our frigate. They are said to come from the coasts of the Canary Islands; others pretend that they are dislodged from the bottom of the sea. This opinion seems to be the most probable, since all the Canary Islands could hardly produce the prodigious quantity which appeared for fourteen or fifteen days past.

On the 31st, in the morning, being Ascension-day, the weather being calm, after saying mass we seized this opportunity of scraping and breaming the vessel. At four in the afternoon we saw

saw a sail which seemed to be steering W. N. W. at the distance of about six leagues. We lost sight of it at night.

On Sunday, the 3d of June, the sea-grass, which had not been seen for a day or two, appeared again in large quantities, and a whale of middle size played round the ship a quarter of an hour, at the distance of gun-shot.

A few days after we saw a bird, which our seamen call *Equéret*, and another called the tailor-bird hovered about our vessel.

On the 13th, we caught a fish with our drag-net called *Grande Oreille*. It resembles the bonito in every particular except the two fins, which are situated near the gills. These fins are falciform, and are at least as large as those of the thunny. Its flesh is not so dry.

On the 15th, at five in the morning, we discovered a sail bearing N. W. of us, which appeared to steer the same course. Upon this we clued up our sails, hoisted our flag and broad-pendant, and made a signal by firing a gun. After sailing as near the wind as possible, in order to wait for her, she likewise hauled the wind, and continued at two cannon-shot or thereabouts to windward. Concluding that they did not hear the first gun, we fired another to windward; when they displayed a flag of peace, and fired a gun. Perceiving afterwards that they took no further notice, we hoisted the ensign with a waft; which she equally disregarded, and always kept to windward nearly at the same distance. As she sailed at least as well as our ship, she doubtless depended upon her sailing. We resolved to give over the chace, as it would have diverted us from our course.

The French Captain could not make any proper excuse for disobeying the King's regulations respecting the marine, by which every ship belonging to the nation is obliged to bring to, when a King's ship gives the signal by firing a gun, and hoisting the broad-pendant on the proper mast, according to the rank of the commander. We went still farther, by hoisting the ensign with a waft, which is a signal of distress agreed upon by all civilized nations.

This

This proceeding therefore, for this reason at least, deserves the highest censure; and sets a very bad precedent. Had we unfortunately been in actual danger, he would have suffered us to perish before his eyes, without giving us that assistance which the laws of humanity require in such circumstances.

The royal navy has ever been jealous of the trading branch. The former entertains prejudices which set it above the seamen's employment, and does not think practice necessary to attain a knowledge of it. The latter, inured to the hardships and fatigues of sea, justly concludes that to excel in the nautic art, requires the practice of a whole life. Hence that party-spirit of which the state becomes the first victim, since the liberty of the Reds, or officers of the royal navy, occasions the servitude of the Blues. If we look into the annals of the last war, we shall find French privateers whose courage and intrepidity seemed to rouse the winds to fight on their side. Could it be believed that a Captain of a vessel (M. de L.) was a calm spectator of an engagement between a French snow and an English privateer, and contented himself with commending the conduct of the Frenchman, who, attentive to every particular, exerted every effort of skill and personal bravery, to prevent the enemy from boarding him. In short he saw her dismasted, and obliged to strike, without firing a gun in her defence. How easy was it for the Commander of a ship of the line well armed to save the brave Captain of the merchantman, and to make himself master of the English privateer! It is plain then that he remained inactive only because it is not the mode to waste any powder to promote the commerce of the nation, or protect a privateer belonging to a good citizen.

It may be urged, in excuse for the conduct of the Captain of the French trading vessel, in not bringing to even when we hoisted our flag of distress, that having probably no more provisions and rigging than were sufficient for his own use, he apprehended that, if we should happen to be in want of them, we should seize his stores by force, if he refused to grant us a voluntary supply. This is an abuse too common in the royal navy, and has given much offence to the trading branch: which, finding itself despised and ill-treated, is glad of every opportunity to retaliate; and I dare say would take some kind of pleasure in their destruction, in hopes of being released by it from the tyranny they experience from the royal navy. It would be for the interest of the state if matters were so precisely regulated by the royal authority, that no person of either party should transgress the order on any pretence whatsoever, but should be punished with the utmost severity. While this animosity, perpetuated by the contempt which the royal navy expresses for the trading branch, and by the abuse of its power, continues to subsist between these two bodies of men, the state must unavoidably be exposed to very great inconveniencies.

We are not disposed to follow the example of others, nor is any one inclined to follow ours. This spirit of singularity, which runs through all our conduct, always tends to our destruction. We imitate the Romans, who employed only their freedmen in maritime affairs, and confined the land service to the patricians. The English have better notions: among them the profession of a sailor is in great esteem; and is the noblest of all the arts, because it is exercised by the principal nobility in the kingdom. The French indeed differ from the Romans, not for the sake of imitating the English, but in order to gratify a number of interested individuals, whose opinion very improperly passes for that of the nation. In France the art of navigation is esteemed a vulgar employment, though the command of ships of the line is a post of honour which can only be filled by a person who is actually a man of some family. Accordingly there is more parade than science or connection in our navy; there is more shew than real skill in our officers, and at the same time their emoluments are not adequate to their expences. In London, the idea of merit and reward is not regulated by fashion and court-influence, but by the good of the state. Nothing is regarded but merit in a sailor whatever his condition may be. If he is a good seaman he is every thing, he is considered as a useful man, is employed

in

in honourable stations, and is rewarded in proportion to his services. It were much to be wished that we would think, or rather act, in the same manner. Virtue and merit ought to be the foundation of true nobility.

This is the source of that spirit of party which is a disgrace to the Reds, an injury to the Blues, and the misfortune of the French government.

The reader, I am persuaded, will excuse this digression, as it is dictated solely by my zeal for the public good, and the love I bear my country. It is certain, notwithstanding the rivalship subsisting between the two nations, that an English Commander would have been so far from acting like the French Captain, that he would have made what haste he could to join us, and to give us all the assistance in his power: which conduct ever ought to be observed between all nations without distinction. We went up to and offered our assistance to the Captain of a Dutch vessel, we had met in October last, which had lost her masts.

On the 16th we saw several whales, and a kind of thornback, which our seamen call *Rouet*. We kept sight of the French ship before mentioned both yesterday and to-day: it continued the same course from the E. ¼ N. E. at the distance of about three leagues from us, and we had proceeded about as far in our course.

On the 18th, at half past five in the morning, we spied a sail coming from the Eastward. At eight it came abreast of us, and we spoke with it. It was the St. Paul de Grandville, Captain Desveau, bound to Newfoundland.

On the 20th and 22d we saw several ships; and on Sunday evening the 24th we steered S. E. ¼ E. with a gentle breeze from N. N. W. to W. N. W. in order to observe the land, which we saw at six in the evening.

On Monday morning, the 25th, we heard the clocks of St. Paul de Leon at seven, being N. and S. of the Isle de Bas; we hoisted our flag, and fired a gun for a boat to come to us, which foon arrived, and carried Meffrs. de Bougainville and l'Huillier de la Serre to Morlaix. The frigate proceeded to St. Malo. At eleven at night we dropt an anchor oppofite the tower of Cape Frehel, the beacon being about a league N. W. ¼ W. of us.

On the 26th, at half paft three in the morning, we got under fail, and about feven came to our moorings in Solidor, where the veffel was difcharged. M. de Bougainville having given the King an account of our expedition, his Majefty ratified the taking poffeffion of the Malouine Iflands, and immediately iffued orders for the Eagle to be got ready to return to thefe iflands.

OBSERVATIONS

# OBSERVATIONS
## ON THE
## STREIGHTS of MAGELLAN,
### AND ON THE
## PATAGONIANS.

THE King of France having approved of the poſſeſſion we had taken in his name of all the Malouine Iſlands, the miniſtry iſſued out orders for the ſupport and improvement of the little eſtabliſhment we had formed there. The Eagle frigate was again fitted out, and M. Alexander Duclos Guyot, who had been ſecond captain in the firſt voyage, was made firſt captain in the ſecond, with the brevet of Lieutenant of a frigate, under the command of M. de Bougainville. Being informed of M. Duclos's ſafe return to St. Malo, and deſirous of knowing in what ſtate he had left the new colony, and what diſcoveries he might have made in the Streights of Magellan, I wrote to him to beg he would inform me of theſe particulars; and received the following anſwer:

"I waited to know what ſervice I ſhould be appointed to, before I did myſelf the honour of anſwering your letter; and therefore begin by acquainting you, that we ſhall ſet out from hence on the 10th or 15th inſtant, for the Malouine Iſlands. But I ſhall firſt put into the Madeiras, to take in wine, and other refreſhments. From thence I ſhall proceed to Port Deſire, on the Patagonian coaſt, to take a view of the country; and then go on to our colony, where after having unladen my proviſions, and landed all my paſſengers, I ſhall return to the

Streights

Streights of Magellan, to fetch a cargo of wood; after which I shall wait for fresh orders from France. This is my destination: M. de la Gyraudais sets out from Rochfort, with a frigate laden with provisions necessary for the colony.

You desire an account of my last voyage, which I shall now give you. We set out from St. Malo on the 5th of October 1765. We had in all on board the Eagle frigate 116 men, 53 of which were workmen, or officers going as passengers to the colony. Among the latter were M. de Perriers, a half-pay captain of the regiment of la Sare; M. Thibé de Belcourt, a half-pay captain of the regiment Dauphin; M. Denis de St. Simon, captain adjutant of the colonies; M. l'Huillier de la Serre, geographical engineer; M. de Romainville, lieutenant of infantry and engineer.

For the first fortnight, we had bad weather and contrary winds. On Sunday the 5th of November, we had a prospect of the Cape Verd Islands. On Monday we passed by the islands of Fogo and Bravo. We did not meet with much storm in crossing the line, any more than under the tropics; and on Saturday the 16th of December, we came within sight of the coast of Brazil, in 31 degrees 30 minutes South latitude, though we thought ourselves, as it commonly happens, still wide of it, from a defect in the charts, which you know throw this coast too far back westward.

We stayed afterwards some time searching for Pepy's island, where it is marked in the charts, and in the neighbourhood, without being able to find it. On Thursday the 3d of January, we had a prospect of the Malouine Islands, and made to land at the Islet, which in our first voyage we called *la Conchée*. On Saturday the fifth instant, we sailed in, and cast anchor at the distance of half a mile from the mouth of the small bay of the colony; where we found every body in good health. We continued unlading till the first of February, when we were ready to set sail. On Sunday the 27th, we had discovered three vessels coming from the West. On the 2d of February, seeing that

they

they did not come into the bay, we set sail for the Streights of Magellan. The weather was rather changeable during our passage. On Tuesday the 12th of February, we had a prospect of Cape Lookout, on the Patagonian coast. After having tacked about, we found ourselves within cannon shot of a lurking rock as large as our longboat, which we had a great deal of trouble to get clear of, on account of the currents, and the roughness of the sea. This rock is not pointed out in our charts. On Saturday the 16th we observed three vessels steering the same course that we did. On the 17th we entered the Streights of Magellan, together with the three ships. On Monday the 18th, one of the three ships working to windward while we were at anchor, she struck on a sand bank. The weather was very fine. We sent our boats to her assistance, with an officer, with anchors and cables; but she soon disengaged herself, and got off without injury. We then found out that they were English *.

On

---

* This was in reality Commodore Byron's small squadron. The fact is told in the printed account of his voyage round the world, in the following terms: "At four in the afternoon, the master of the storeship *(the Florida)* came on board the Dolphin, bringing a packet from the Lords of the Admiralty to the Commodore.—He had likewise been several days in search of Pepys's island, but was like us obliged to desist.—To our great surprize in the morning of the second day, after we left the harbour in company with the Tamer and storeship, we discovered a strange sail, which indeed put us into no small consternation. The Commodore was inclined to believe, that this ship was a Spanish man of war of the line, who having got intelligence of our voyage, was come to intercept us; and in consequence of that surmise, boldly gave orders, that all on board the Dolphin and Tamer should prepare for a warm reception, by firing all our guns, and then boarding her from both ships; but while we were bringing to, and waiting for her, we found it grew dark, and we soon lost sight of her till the next morning, when we saw her at anchor, at three leagues distance, and therefore continued sailing towards Port Famine. We however found that she still followed us, though at a great distance, and even came to an anchor when we did. On the 20th we were chiefly employed in getting up our guns; we soon got fourteen upon the deck, and then came to an anchor, having the Tamer astern, with a spring on our cable.

Thus busily were we employed in taking all the measures prudence could suggest, to defend us from an imaginary danger; when an unlucky accident, which happened to the storeship, shewed that we had nothing to fear, and that the vessel, against which we were arming ourselves, ought not to be considered as an enemy;

On Wednesday the 20th, the English anchored in Port Famine, and we sailed on till the 21st, when we cast anchor at the distance of five leagues from the English, and called the place the Eagle's bay, as it has no name on the charts. The next day, being the 22d, M. de Bougainville discovering a very fine bay or port, at the distance of one league and a half to the South, we went there and fastened the ship to four trees very much under shelter, at the distance of a league from the French bay: We called it Bougainville bay. We took in some very fine wood here and shipped it conveniently, by hauling on board with a hawser the wood cut upon the shore. We stayed here till the 16th of March, it being all the time very fine weather. On the 25th of February, two English vessels, going to the South Seas, passed by us. On the 16th of March in the morning, after having left a French flag, hoisted upon a hut, and several cloaths, kettles, hatchets, and other utensils necessary for the savages, we set sail. After having gone a league a calm came on, and we cast our anchor in Eagle's bay. On the 17th it being calm, M. de Bougainville met some of the savages as he was out a shooting. He went up to them, and they appeared very gentle. On Tuesday the 19th we set sail again; and on the 20th in the morning, the wind being against us, we anchored in Port Famine. On the 21st in the morning, some of the savages calling out to us, we went up to them. They expressed a great desire of coming on board: we therefore took six of them along with us, whom we entertained, and who did not appear to be much surprized. They are a set of men much like

enemy; for while the storeship was working to the windward, she took the shore on a bank about two leagues from our ship. About the same time, the strange ship came up with her, cast anchor, and immediately began to hoist out her long-boats, to give her assistance. But before they had come to the storeship, our own boats had boarded her, and the commanding officer had received orders not to let them come on board, but to thank them in the politest manner for their intended assistance. We afterwards found this to be a French vessel; and having no guns that we could see, supposed it to be a merchantman, who had come to those parts for wood and water.—On the 21st we got into Port Famine, where we moored our ships."

like the Indians of Mon o, ha no o er dreſs than the ſkins of Sea-Wolves, Gu es, ar Vicunas; they appear very poor, have no taſte for e, but are very fond of fat. We dreſſed them in red cloaths, and gave them ſeveral neceſſary domeſtic utenſils; we then accompanied them to land; crying out all the way *Vive le Roi de France*, which they repeated after us very well. We left a flag diſplayed. They expreſſe much good-will towards us, giving us their bows and arrows. When we ſaw them they were painted white, and in ſpots, but as ſoon as we had given them ſome red lead, not cinnaber vermillion, they immediately painted themſelves with it; and ſeemed to be fond of this colour. As we were returning to the ſhip, they ſaluted us with *Vive le Roi* in French, having remembered that expreſſion; and then they hollowed after their own manner, ſtanding all round the flag. As we got farther from them, they raiſed their ſhouts, and increaſed their fires.

This is nearly all I can tell you of theſe inhabitants of Patagonia. We did not land on the Terra del Fuego. I believe theſe are nearly the ſame kind of people as thoſe who croſs the Streights, in their canoes made of the bark of a tree. The firſt time we ſaw them, they had kinds of hatchets; but they took care to conceal them afterwards, as well as their wives and children.

At length, on Saturday the 23d of March, we ſailed out of that famous ſtreight ſo much dreaded, after having experienced there, as well as in other places, that it was very fine and very warm; and that three-fourths of the time the ſea was perfectly calm.

It is remarkable that the ſea ebbs as it enters on the northern ſide: we had a proof of this every day: in the middle the currents are diſtinguiſhable, but in the narroweſt parts of the entrance they are very ſtrong; they run at leaſt two leagues and a half, and ſink about four fathoms.

There is no wood at the entrance of the Streights, neither on one ſide nor the other. There are nothing but immenſe plains.

About

About four and twenty leagues up the country, both on the coast of Patagonia, and on the Terra del Fuego, the woods begin. We found very little game, and that much followed by the natives, very little fish, and in the places where we had been, none of those beautiful shell fish so much admired.

At length we steered our course in order to pass to the South of the Danicant islands. On Tuesday the 26th, we came within sight of land, which was the country to the West of the Malouine Islands, about fourscore leagues distant from Cape Virgin, which forms the entrance of the Streights. We afterwards sailed fifty leagues to come back to cast anchor in the port; so that we may reckon that we had passed by fifty leagues of the coast to the southward, which is not however its greatest length, as there is a streight which divides the North and South lands without any woods. On the 29th of March we cast anchor in the same place where we did before, having almost always had fine weather. We unladed our wood, and on the 27th of April we set sail for France, leaving 79 persons in the Malouine Islands. Our passage was rather tedious, by reason of the calm weather which obliged us to put into harbour, on account of the few provisions we had remaining, having left as many as we could behind us. On the 18th of July we put into the harbour at Angra in the island of Tercera, where we supplied ourselves with plenty of every thing, having found there all we wanted. On the 25th we left this harbour, and on the 13th of August arrived at St. Malo.

I am, SIR,

St. Malo,
1st September, 1765.

Your very humble Servant,

ALEXANDER DUCLOS GUYOT.

I was

I was not at Paris when M. de Bougainville returned, being gone to Montbrifon in Forez. He fent me the following letter, which M. de Bougainville de Nerville his coufin, who was left commander at the Malouine Iflands, had commiffioned him to deliver to me. It was accompanied with a letter from him, which I fhall give at the end of this.

If I had thought, Sir, you would have had the complaifance to go and keep my mother company in her folitude, I fhould not have omitted mentioning you to her, and defiring that favour of you. She fays fo many handfome things of you, and you fpeak fo well of her, that I have reafon to conclude you equally fatisfied with each other. I am very glad to find that her company is fo agreeable to you, and at the fame time am much flattered in thinking myfelf fometimes the fubject of your converfation.

I fhall now fay fomething to you about our fituation. I have nothing particular to tell you about the winter we paffed here. It has not been fevere; for there never was fnow enough to cover one's fhoe-buckles, nor a fufficient depth of ice to fupport a ftone as big as one's fift; and if it had not been for the rain, which runs through our tents as through a fieve, we fhould have had very little occafion for fire, which we were now obliged to make in order to dry ourfelves. You would not have known our colony again had you returned with M. de Bougainville. In the firft place you would have found us all very fat, the air being very healthy. You would have found all along the place where we live a fine walk of fmooth even ground, and upwards of twenty feet wide; a new magazine raifed again upon the border of the fea; a fort completely repaired placed on a level, with platforms made with flat ftones under the cannons; a new powder magazine, a bakehoufe, and a forge. By the account we kept, we killed above 1500 buftards in the feafon; for there is a time when they leave this country and go away to other parts, except a few ftraggling pairs whofe eggs we never could find; but only their young ones which were always fix in number.

One brood of these was brought me, and was taken care of by one of our hens as her own. I was in hopes of sending them to France, but since my cousin's arrival here, they have experienced a number of evils, and have at length all perished by the mischievous tricks of the ship-boys who came to land: so that I must put this off till another season. We have made the discovery of a bird much more beautiful than the bustard, which is a kind of swan, as large and as white, but whose neck is as black as jet, and his bill red. We have not been able to kill any of them, as they are extremely wild. By other discoveries which I have made in the island more than twenty leagues to the West, it appears that the part we dwell in is detached from other adjacent islands, or joined only by an Isthmus. We may perhaps come at the true knowledge of this by means of the schooner which is to be left with us. The study of natural history, which we have not neglected, has furnished us with several of those conchæ called *Poulettes*, or *Gueule de Raye*.

There are few of those you sent me the drawings of to be found in good preservation. The Patellæ, you know, are common here. We have great expectation from our agriculture, our kitchen garden having succeeded very well. With regard to the corn, it produced in the dry land some beautiful ears; but they were fine only in appearance, having no grain within them. Our lands having been yet unsown require a longer time for cultivation, and must even be improved with good dung. We have not a sufficient quantity of beasts to make any trials with them. Four of our heifers and our three horses are always in the open field; and we have never been able to catch them again, but their wandering disposition has made us acquainted with one of the great advantages of this country: which is, that cattle may remain in all seasons, day and night, in the open fields, without being in want of either pasture or litter. We often meet with one or other of them when we go out a shooting; they are as fat as hogs, and their liberty seems to agree very well with them. I return you many thanks for

the

the trouble you have taken in executing my commiſſions, and have received the things. I am making up a cheſt of the ſhells, ſeeds, and ſtones of this country; if you happen to be in the way when my couſin arrives he will ſhew them to you. They ſay you have put a ſhell into the cabinet of the Abbé of St. Germain, which is the only one of its kind. If that ſhell has been found here, be ſo kind as to ſend me a drawing of it.

From the Malouine Iſlands, 25th of April 1765.      DE NERVILLE.

The following is M. de Bougainville's letter.

I am at laſt returned, my dear fellow-traveller. At my arrival I found I ſhould not be able to ſee you, which gives me a great deal of concern. Be aſſured that no one intereſts himſelf more than I do in every thing that concerns you; and that I would have given any thing in the world, if you would have accompanied me in the ſecond voyage. We have made an alliance with the Patagonians, who have been ſo ill ſpoken of, and we have found them neither taller, nor even ſo wicked as other men. I ſend you a letter from my couſin, who has behaved admirably well. None of our people have ever been ſeized with a fever. The winter has neither been ſevere nor long, and the eſtabliſhment ſucceeds very well. I brought them this year my ſhip full of the fineſt wood in the world, which I had from my friends the Patagonians. I have not at preſent time to enter into any more particulars, having not a moment to loſe. I believe I am going to be ſent into Spain, to ſettle ſome things with that Court relative to our new eſtabliſhment. I beg you would let me hear from you,

Paris, Auguſt 26, 1755.      and am, &c.

DE BOUGAINVILLE.

M. de

M. de Bougainville was sent into Spain and settled matters between that Court and the Court of France, respecting the cession which the latter made to the Spanish of the Malouine Islands; and M. de Bougainville set out from Nantz in 1766, on board a French frigate, and went to Buenos Ayres, taking a Spanish Governor from thence, and some troops of the same nation, to put them in possession of the aforesaid islands. Before he went away, he communicated to me the observations he had made on the Streights of Magellan, together with a correct chart of these Streights, which is among the plates, as well as a chart of the East, North, and South coasts of the Malouine Islands, which they had passed by in going and coming back through these Streights. By this chart, one can judge only of the extent of the Malouine Islands to the North and South, the western part not having yet been discovered. The English who settled themselves in 1765 at Port Egmont, situated more to the West than the French establishment, may hereafter give us some informations with regard to those parts yet unknown.

M. Alexander Duclos Guyot, and M. Chenard de la Gyraudais, having communicated to me the journals of their voyage they made together to the Streights of Magellan in 1766, with leave to make extracts from them; I have thought necessary to give these to the public, as well on account of the useful observations they contain relative to currents, the nature of the sea, and the coasts which form the Streights, as to settle the doubts of many learned men and others, upon the real existence of the Patagonian giants.

Extract of the journal of M. Alexander Duclos Guyot, Lieutenant of a frigate, on board the Eagle frigate, in the Streights of Magellan, in 1766.

On the 24th of April, we set sail from Acarron bay at the Malouine Islands. On the 26th, one of the Sebald islands that
lies

STREIGHTS OF MAGELLAN.

lies moft to the North Weft, bore S. W. ¼ S. of us, diftance 40 miles.

On the 28th in the morning, we faw a great quantity of whales and pinguins. At noon Cape las Barréras bore Weft of us nine leagues.

On the firft of May, at half an hour paft feven, we fteered W. S. W. in order to have a view of the land of Patagonia. At nine o'clock, bearing round the bank which is at the entrance of the Streights of Magellan, the fea was changed, its waters being like thofe of a river made muddy by rains.

On Saturday the 3d of May, at eight o'clock, Cape Virgin bore N. N. ¼ N. W. three leagues and a half, or four leagues. The moft weftern part of the Terra del Fuego S. W. ¼ S. Cape Santo Spirito S. S. E. Cape Poffeffion W. ¼ S. W. I think there are not lefs than feven leagues from one point of land to another at the entrance of the Streights.

On Sunday the 4th, at break of day, we were about four leagues S. E. of Cape Poffeffion. There is a ridge of rocks and a fand bank near Cape Orange. It extends a great way, fo we were obliged to coaft the land of Patagonia. Here we faw a fire upon the fhore, and drawing nearer to it perceived fome men on horfeback, and many others on foot. When we came oppofite to them, they called out to us, but we did not underftand their language. We anfwered them with fhouts, and hoifted our flag. Five of them followed us about two leagues round the coaft, but night coming on we loft fight of them. They feemed to be good horfemen, managing their horfes well, which were very active.

We hardly perceived any currents in the narrows, where it was almoft a calm. This entrance in its narroweft part is a full league over. At five o'clock in the evening, we anchored in Boucaut bay, in nine fathoms and a half water, with a bottom of rotten fhells.

REMARKS

# REMARKS on the TIDES.

IN the laſt voyage, I had obſerved, when we came into the firſt narrows, that the tide was coming in, and I reckoned it was the beginning of flood. I did not however perceive on the ſhore that the ſea roſe conſiderably; at which I was the more ſurpriſed, as all ſailors agree in ſaying that it does; neither was the ſhore wet, as it generally is when the ſea retires. On coming out we were two hours and three quarters making ſeven or eight knots, without getting on half a league. When the current diminiſhed, and we had ſailed half-way up the Streight, I perceived on its banks that the water had juſt fallen at leaſt four fathoms perpendicular. This obſervation induced me to imagine that when it is flood the ſea goes out on the northern ſide; but on the contrary, when it is ebb, it comes in, and bears to the South.

When we went along Cape Orange, we perceived a very extenſive flat ſandy ſhore, which we took for the open ſea at coming in, being concealed, as all the ridges and banks of Cape Orange are, which we could not ſee. This confirms me in my opinion, which is contrary to the ſentiments of all thoſe who have ſailed in theſe Streights before me. This day the tide was coming out, and was againſt us for ſome time; nevertheleſs the tide was very high when it began to bear to the South.

Then all the banks and ridges were concealed, as well as the flat ſtrands, and ſhores which we had ſeen wet when we came out. I obſerved, that the tide bore in till nine o'clock. The ſea had then fallen four feet perpendicular: afterwards coming out again it roſe three fathoms; then there was a little interval without any ſtream, notwithſtanding which it ſtill roſe one fathom: afterwards the ſea took its courſe again, when it neither roſe nor fell while we went two-thirds of a league in an hour.

It

It afterwards fell without any current; which made me think the currents were not regular; and that in bays, the turn of the tide is caused by the swell. I suspend the determination of this point, till it is confirmed by farther observations.

We perceived about three o'clock in the afternoon, that the sea began to enter into the narrows, the Moon being 26 days old; which would make the situation of the narrows E. and W. so that it would be high water there at twelve minutes past six o'clock on the day of new and full moon.

On Tuesday the 6th, the savages appeared about nine o'clock in the morning, and were kindling a fire on the shore by the small river Baudran. We hoisted our flag, and M. de la Gyraudais his broad pendant. Afterwards we both put our yawl and longboat to sea with men armed with muskets and cutlasses. In M. de la Gyraudais's longboat was an officer with presents for the savages. In my yawl, we had seven sailors and three officers under the command of my brother. At eleven o'clock we saw them land, and some men on horseback who received them; which appeared to me a good omen of peace. Nothing particular happened till twelve o'clock.

My brothers account was, that the savages, who are natives of this country, were not the same as those we saw last year in Savage bay, and that they spoke a different language. There were six men and one woman, who had but six horses, each guarded by a dog who never leaves them.

They received our people very well, coming up to them to shew them where they should put into the shore and land. They did not appear surprised nor shew the least sign of emotion. We measured the shortest of them, and my brother found him 5 feet 7 inches high French measure. The rest were considerably taller. They were covered with the skins of deer, guanacoes, vicunas, otters, and other animals. Their arms are round stones, whose ends are lengthened out and pointed. The round part is fixed to the end of a string composed of several narrow straps, twisted and interwoven into a round form like

P p 2 the

the ſtring of a clock, and making a kind of ſling. At the other end of the ſtring is another ſtone in form of a pear, not more than half as big as the other, and appearing as if it was wrapt up in a bladder.

They uſe theſe weapons chiefly to catch animals; at which ſport they are very dextrous, as they ſhewed our people by an experiment made in their preſence. They have alſo other ſlings nearly of the ſame kind of conſtruction. They manage their horſes with great dexterity, and have a kind of ſaddle, very much like that we uſe for packhorſes. Theſe ſaddles are made with two pieces of wood, covered with leather and ſtuffed with ſtraw. The bit of the bridle is a ſmall ſtick, and the reins are twiſted as the ſtrings of their ſlings. They wear a kind of buſkins or half boots, of ſkin with the ſhag on, and two pieces of wood fitted to each ſide of the heel, joined together in a point, which ſerve them for ſpurs. Their breeches are very ſhort drawers, much reſembling thoſe of the ſavages of Canada, and are of a very good cut. It is evident they have had ſome intercourſe with the Spaniards, from their having a very thin two-edged knife, which they place between their legs. Their buſkins are made like thoſe of the Indians of Chili. They pronounced ſome words which were either Spaniſh, or derived from that language. On pointing out the perſon who ſeemed to be their chief, they called him *Capitan*. When they wanted to ſmoke and aſked for tobacco, they ſaid *Chupan*.

They ſmoke in the ſame manner as the inhabitants of Chili, throwing out the ſmoke by their noſtrils; and are extremely fond of a pipe. While they were ſmoking they cried *Buenos*, ſtriking themſelves upon the breaſt.

We gave them ſome new bread, and ſome ſea-biſcuit, which they eat with great appetite. The preſents we made them conſiſted in ſome pounds of that red which we call vermilion; and ſome red woollen caps, which however not one of them could put his head into: theſe caps though very large for heads of a
common

common fize, were ftill too fmall for them. We alfo gave them fome bedding, fome hatchets, fome kettles, and other utenfils.

My brother put his pocket-handkerchief round the neck of the chief; who having accepted of it, immediately loofened his girth, made of ftraps twifted together like the girth of a faddle, having at each extremity a ball of ftone half inclofed with leather. There was alfo another ftone fixt to the middle of the belt, and a whetftone. He gave this belt to my brother, and faftened it round his waift, expreffing much friendfhip for him. We gave them to underftand we were going on much farther in the Streights, and they made us comprehend by figns, that they would go to bed as foon as the fun did, fhewing us at the fame time that they would lie down, and making a noife as if they were fnoring in their fleep.

As foon as our boats had quitted them and got out to fea, they mounted on horfeback, and directed their courfe towards the place to which we had made them underftand we were going.

They feem to be crafty, bold people, being more inclined to receive than to give. They wrap themfelves up in beafts fkins fewed together, as the Spaniards do in their clokes. Our people killed fome partridges; faw fome wolves, foxes, and a great number of rats, but nothing curious.

On Thurfday at noon we caft anchor under the low lands of Cape Gregory, in 25 fathoms of water.

After dinner we put our yawls to fea to go a fifhing and fhooting. They came back in the evening without having taken or killed any thing, excepting one mangy vicuna, which M. Gyrauduis fhot. There are numbers of vicunas in this country, which is very beautiful. Our people faw a great quantity of foxes, wolves, and rats, and met with fome few thickets of yellow wood, but no water.

On Friday the ninth we fet fail at day-break. At ten o'clock we got into the fecond narrows, and fteered our courfe in order to pafs between the iflands of St. Elizabeth and St. Bartholomew. We afterwards anchored at 11 o'clock in the bay of Cape Noir,

its

its point bearing N. N. W. 5 degrees N. where the wood begins to appear.

In visiting the woods we found none but what was fit for fuel, and some yellow wood. The soil appears pretty good as well as the bay; into which we might have advanced much farther, the bottom being even: at 8 or 9 fathom of water, a fine sand, and muddy nearer the land. In this bay one may be under shelter from the N. N. E. by the W.

We took in fishing only one large *Cornet*, some *Grai-dos*, with a golden fish, which was a kind of smelt. Our shooting parties were much less fortunate. By the great quantity of bustard's excrement we found scattered about in the bushes, we imagined, that that bird must be very plentiful here in the season. There is no fresh water here; but there is a lake at the distance of a mile from the bottom of the bay.

On Saturday the 10th, at four in the morning, the sea running eastward, fell twelve fathoms perpendicular. This appears contrary to all my fore-mentioned observations; but it might proceed from some cross tide.

We continued along the coast of Patagonia, and found by our soundings the depth of water increase to 35 fathoms, muddy bottom, as we advanced towards the South. The coast is here also bordered with finer wood, which is found in greater quantities.

Having sailed seven leagues in this direction, we came to the opening of a small bay, where we met with a point, even with the surface of the water, and extending half a league out.

We had scarce sailed one quarter of a league, after finding no soundings with a hundred fathoms, when all at once we met with no more than seventeen fathoms depth of water, and a little farther on, only eight fathoms, then five, then four and a half, with a fine sandy muddy bottom. Soon after the depth increased to five and twenty fathoms. It is to be observed that it was high water. Perhaps the shallowest of these places would not have been covered at low water. There is no

wood

wood upon this point, which is about seven leagues from Cape Noir; and the bank is one league South East of this point. This bank is not marked on the charts of the Streights; although it is very dangerous, being in the middle of the bay; which I imagine to be that called Freshwater, by its distance from Port Famine. There are two small rivers here, and some very fine wood; and it answers exactly to the description given of it by the Englishman, who named it Freshwater bay.

We anchored soon after in Port Famine, which we founded, and found it good in every part. One may coast St. Ann's point at two cables length without danger, if forced to it by the wind; the least depth of water there is five or six fathoms, which increases gradually to twenty-five at the distance of a quarter of a league: but one must not anchor here, because the bottom is rocky, and there is a strong current. At the South West of this point there is a bank one cable's length from land, which is not three feet under water at low tide.

When the wind will allow of it, it is better to keep out a full mile from St. Ann's point, on account of the current; and lest there should still be some lurking rocks under water, which may have escaped our notice: one may cast anchor in eight or ten fathoms water, rather towards St. Ann's point, than towards the South; for here the depth of the sea suddenly diminishes even at high water, as well as in the bottom, where, at low water, there appears a shallow, uncovered for more than a quarter of a league.

On Saturday the 17th, we sounded the small bays to the North of St. Ann's point, where we found some banks, extending far out.

On Sunday the 18th, we sent after dinner all our carpenters on shore, to cut some wood for burning and building; which was the reason of our being sent here, as well as to fetch away some trees for planting.

On Wednesday the 28th, M. de la Gyraudais being laden and ready, set sail at seven in the morning to return to the Malouine Islands.

On Friday the 30th, in the morning, I perceived fome favages upon the fandy ifland, which forms the South entrance of the bay where we had left them the year before. I went to them, and knew them to be the fame favages. They were two and twenty men, without women or boats. Having no prefents to give them, and not being able to make them comprehend me, I embarked again.

On Sunday the 1ft of June, early in the morning, the favages made fome figns to us; but the bad weather prevented us from coming to them. They made us underftand, that they wifhed we fhould get into the river with our yawl.

On the 2d, two of the favages appeared at the bottom of the bay, calling out to us in their language. I fent an officer in the yawl, to afk them if they would come on board. On the arrival of the yawl they fled towards the river beckoning us to follow them. The officer thought it more prudent not to do it, and came on board again. At eleven o'clock we faw them come out again in fix canoes. They croffed the bay, paffing within mufket-fhot of us, but would not come on board: they went and landed in a little creek under St. Ann's point. As I had put fix men in this place to cut fire-wood, and the favages were very numerous, I immediately armed the yawl and the longboat, and went to meet them. At my arrival, fome of them were employed in building their huts; others were fifhing for fhell-fifh, mufcles, patellæ, fea-urchins, crabs, bucinna, taking all thefe only from the rocks. Notwithftanding this they have nets made with cat-gut.

After having renewed the alliance made laft year, I diftributed prefents among them, confifting in fome pounds of vermilion, fome woollen bed-cloaths, fmall looking-glaffes, chalk, knives, fome clokes, a hatchet, bread, &c. They would not tafte any wine. I did not chufe to offer them brandy, left their acceptance of it might be attended with dangerous confequences.

Their company appeared to confift of twenty-fix men or boys, and forty women and girls, among whom were a great number ef young people. The Chief of them is called Pacha-chui. He is diſtinguiſhed from the reſt by a cap of birds ſkins with the feathers on. When he receives any viſits he puts it on his head, which is, no doubt, meant as a mark of his dignity. The preſence of the men, who ſeemed exceſſively jealous, obliged the women to aſſume an appearance of great modeſty.

I queſtioned the Chief as well as I could about his religion. He gave me to underſtand, at leaſt I thought I comprehended by his ſigns, that they neither worſhip the ſun, moon, men, nor animals, but only the heavens or the whole univerſe; this he repeated ſeveral times, always lifting up his hands joined together over his head.

During this time they continued throwing upon the fire, without any ceremony, all the wood cut down by our people. This obliged me to ſend my ſix men to cut wood at a greater diſtance from theſe ſavages, to avoid quarrelling with them.

They exchanged with our people ſome bows and arrows, and ſome necklaces of ſhells in return for cloaths. I then left them, and invited them to come on board. Four of them accepted my invitation. I made them dine with me, and entertained them in the beſt manner I could. They preferred bacon to every thing elſe. Their deſert was a candle to each, which they devoured with great eagerneſs. When dinner was over, I had them dreſſed from head to foot, and gave them ſome trifles with which they appeared very much pleaſed; and then ſent them to land.

In the afternoon I returned to the huts of the ſavages. The Pacha-chui came to meet me, and made me a preſent of a kind of flint to ſtrike fire, like thoſe which are found in Canada, appearing to be a marcaſite of yellow copper. He afterwards diſtributed the preſents I had made them in the morning.

One of them was continually muttering; I aſked him the reaſon of this. He gave me to underſtand that he was ſaying his prayers, by pointing up to the heavens as the Pacha-chui had done in the morning. This ſeemed to imply that they worſhipped

shipped some divinity, but I could not comprehend what the divinity was, nor under what title he was adored.

Both men and women have no other dress than the skins of sea-wolves, vicunas, guanacoes, otters, and lynxes, which they throw on their shoulders. Most of them are bare-headed. A bird's skin with the feathers on, covers their private parts. The men call themselves *Pach-pachevé*; the women *Cap-cap*. They taught me these names by shewing me first their persons, and afterwards the parts which distinguish the sex. Both men and women are thin. Their canoes are ill-built, in comparison with those of the savages of Canada. The women are the persons employed in rowing and fishing. They have a number of dogs, resembling foxes; which they call *Ouchi*; and their canoes, *Sborou*.

It is to be observed, that the morning tides are always equal every morning; rise very little in open sea, and are only as the neap-tides.

On Wednesday morning the 4th, the savages made no scruple of burning five or six cords of wood, which our people had cut down, but they assisted in bringing the rest on board.

At noon the Pacha-chui came on board our frigate, attended by eleven men. I made him dine with me, and gave the others some biscuit, and a piece of tallow; and for their drink three pints of the oil of sea-wolves. They ate and drank all up with a most excellent appetite. I afterwards dressed the Pacha-chui, and giving some trifles to the others, sent them all on shore.

On the 6th, all the savages, pleased with the reception I had given their comrades, came in four canoes to pay me a visit. But as they had large fires in their canoes, I would not suffer them to come on board, at which they seemed displeased. I ordered them some biscuit and oil; and after dinner sent them back without giving them any reason for it.

On Sunday the 8th, the savages began to be troublesome: they stole several hatchets, some provisions, and cloaths from us. As they seemed inclinable to theft and fraud, I took the reso-

lution

lution to let nobody lie on shore, and to submit to the inconvenience of having all the utensils and tools brought back every night.

On Monday the 9th, the savages stole again some harpoons, hatchets, iron-wedges, and mauls. I complained of this to the Pacha-chui, and desired our tools might be returned, but to no purpose. I then gave them to understand, that if they persisted in these practices, we should treat them in a different manner.

Their boat, which had crossed the bay last night, now brought them a dying man, about forty years of age, who was exceedingly emaciated.

In the afternoon, our wood-cutters represented to me, that they lost a great deal of time in coming back to lie on board, and then returning in the morning to the wood: they therefore asked leave to lie on shore. I consented to this, desiring them at the same time, to treat the savages mildly if they came to visit them.

For this purpose, I placed a discreet person at the head of them, and with him his brother, a man of a mild disposition, and who, from being used to live among the savages of Canada, was in some measure acquainted with their manners: and after recommending it to them to keep a strict watch lest they should be surprized, I returned to the ship.

On Thursday the 12th, about four o'clock in the morning, we heard some noise among the savages. Three of their canoes, with a great number of women in them and some men, came up to our frigate. I gave them some pieces of bread, and some oil of sea-wolves, the greatest part of which they put into a kind of bladder they had brought on purpose, and drank off the rest. I would not suffer them to come on board, on account of their being so much addicted to theft, and because they had got large fires in their canoes. This day I observed, contrary to the common custom, that the men were not painted: only some few of them were painted black, which gave them a very frightful appearance. The women were all spotted with black, having their faces and necks bloody, as if they had scratched themselves

with

with thorns. Two of their canoes doubled St. Ann's point going to the North.

On Sunday the 15th, in the morning, I went to pay a visit to the savages. Not seeing the sick man, I asked them what was become of him; they made me comprehend he was dead. The cries we had heard on Thursday morning were probably the marks of their mourning. They seemed all very much afflicted, and were all painted black, contrary to the usual custom; and the women appeared scratched all over, as if they had been torn with pins. I observed that they shewed much regret for the dead man. I asked them by signs what they had done with him. They answered me only by lifting up their hands to heaven, repeating the same signs several times, in order I suppose to make me understand the deceased was there: from whence it may be conjectured that they believe in a future state. They would never tell me what they had done with the dead body. I am inclined to think they had transported it in one of their canoes, with which they had doubled St. Ann's point. I distributed some biscuit and oil of sea-wolves among them.

On Monday the 16th, I perceived two boats of savages coming towards us, and all the rest going out of the bay. I put myself into our yawl, taking some bread and oil along with me. When I came near them, I made them a sign to follow me to land which they did very readily. I gave them the bread and oil. They broke up their camp, and those who staid behind were gathering up the remains of it. They made me understand that they were going to live at the distance of a league from that place, in one of the small bays to the North of St. Ann's point, because the shell-fish became scarce in the place where they were. The Pacha-chui was in one of the two boats, and was coming with an intention to thank me, and to apprize me of his departure.

I then ventured to ask him, if any of his young people would come away with us, making him understand as well as I could, that I would bring him back in a twelvemonth. He answered

by

by figns that he confented, and immediately prefented one of them to me, who feemed fatisfied. We then left each other, and I brought away my young favage with me, to put him on board. I dreffed him, and entertained him as well as I could. The Chief went out of the bay to join his troop.

On Tuefday the 17th our favage feemed to be pleafed with us; and even looked contented and chearful. About ten o'clock, feventeen favages coming by land from a fmall bay which lay North of us, and where they were encamped, paid a vifit to their companion. We went to meet them, taking him along with us; and I gave them fome bread and oil for their breakfaft. As we were going back, another of them afked leave to come on board to ftay with his comrade. As the offer was voluntary I took him along with me.

Towards fix o'clock in the evening, I perceived that our two favages were fo melancholy as even to fhed tears, and that th.y were conftantly looking towards land. I was not at a lofs to find out the caufe of this uneafinefs; and thought it natural that they muft on reflection regret the refolution they had taken. Notwithftanding my defire of bringing them away, in hopes that I might afterwards receive fome ufeful information from them, I determined to fend them back, and reftore them to that liberty which they certainly imagined they had loft. I made them get into our yawl, and had them conducted back to land. They expreffed much joy when they came on fhore, and defired they might go to their families.

On Wednefday, at 9 o'clock, they came to afk for fome bread and oil. I ordered fome to be diftributed to them, and having affifted in loading our longboat, they went back to their firft encampment. At four o'clock in the afternoon they left us, making me underftand that they were going to reft, becaufe the moon, which they call *Sercon* was up; but that they would come beak, and bring with them the two young men who had been on board of us. When we got back to our fhip, we heard two guns fire; the fignal agreed upon between us to call for help, in

cafe

case we should be attacked by the savages. I then suspected that our people were engaged with them. I immediately had our boats armed, and sent them to their alliance, but it was too late: the victory was already gained, and the savages routed when we landed. The affair happened in the following manner:

Twenty, or six and twenty savages, as we were told, came down secretly and silently through the wood behind the workshop; and three of them entered suddenly into the hut where our people were, who thinking that the savages seemed to have some mischievous design, placed themselves at the entrance of the hut to hinder the rest from coming in. They then attempted to force their way, and not succeeding fell upon our men, some attempting to seize their legs, in order to throw them down, and probably to bind them, being provided with large straps in form of slings, having at the end a dart about six inches long, made of a jagged bone; the rest beat them with large sticks. Our people, though they were surprized at so sudden a declaration of war, were not discouraged. They seized their cutlasses, and exerted themselves bravely against their enemies, destroying as many of them as they could; by which means they threw the savages into confusion and routed them: our people however were but seven against twenty-five: three savages remained dead upon the field of battle, exclusive of the wounded; three of our people were wounded; the master carpenter received several blows upon the head with a stick; another was dangerously wounded in the head with a cutlass; and his brother was cut on the hand with the same instrument, which has quite disabled him. The wounded were dressed as soon as they came on board. One of the three was afterwards trepanned.

On Friday the 20th, in the morning, I sent the longboat to fetch away the timber, and to bury the three savages in the same grave. After having raised the ground to a certain height, we placed their skins or cloaks, with their shoes on the top, that the other savages might find out the place where their dead companions lay; and that they should not think we had eaten them;
which

which perhaps they might do, if they were unable to find the dead bodies.

On Sunday the 22d, we were at the entrance of the narrows; and at eleven o'clock we saw several fires on the low lands of Cape Gregory. In coasting these, we discovered about 90 or 100 men, most of them on horseback, who followed us to the place of anchorage; thinking, without doubt, that we should anchor there. But I was prevented by the wind blowing fresh, and the weather being favourable for sailing out of the Streights. We made twelve leagues since morning, the savages making signs to us all the while. At nine o'clock in the evening we cleared Cape Virgin, and left the Streights.

---

*Remarks made in 1766 in the Streights of Magellan, from Cape Virgin to Cape Roud; by M. de la Gyraudais, Lieutenant of a Frigate, at present Captain of a fire-ship.*

CAPE Virgin is of the same height as Cape Fréhel, in the road of St. Malo, and has the same form. At two leagues and a half westward, it sends forth a low point, which extends a league out at sea to the South; with a ridge of rocks, which is covered by the tide at two cables length from this point; and against which the sea breaks with great violence. This ridge is not marked upon the chart of the Streights, any more than a bay in which we anchored. The coast is rather high and sound, from Cape Virgin to Cape Possession. One may sail along it at the distance of half a league without any danger. Possession bay is large. It shelters ships from the wind, from the W. S. W. to the N. E. passing by the N. It may easily be known by M. de Gennes' plan, which is accurate in the distances, and the bearing of the lands; except with regard to Lion's island, which he does not place sufficiently to the W. S. W. by one league and a half at least. Over Possession bay, there is a large cape, and

to

to the S. W. of this, four small hummocks situated near each other.

From this bay till one gets beyond the first narrows, the coast is low and found on the starboard side going in. After this comes the bay Boucaut, formed by the first narrows, and Cape Gregory which is pretty high. Two leagues in land there is a mountain, running N. E. and S. W. and a very high even land, which is seen a long while before one enters the first narrows.

After passing the second narrows, the land rises, and there are several hollows from this to St. Elizabeth's island; and from thence to the main land, which must be coasted as near as possible, particularly on the flood; because the tide throws with prodigious force against St. Bartholomew's island. The passage is between these two islands to Cape Noir, which is high; and where there is very convenient and good anchorage, called by M. de Gennes, Freshwater, though it is not so. Here we begin to find wood. Freshwater is six leagues beyond, in a creek, the starboard point of which is very low, and where there is no wood. Here in sounding across we had no ground at fifty fathoms. Two minutes after we saw the bottom, and at four fathoms fine grey sand. We followed this bottom a quarter of a league farther, taking care to keep rather wide of it. I would advise not to go nearer to it than the distance of two leagues. From thence to Port Famine the land is high, as it is also to the bay of Cape Rond.

*Observations on the Terra del Fuego side, from the entrance of the Streights.*

FROM the side of Cape Virgin, to two leagues and a half within, the land is high and found. Here there is a very low point, extending one league out at sea S. E. and N. W. To the N. and S. of this point, and one league wide of it, is a shoal
bottom;

bottom. The coaſt afterwards forms a hollow, not to be ſeen but in fine weather, as far as Cape Orange, which makes the entrance on the larboard ſide of the firſt narrows. Here is a ridge of rocks which covers at high water, and extends N. E. S. W. to the diſtance of two long leagues from this cape. From hence to the ſide of the ſecond narrows, the land forms another hollow; and from the ſecond narrows to the ſide of Cape Rond, the land is very high, and forms an appearance of four hills. Between theſe poſſibly there may be ſome bays. M. de Gennes has not marked the two low points of land, placed before, and on this ſide of Cape Rond, at one league and a half or two leagues diſtance.

---

*Extract of the Journal of the ſame M. de la Gyraudais commanding his Majeſty's Pink, l'Etoile, going from the Malouine Iſlands to the Streights of Magellan.*

I Believe there is a greater diſtance between the Malouine Iſlands and the main land of Patagonia, than is marked upon the charts; for the Eagle found herſelf by her reckoning eighteen leagues ahead of the ſhip, as well in going as in coming back. We ſounded frequently, and found ſixty fathoms, mixed bottom, with white coral, and a gun flint, which was remarkable enough. Here we ſaw ſeveral whales, ſome ſea-larks, larger than common, ſome pinguins, divers, petterils, oſpreys, and large gulls.

From the twentieth to the firſt of May we had thick weather, which hindered us from ſeeing land, when we were more than half a league diſtance from it: the ſea ſeemed agitated as if we had been in a race. The water was here diſcoloured at eight leagues from the ſhore, but more ſo at the mouth of the Streights. At ten, the weather clearing up, we ſaw land, diſtance four leagues.

leagues. By our reckoning we still found the Malouine Islands farther off from the main land, than is laid down by our charts. On the fifth instant, about four in the afternoon, we saw a fire on the coast of Patagonia. Upon coming nearer, we saw seven men with their horses. We could not discern whether they were naked or clothed. When they perceived that we had got beyond the place where they had made their fires, they followed along the coast, mounted upon their horses, and dogs after them. Seeing that we continued our course, they shouted, but we could not comprehend their meaning. The wind and tide being in our favour, we lost sight of the Patagonians and passed the first narrows. It was a league and a half over. Between five and six we anchored in the bay Boucaut, at three leagues from Cape Gregory, with ten fathoms water, muddy bottom of sand and small shells, at the distance of a full league from the land. One should not cast anchor in lesser depth of water; for the sea fell three or four fathoms in the nighttime. The coast is well laid down in M. de Gennes' plan.

From the 6th to the 7th, in the night, we again saw fires on the Patagonian coast. At eight o'clock this fire was of one side of us, and we distinguished some Patagonians on shore, by means of our spying glasses. The Eagle and myself put out our yawls to sea, and sent them with fifteen men well armed, including the officer, to the spot where we saw seven of the savages. They paid our people some compliment in their own language. Our seamen could not understand them; but imagined their faces and behaviour expressed a satisfaction at seeing us. After the first compliments, they conducted our people to their fires.

Here they examined the Patagonians at their leisure, and found them to be men of the highest stature: the least of them was five feet seven inches *(French measure)*, and of a bulk beyond the proportion of their height, which made them appear less tall than they are. They have large strong limbs, and broad faces; their complexion is extremely tanned, their forehead high,

their

their nose flat and broad; their cheeks are full, and their mouth large; their teeth are very white, and well ranged, and their hair black. They are stronger than our Europeans of the same size.

The words they pronounced were, *Echoura, Chaoa, Didon, ahi, ahi, obi, Choven, Quécallé, Machan, Naticon, Pito*. These were the only words our people could gather, while they were warming themselves at their fires.

M. de St. Simon, an officer, who by order of the ministry embarked with us for the Malouine Islands with presents for the natives, acquitted himself extremely well of his commission. He gave them some harpoons, bludgeons, bedding, woollen caps, vermilion, and in short every thing he thought would be most agreeable to them. They appeared very well pleased.

They are clothed with the skins of guanacos, vicunas, and other animals, sewed together in form of square clokes which reach below the calf of the leg almost to the ancle. They have a sort of buskins or half-boots, made of the same skins, with the shag on the inside, as it is also in their clokes, which are very well sewed together in regular compartments, and painted on the outside with blue and red figures, bearing a resemblance to Chinese characters. The figures however are almost all alike, and divided by straight lines which form sorts of squares and lozenges [*]. They have something like hats ornamented with feathers, much in the same manner as ours. Some of these hats resemble very much the Spanish caps.

Several of our people went a shooting at some distance, where they killed a few partridges, and saw some carcases of vicunas.

[*] M. de la Gyraudais received as a present from these Patagonians, when he visited them at his return to the Malouine Islands, several of their clokes, some of their weapons, some slings armed with stones, and some necklaces of shells from their women. He brought them to Paris, and gave part of them to M. d'Arboulin, who had some of them presented to the King, and kept the rest. I examined them at leisure, and although I am rather more than five feet seven inches (French measure) one of these clokes thrown on my shoulders, (as the Patagonians wear them) trailed on the ground at least a foot and a half.

The country they went over is uncultivated, barren, and dry. There is nothing but heath upon it, and very little grafs. The horfes of the favages feem to be very bad, but they manage them with great dexterity. The Patagonians made fome prefents to our people who were returned from fhooting. Thefe were round ftones, of the fize of a two-pounder ball. They are placed in a ftrap of leather, faftened and fewed to the end of a ftring of catgut twifted like a rope. It is a kind of a fling, which they ufe very dexteroufly for killing animals a hunting. On the end, oppofite to that which fixes the round ftone, there is another ftone placed, half the fize of the former, and clofely covered all over with a kind of bladder. They hold the fmall ftone in their hand after having paffed the cord between their fingers; and then making a turn with the arm, as in cafting a fling, they throw the weapon at the animal, whom they can reach; and kill at the diftance of four hundred feet.

The complexion of the women is tolerably clear, for they are much lefs tanned than the men, yet they are proportioned to them in fize. They are alfo dreffed in a cloke, wear bufkins; and a kind of fmall apron, which only hangs down half the length of their thighs. They certainly pluck out their eyebrows for they have none. Their hair is dreffed in front, and they have no hats.

Thefe Patagonians are ignorant of the paffion of jealoufy, at leaft there is reafon to think fo, from their encouraging our people to handle the breafts of their wives and daughters, and making them lie promifcuoufly with them, when I paid them a vifit on my return to the Malouine Iflands.

We gave them bread which they ate, and fome tobacco for chewing and fmoking. By their manner of ufing it, we faw plainly it was no novelty to them. They would not drink any wine. When we had been five or fix hours with them, they grew more familiarized. They were very curious, fearched our pockets, were very defirous of feeing every thing, and examined us with attention from head to foot.

We

We mounted their horses, which were equipped with bridle, saddle and stirrups. They use both whip and spurs; and seemed satisfied and well pleased to see our people ride their horses. When I had a gun fired for signal to bring our people back, they shewed not the least emotion or surprise. When we went away they entreated us much to stay with them, giving us to understand by signs, that they would supply us with food, and though they had nothing to offer us at present, yet they soon expected some of their people to return from sporting. We answered them also by signs that we could not possibly stay; and that we were going directly to a certain place, which we attempted to point out to them, endeavouring at the same time to make them comprehend that we wished them to bring us some oxen and horses. We know not whether they understood us.

On the eighth, having set sail from Bay Boucaut, and anchored under Cape Gregory, we went a shooting on shore, and the soil appeared the same as on the last spot. After we had walked about a league, we met with two herds of vicunas, each consisting of three or four hundred, of which we could not kill more than one with a musket charged with ball. I also shot a *Stinkingsem*, which I left on account of its offensive smell. I likewise fired at a wolf, but all these animals are very wild, and will not suffer any one to approach them.

At half past six in the morning of the ninth, we got under sail in very pleasant weather. M. de Gennes in his draught lays down the second narrows East and West corrected by the globe; but he has marked it two points too much to the West. I would advise to keep the Patagonian shore till you come to the North and South of Elizabeth's island; on account of the strong tide which runs upon St. Bartholomew and Lyon islands, and upon some shoals lying off those islands. We coasted close to Elizabeth's island, till we came to Cape Noir, where we anchored in eight fathoms water, sandy and muddy bottom, with broken shells.

From

From Friday the ninth to the tenth, we kept along the Patagonian shore, at the distance of a league and an half. The coast appeared woody, but on the return of our boat we were told the wood was not good for much. Being near a low point we sounded, and no ground at fifty fathoms. An instant after we saw the bottom, which was sandy, and at four fathoms water; this obliged us to haul off.

From the 10th to the 11th we had much wind, and foggy weather, with a very rough sea. As we were no more than five leagues from Port Famine, I determined to go and anchor there. The Eagle followed us, and we soon had reason to be pleased with this resolution, for a quarter of an hour after we came to anchor, we could not discern any object at the distance of half a cannon-shot from us, and the wind still continued blowing very hard.

From the 11th to the 12th, the fog and rainy weather continued. Having walked round the bay, we met with some fine wood, and discovered a very rapid river, on the larboard point of the mouth of the bay. This stream makes the sea as dirty and as turbid, as a river overflowing from abundance of rains.

On the water side there were seven or eight huts belonging to the savages, which they had but lately quitted. I fired a gun, and hoisted our flag, in order to attract the savages from the neighbouring parts.

From the 13th to the 14th there was a high wind, followed by a prodigious violent storm, which ended in a great fall of rain, succeeded by snow and hail, which lasted till noon, when the weather grew calm.

From the 16th to the 17th, we met with some very fine wood, and sent an officer and thirty men on shore, to pitch a tent, and cut roads through the woods. We were constantly employed in cutting and shipping our wood till the 17th, when we unmoored, leaving the Eagle to complete her cargo, and bring up ours to the Malouine Islands.

From the 29th to the 30th, at ten in the morning, we saw a fire on shore, which the savages had kindled on our account. We steered towards the fire, and saw some men and horses.

From the 30th to the 31st, the night coming upon us unawares, we came to our anchorage by the light of two fires which the savages had made for us, one upon a mountain, the other upon the sea-side. We anchored in nineteen fathoms, black muddy bottom, with small shells.

At day-break the savages shouted, in order that we should come to them. I put my yawl and longboat to sea well armed, and with presents. I went on shore, where I found three hundred savages, including men, women, and children. Not expecting to meet with so many, I was obliged to go on board again to fetch some more presents.

From the 31st to Sunday the first of June 1766, the wind having driven our yawl from shore, which was empty, our people were under some anxiety for fear of losing it. The savages perceiving this, one of them who was on horseback, spurred his horse, and plunged with him into the sea, to swim after the yawl. He got hold of it, and brought it back to our seamen. Perhaps we who pique ourselves so much upon our politeness, affability, and humanity, and who call these Patagonians savages, would hardly have done so much for them, in a similar circumstance.

At seven in the morning the longboat went to shore with the rest of the presents, which the stormy weather had prevented us sending sooner. It came back with thirteen of our people who had stayed with the savages since yesterday morning. They told us that these Patagonian giants had treated them with the utmost civility according to their manner, and given them marks of the sincerest friendship, even so far as to invite them to lie with their wives and daughters; that they had given them some flesh of the guanacos, several of their clokes, and some of their slings; and the women some of their necklaces made of shells.

They

They also made me a present of twelve horses; which I could not keep for want of forage.

The piece of civility most troublesome to our folks, was that of being obliged to lie promiscuously among the Patagonians; who often lay three or four together upon one of our people, to keep the cold from them; so that their muskets and other arms became useless. They would therefore have had no resource left but in their pocket-knives, which would not have been of much service for defending them, in case of necessity against five or six hundred men, including women and children, and all of them proportionally of an enormous stature, both in height and bulk. Each man or woman, had one or two dogs, and as many horses. They seemed to be of a mild disposition, and very humane. It would be easy to establish a very profitable trade with them, for their horses, and for the skins of vicunas, which are so much valued, and bear so high a price in Europe. The skins of guanacos are also excellent, though not so fine.

From the 7th to the 8th, a very high wind, rainy and thick weather. The sea was terrible, the wind blowing always by squalls.

From Sunday the 8th to the 9th, the sea was very rough, with rain, hail, snow, and fogs. At nine we saw land without knowing what it was: at noon we found it to be Sebald de Wertz islands, which bore S. E. distance ten leagues.

On the 15th we cast anchor in Acarron bay, in the same place from whence we set out.

F I N I S.

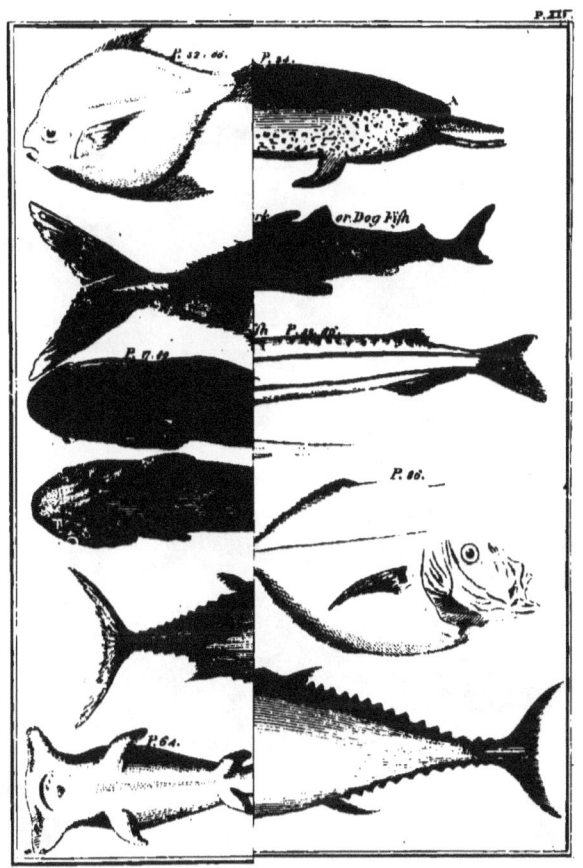

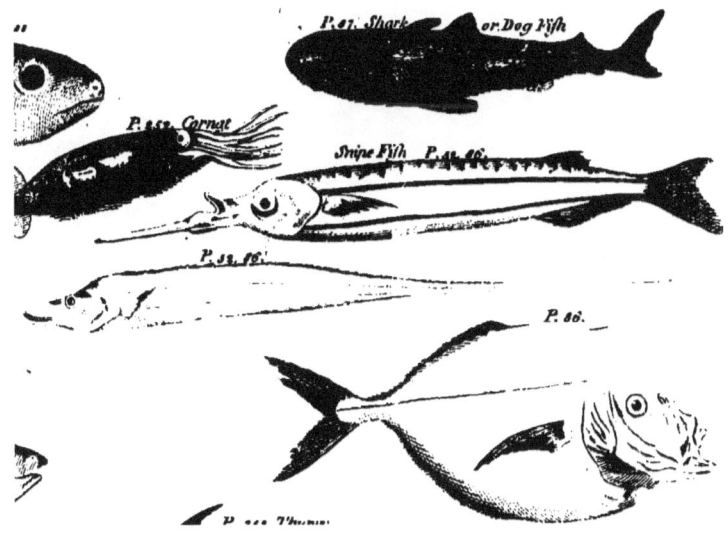

Head of the Quebranta Huessos.

www.ingramcontent.com/pod-product-compliance
Lightning Source LLC
Chambersburg PA
CBHW020317240426
43673CB00039B/842